Analyzing Qualitative Data with MAXQDA

Udo Kuckartz · Stefan Rädiker

Analyzing Qualitative Data with MAXQDA

Text, Audio, and Video

 Springer

Udo Kuckartz
Berlin, Germany

Stefan Rädiker
Verden, Germany

Translation from the German language edition:
Analyse qualitativer Daten mit MAXQDA by Stefan Rädiker, Udo Kuckartz
Copyright © Springer Fachmedien Wiesbaden GmbH, part of Springer Nature 2019. All
Rights Reserved.

ISBN 978-3-030-15673-2   ISBN 978-3-030-15671-8   (eBook)
https://doi.org/10.1007/978-3-030-15671-8

This Springer imprint is published by the registered company Springer Nature Switzerland AG.
The registered company address is: Gewerbestrasse 11, 6330 Cham, Switzerland

Preface

"To begin at the beginning" is the opening line of the play *Under Milk Wood* by Welsh poet Dylan Thomas. So, we also want to start here at the beginning and start with some information about the history of the analysis software MAXQDA. This story is quite long; it begins in 1989 with a first version of the software, then just called "MAX," for the operating system DOS and a book in the German language. The book's title was *Text Analysis Software for the Social Sciences. Introduction to MAX and Textbase Alpha* written by Udo Kuckartz, published by Gustav Fischer in 1992. Since then, there have been many changes and innovations: technological, conceptual, and methodological. MAXQDA has its roots in social science methodology; the original name MAX was reference to the sociologist Max Weber, whose methodology combined quantitative and qualitative methods, explanation, and understanding in a way that was unique at the time, the beginning of the twentieth century. Since the first versions, MAX (later named winMAX and MAXQDA) has always been a very innovative analysis software. In 1994, it was one of the first programs with a graphical user interface; since 2001, it has used Rich Text Format with embedded graphics and objects. Later, MAXQDA was the first QDA program (QDA stands for qualitative data analysis) with a special version for Mac computers that included all analytical functions. Since autumn 2015, MAXQDA has been available in almost identical versions for Windows and Mac, so that users can switch between operating systems without having to familiarize themselves with a new interface or changed functionality. This compatibility and feature equality between Mac and Windows versions is unique and greatly facilitates team collaboration. MAXQDA has also come up with numerous innovations in the intervening years: a logically and very intuitively designed user interface, very versatile options for memos and comments, numerous visualization options, the summary grid as a middle level of analysis between primary data and categories, and much more, for instance, transcription, geolinks, weight scores for coding, analysis of PDF files, and Twitter analysis. Last but not least, the mixed methods features are worth mentioning, in which MAXQDA has long played a pioneering role.

This list already shows that today MAXQDA is much more than text analysis software: the first chapter of this book contains a representation of the data types that MAXQDA can analyze today (in version 2018) and shows which file formats can be processed. The large variety of data types is contrasted by an even greater number of analysis methods. The variety of possibilities is fascinating on the one hand, but also poses us, as authors of this book, the question of what content we should select, which methods and procedures we should describe, and with what degree of detail? It makes a huge difference whether videos from school lessons are analyzed in the context of didactical classroom research, whether narrative interviews are analyzed in biographical research, or whether mixed methods evaluations of development policy measures are carried out. In all the three cases, a specific method is required, each of which would deserve its own treatise, its own step-by-step guide—and, of course, there are many other fields of application in addition to these, such as nursing research, environmental research, and technology research. We have tried to deal with as many topics as possible; above all, we focus on those aspects that have a multi-use character and play the same role in many fields of application, in many types of data and methods. This includes, first and foremost, questions relating to the formation of categories, to which we pay particular attention.

Structure of the Book

In the *first main part*, the basic functions of MAXQDA are presented after a methodical introduction. The structure follows the logic of the research process. The first chapter "Analyzing qualitative data with software" contains a short methodological introduction and gives an overview of the analysis options. The following chapters deal with the management of the interface of MAXQDA (Chap. 2), preparation and import of data (Chap. 3), and handling and transcription of audio and video data (Chap. 4).

Reading, reflecting, and exploring are the beginning of intensive work with the data (Chap. 5). The central analytical activity of coding is the subject of Chap. 6 (text data and PDF) and Chap. 7 (video data and images). The following Chap. 8 "Building a coding frame" focuses on the important question of the construction of the category system. Following the logic of a step-by-step guide, the ninth chapter then deals with the question of how coded segments can be retrieved and which forms of further work follow, for example for the differentiation of codes. Chapter 10 "Using variables and quantifying codes" is of particular interest for mixed methods approaches, but the chapter is also important for all those who have collected additional data, such as sociodemographic information, in the context of problem-oriented interviews and want to combine it with qualitative data. Chapter 10 concludes the basic part of the book. Up to this point, the chapters should be read sequentially, as they are largely based on each other. This recommendation applies in particular to readers who do not yet have any knowledge of computer-assisted analysis of qualitative data.

The *second main part* of the book is problem oriented (Chaps. 11, 12, 13, 14, 15, and 16); special analysis problems are discussed here. While the first main part could best be read sequentially from front to back, the chapters of the second application-related part can be read independently of each other. For example, when it comes to how to create a literature review, it is sufficient to read only Chap. 14 after the first part. By structuring this part of the book to focus on applications, we hope to avoid the acquisition of "lazy knowledge," which one unfortunately forgets very quickly according to experience. Here, in the second main part of the book, special types of analysis or special data types are discussed: Chapter 11 deals with paraphrasing techniques, case-oriented summaries, and case comparisons. Chapter 12 is devoted to the questions of how to discover relationships, how to perform group comparisons, and which forms of presentation and visualization of the results are possible with MAXQDA. Chapter 13 is devoted to mixed methods approaches, in particular the possibilities of integrating qualitative and quantitative research. The following two chapters deal with special forms of analysis: literature reviews (Chap. 14) and focus group analysis (Chap. 15). Chapter 16 focuses on a very popular form of mixed methods research, namely the analysis of (online) survey data with closed and open questions.

The *third main part* of the book, covering the last four chapters, is again devoted to general topics that are independent of specific types of analysis: Chapter 17 deals with the visual representation of relationships, for example in the form of information graphics, concept maps, causal networks, and models; Chap. 18 deals with the possibilities for teamwork, including the technical implementation of collaboration; and Chap. 19 deals with the question of the question of consistency when different people share the work of coding the data material. The final Chap. 20 is devoted to questions of documentation and archiving that arise at the very end of a project such as how the analytical work, for example, the coding frame, can be documented.

This book is consciously written with the goal of optimal handling of MAXQDA. Although reference is made to methodological literature, anyone who wants to learn how a qualitative content analysis works, for example, or which methods of video analysis exist, should fall back on the multifaceted methodological literature. In this book, we convey the knowledge necessary to implement existing methods with MAXQDA as comprehensibly and clearly as possible.

We would like to take this opportunity to thank Sean Ohlendorf for translating this book into English. We are very grateful for the insightful comments and suggestions provided by Graham Hughes. In addition, we would like to thank Denise Gider, Malte Hilker, and Aikokul Maksutova as well as Anne Kuckartz, Isabel Kuckartz, Jonas Ringler, Fabrice Mielke, and Ann-Kathrin Fischer for their comments.

Berlin, Germany   Udo Kuckartz
Autumn 2018   Stefan Rädiker

Contents

Introduction: Analyzing Qualitative Data with Software

The umbrella term "qualitative data" covers a wide variety of data types. Using computer software to analyze these various types of data is a relatively new area of methods development. Indeed, computer-assisted analysis of multimedia data—such as videos—has only recently come to the fore, thanks to rapid technological developments. Today (almost) everyone can collect and analyze this kind of data (e.g., via video recordings on their smartphone). This chapter provides an overview of types of data that can be analyzed with MAXQDA, which file formats the software can process, and the scope of its features and functions. We will also discuss the relationship between qualitative methods and computer software as an analytical tool in practice of research. Does the inherent logic of computer software favor certain social science methods? Or can computer-assisted qualitative data analysis be regarded as an independent method that replaces other traditional (especially interpretative) methods?

> **In This Chapter**
> - Get to know a variety of qualitative data types
> - Gain an overview of the range of data types and formats that MAXQDA can analyze
> - Gain a first impression of MAXQDA's features and functions
> - Understand the debate concerning QDA software as an analysis tool or method

What Is Qualitative Data?

MAXQDA is a software for the analysis of qualitative data and therefore belongs to the family of CAQDAS, the acronym for "Computer Assisted Qualitative Data Analysis Software." Recently, the shorter term QDAS (Qualitative Data Analysis

© Springer Nature Switzerland AG 2019
U. Kuckartz, S. Rädiker, *Analyzing Qualitative Data with MAXQDA*,
https://doi.org/10.1007/978-3-030-15671-8_1

Software) has occasionally been used; we will stick to the term CAQDAS through-out this chapter. At this stage, however, you may be wondering what exactly qualitative data is. The term "qualitative data" comes from the social sciences and is an umbrella term for all nonnumerical, unstructured data. While most people can immediately imagine something under *numerical data*, this is not done so easily in the case of *qualitative data*. Numerical data, that is, numbers—whether large or small numbers—with varying degrees of accuracy; this data is usually collected by means of measurements and analyzed using statistical methods. Appropriate software such as SPSS, STATA, SAS, or SYSTAT is available for these analysis methods.

While the field of numerical data is very simple, the opposite applies to qualitative data. There is an incredible amount of *qualitative data*, ranging from interview and focus group transcripts to photographs, documents, films, and audio and video recordings. However, the term "qualitative variables" used in quantitative social research must be distinguished from qualitative data; this refers to variables with nominal-scale levels, such as the variables "Gender," "Marital status," or "Party preference." These variables are often also called *categorical variables*, because their characteristic values can be assigned to categories ("Democrat," "Republican," etc.).

It makes sense to distinguish between methodological and technical aspects when considering different types of qualitative data. Methodologically, a distinction is made between narrative interviews, episodic interviews, ethnographic interviews, problem-oriented interviews, etc. For example, I can conduct an open-ended inter-view with a person using an interview guide. While the topics on which I would like to ask base my questions have been fixed in advance, apart from that, the interview is completely open. Technically, all these distinct types of data can be recorded in an MP3 or other audio file format. After the audio recording has been transcribed, the interview is saved as a text file in a specific format, e.g., RTF, DOC/X, or PDF. This technical side is not unimportant if you want to analyze the interview in MAXQDA or another QDA program. Some QDA software can only analyze texts in TXT or RTF format, while other programs can also handle documents in PDF format (sometimes only the words contained in a PDF file, but not the images, tables, or any other non-textual content). Other programs can also analyze audio and video files, and finally there are programs like MAXQDA or ATLAS.ti that allow synchronized playback and analysis of transcripts and their respective audio or video files.

So, if you consider the type of data analyzed, quantitatively oriented researchers have it relatively easy because they deal with only one type of data, namely, numbers. Qualitative researchers, in contrast, are confronted with a variety of data types; referencing the term "biodiversity," you could even use the expression "quali-diversity," a vast, hardly manageable plurality of data types and modes of data collection.

Table 1.1 Data types and formats that can be analyzed in MAXQDA

Data type	Examples from empirical social research	Importable data formats in MAXQDA
Existing texts of all kinds	Interview and focus group transcripts, research diaries, notes, etc.	RTF, RTFD (Mac), DOC/X, ODT, TXT
Paperwork	Research reports, articles from journals	PDF
Audio recordings	Structured interviews, narrative interviews, episodic interviews, focus groups, etc.	MP3, WAV and other formats
Video recordings	Ethnography, field research, educational research, etc.	MP4, MOV, 3GP, 3GGP, MPG, AVI, M4V, AVCHD
Surveys	Import survey data from Excel with automatic coding. Import of variables from SPSS files	XLS/X, SAV
Data from online survey tools	SurveyMonkey, Qualtrics, LimeSurvey, 2ask, etc.	Via API from SurveyMonkey, XLS/X, HTML
Spreadsheets	Import of spreadsheets	XLS/X
Data from social media	Twitter, Facebook, etc.	Via API from Twitter, PDF (von Facebook-Seiten)
Photographs, pictures	Ethnography, field research, urban research, educational research	PNG, JPG, JPEG, GIF, TIF
Bibliographic data	Exports from literature management programs (Endnote, Citavi, Zotero, etc.) and online literature databases	RIS, TXT
Web pages	Websites of organizations, web forums, etc.	PDF, PNG
MAXApp projects	Import of projects created with MAXApp (iOS/Android)	ZIP, XML
Pre-structured data	Semi-structured interviews with open and closed questions, database exports, etc.	RTF, RTFD (Mac), DOC/X, ODT, TXT
Texts and tables entered directly in MAXQDA	Field notes, observation protocols, etc.	–
Audio and video recordings transcribed in MAXQDA	All types of interviews and group interviews; video recordings, e.g., of lessons in school classes	–

What Types of Data Can Be Analyzed with MAXQDA?

In accordance with the variety of qualitative data described above, the list of all data types that can be analyzed with MAXQDA is very extensive. Table 1.1 provides an overview of data types and data formats without claiming to be complete.

The last two rows of Table 1.1 are different from the others, because in these cases the data is not available in advance; it is generated using MAXQDA. You might enter an observation protocol or a field note directly into MAXQDA while conducting field research, for example, or transcribe audio/video files with the program.

You can choose between 15 different languages for the MAXQDA interface. Regardless of which interface language you choose, MAXQDA can process all texts that comply with the Unicode standard; this means that texts in (almost) all languages, for example, Chinese, Korean, or Arabic texts, can be processed. This also applies to all category names, document names, notes, and summaries entered in MAXQDA.

The Analytical Functions of MAXQDA

MAXQDA is able to analyze all the data commonly collected in the context of empirical social research. Of course, the software can also be used for tasks beyond social science research. It is particularly well suited, for example, to conducting literature reviews, as is standard practice in all scientific disciplines. MAXQDA can also be used to systematically index and automatically code large volumes of text: companies can manage their board meeting minutes, pastors their sermons, and criminal investigation offices their interview records.

What can you do with MAXQDA and what features and functions does it offer? The functional overview, which is available on the MAXQDA website at www. maxqda.com/products/maxqda-features, comprises 11 sections:

1. Data types (import and analysis)
2. Data management and usability
3. Transcription
4. Qualitative data analysis
5. Mixed methods
6. Visualization
7. Teamwork
8. Report and publish
9. Languages
10. Quantitative text analysis
11. Statistical data analysis

With a volume of almost 20 pages, the list of individual functions is far too long to be reproduced in full here, especially since many functions are described in detail in the other 19 chapters of this book. Here, at the outset of working with the software, we will restrict ourselves to an initial overview of the basic functions for qualitative data analysis (point 4 of the list above); these are displayed in Table 1.2.

MAXQDA can support your work throughout every phase of a project. A central feature of MAXQDA and all QDA software is the option of working with codes (categories) and assigning codes to selected parts of your data—be these words or passages of a text, sections of an image, or scenes in a video. Since the beginnings of

Table 1.2 MAXQDA's basic functions for qualitative data analysis

Analysis function	Description
Coding	Assign codes to parts of a document (text passage, part of an image, video clip). Form categories inductively from the text, e.g., by in vivo coding, coding with colors as you would with a highlighter, coding with symbols ("emoticode"), assigning shortcuts for frequently used codes
Text search and automatic coding	Search for terms in all or selected documents of a project. Automatically code their locations with flexible determination as to the context to be coded (e.g., complete sentences, paragraphs)
Hierarchical category system	Work with a hierarchical category system (code system)—subcategories of up to 10 levels. Organize the category system and its layers via drag and drop. Use code favorites and code sets as a compilation of codes. Optional weighting of and comments on coded segments
Memos und comments	Attach memos to documents, codes, or data segments with your own comments, ideas, and hypotheses. Option to write free memos. Eleven different memo types and memo labels help you organize your memos. Search for and filter memos in table overviews. Search for terms in all documents or memos of a project
Paraphrasing	Select part of a text and summarize the content of this text passage in your own words
Thematic summaries	Summarize text passages to which the same code has been assigned on a case-by-case basis, i.e., write a summary of the statements on a specific topic for each document
Code search	Search for coded data segments by selecting ("activating") documents and codes. Interactive lists with results, simultaneously display segments in their original document. Filtering possible by activation, variables, colors, and weights
Classification with Variables, mixed methods	Assign demographic and other standardized information as variables for documents. Group and search data using variable values. Within the framework of mixed methods studies that combine quantitative and qualitative data
Links and references	Link individual text passages or image sections with each other and with external files, web pages, or geo-references
Logbook	Record valuable information on the working process of a research project in a research diary

QDA software development in the 1990s, the analytical technique of coding data segments has played a central role in qualitative analysis; however, there are also analytical approaches that are not category-based (Silver & Lewins, 2014, pp. 18–19). In this way, QDA software can also serve to support purely hermeneutic analyses by allowing quick searches for words and word combinations, as well as the display of references in context. Additionally, the ability to link points in texts and images together, thereby creating a hyper-structure across these documents, also works without categories and requires no coding of the data.

Methods for Qualitative Data Analysis

"What is, and to what end do we analyze qualitative data?" is a question one might pose, in the style of Friedrich Schiller's inaugural lecture in Jena. The answer would not come so easily, however, because there are many, indeed a great many qualitative methods: the program for the annual Magdeburg Methodological Workshops on Qualitative Education and Social Research (www.zsm.ovgu.de), for example, lists more than 40 methods. The list of methods that are the subject of the workshops at the Berlin Method Meeting (www.qualitative-forschung.de/methodentreffen/) is hardly any shorter:

> Psychoanalytically oriented social research, interpretation as co-construction, grounded theory methodology, qualitative content analysis, documentary method, sociological hermeneutics of knowledge, sociological hermeneutics of knowledge, biography and narration analyses, biographical case reconstruction, objective hermeneutics, observation protocols, triangulation, artifact analysis, sociological discourse analysis of knowledge, sequence analysis in text interpretation, figurative hermeneutics, film and television analysis, life-world analytical ethnography, auto-ethnography, systematic analysis of metaphors, grounded theory and situational analysis, biographical case reconstruction.

All these are methods which are described in varying degrees of detail in the relevant literature and are used to a varying extent in the practice of social research. It is also clear that the listed methods involve very different levels of abstraction. Scholars have often tried to create a typology of qualitative methods according to criteria of proximity to or distance from one another. The typology developed by Renata Tesch, for example, is well known; it groups methods according to their underlying research interest and distinguishes between four main types (Tesch, 1990, pp. 72–73):

- Research interest is focused on the characteristics of language.
- The research interest is directed toward the discovery of regularities.
- The research interest is focused on understanding the meaning of texts and actions.
- Research interest is focused on reflection.

Typologies of this kind are always confronted with the difficulty of plausibly assigning concrete methods such as grounded theory method, discourse analysis, or content analysis. Often there is not enough differentiation between method and methodology. As a sub-discipline of scientific theory, methodology deals with the inherent logic of methods, i.e., the question of which method is appropriate for certain research problems. Methods, on the other hand, designate planned procedures for achieving a certain goal, for example, the way in which a hypothesis is examined. Even though they may only be of limited use, typologies like the one by Tesch listed above give a certain overview and put the criteria of comparison up for discussion. Indeed, in their book focusing on QDA software, Silver and Lewins (2014, pp. 23–33) refrain from grouping and typifying the variety of methods and methodologies and instead sketch out five *strategies of analysis* that they believe are effectively supported by QDA software, namely, discourse analysis, narrative analysis, framework analysis, grounded theory method, and thematic analysis:

1. *Discourse analysis* refers to a wide range of language-based approaches to the analysis of texts, ranging from descriptive variants to Foucault's discourse analysis and critical discourse analysis. The data can be collected using various methods such as interviews and group discussions or is already available in the form of papers, articles, reports, speeches, etc. There are different approaches to discourse analysis in different disciplines, the common feature of which is that interest is directed toward language, words, sentences, and linguistic structures.
2. Silver and Lewins also see the field of *narrative analysis* as characterized by diversity. It is also about language and the analysis of texts, mostly interviews, diaries, existing narrative sources, and more. The methodologies and methods used in these fields (such as oral history) are numerous; Silver and Lewins name grounded theory, hermeneutics, and phenomenology.
3. *Framework analysis* is a special analysis technique that is category-based and organizes the key research topics in a matrix into which thematic summaries are entered. Silver and Lewins themselves point out the similarities of this relatively unknown approach with grounded theory, thematic analysis, and code-based methods.
4. *Grounded Theory* is a research style dating back to Glaser and Strauss (2009, firstly 1967). It is more of a methodology than a method. Since its beginnings, grounded theory has focused on the method of constant comparison. It is based on a multistage process of coding and working with memos. From initial open coding, one works in an interplay of new data collection, analysis, and memo writing up to codes of higher abstraction and higher importance. Grounded theory method has also diversified in recent decades, and there are now various variants, ranging from Corbin's more traditionally interpretative approach (Corbin & Strauss, 2015) to Charmaz's constructivist orientation (2014).
5. The *thematic analysis* is, as Silver and Lewins see it, a technique used in many approaches rather than as an independent method. In contrast to Foucault's discourse analysis or grounded theory, for example, the method of thematic analysis is not accompanied by certain basic methodological or epistemological assumptions. Thematic analysis is flexible, is used in many disciplines, and aims at a detailed description of the data rather than theory development.

These five strategies presented by Silver and Lewins clearly exhibit varying degrees of abstraction and have different theoretical foundations, sometimes a very far-reaching theoretical foundation such as Foucault's discourse analysis. This difference in the level of abstraction applies all the more to the two other strategies presented by Silver and Lewins, mixed methods research and visual analysis, which they describe as *broader approaches*. While mixed methods research sees itself as a methodology—Johnson, Onwuegbuzie, and Turner (2007, p. 129) even speak of a "third methodological paradigm"—the analysis of visual data material can certainly take place within the framework of grounded theory method, discourse analysis, or mixed methods.

This division into five strategies and two broader approaches, as well as the typology of Tesch, is obviously based on the observation that these various methodologies, methods, and techniques are all used to varying extents in empirical research and can all benefit from the support of QDA software. However, these groupings are not necessarily convincing in terms of their classification system. They are more like playlists on YouTube, which summarize similar things according to certain criteria but do not claim to create a system covering the entire field.

As you can see, there are diverse answers to the first part of the question, "What is, and to what end do we analyze qualitative data?," as asked at the beginning of this chapter. In fact, the answers are so diverse that it might be advisable to write whole separate texts, such as "Grounded Theory with MAXQDA," "Ethnography with MAXQDA," or "Critical Discourse Analysis with MAXQDA." However, this strikes us as a bit too ambitious at this stage. Instead, we will stick (for now) to providing you with a book about data analysis with MAXQDA that is method-spanning, but nevertheless method-oriented, and avoids giving too concrete instructions as those you might expect to find in a software reference manual.

Only a few of the methods described above try to answer the second part of the question based on Schiller's lecture, namely, to which end qualitative data analysis is to be carried out. This question extends beyond the area of methods and into the areas of methodology, epistemology, and ontology. In this book, which is primarily concerned with methods, we will exercise some caution regarding the further layers of epistemology and ontology over and above these methods. Nevertheless, we think it is worth pointing out that social science methods that utilize modern digital technologies presents tremendous opportunities for interdisciplinary work, the recognition of interrelationships and the development of theories. Of course, the methods described in this book cannot with certainty prevent you from getting lost in details, but at the very least they offer you the chance to develop far-reaching theories and thereby contribute to social transformation.

Is MAXQDA a Method?

Since the beginnings of software for computer-assisted qualitative data analysis, the methodological status of QDA software has been a matter of controversy. The following positions mark the two extremes of a broad spectrum of positions and opinions.

On the one hand, there is the position that CAQDAS imposes a certain method on the user. Working with categories is especially favored, for example, and interpretative methods are strongly disadvantaged. In other words, according to this view there is a kind of hidden curriculum with which CAQDAS provides a very specific direction of analysis that, in turn, is diametrically opposed to the classical qualitative approach to analysis. This view can already be found in the early 1990s with Barney Glaser, co-author of grounded theory (Glaser, 1992). Here, QDA software is essentially regarded as "devil's work" from the neoliberal world of thought, which brings about accelerated efficiency and thus serves as the death knell of the "good old times." This line of thought can still be found in current publications, such as those of Jo Reichertz (2014, 2016).

Other authors such as Kelle, Prein, and Bird (1995) and Fielding and Lee (1998) have opposed this argumentation by referring to the actual practice of empirical social research, which clearly demonstrates that CAQDAS is used within very different methods and methodologies. Against this background the metaphor of the toolbox is mentioned again and again, according to which CAQDAS is a method-neutral toolbox, from which you can choose the suitable tools depending on your preferred method. Real research practices are presented as proof of this, in which, for example, proponents of grounded theory as well as those of discourse analysis and those of qualitative content analysis all work with the same software.

Of course, there are a multitude of gradations between these two opposing positions of "devil's work" or the "toolbox." The advocates of QDA software, to which we also belong, have naturally mostly taken the second position (that of the "toolbox"). After more than a quarter of a century of QDA software development and the advent of Industry 4.0, autonomous driving, and enormous advances in artificial intelligence research, however, the time has come for us to critically rethink this position. The metaphor of "QDA software as a toolbox" does not adequately reflect the scope and depth of digitization and the changes in the research process CAQDAS has prompted. A toolbox, as a quick Google search for images will demonstrate, contains traditional *mechanical tools*. However, the computers and software of today cannot be compared to tools such as hammers, pliers, and screwdrivers. These are very complex algorithm machines. A magnetic resonance scanner used in medical diagnostics is also a tool but has a completely different status in the diagnostic process than a "clinical thermometer" or a "stethoscope"; in this context, the discussion as to whether CAQDAS is a separate method or merely a tool seems to be an idle discussion. However, if faced with answering the question "tool or method" as an either/or choice, regarding it as a method seems to us to be rather more appropriate than the tool metaphor, which plays down the effects of QDA software on the social practice of research (Zhao, Li, Ross, & Dennis, 2016).

In this context, it seems necessary to take another closer look and ask: what is a method? You will find several definitions, including the following from an online glossary:

> Methods are well-founded procedures used according to plan to achieve defined goals (usually within the framework of defined principles). Methods can be subject-specific. Methods include notation, systematic instructions and rules for checking the results.[1]

---

[1] Arbeitskreis "Informatik-Begriffsnetz" der Gesellschaft für Informatik e.V. (GI) referring Hesse et al. (1992), translated by the authors http://www.informatikbegriffsnetz.de/arbeitskreise/vorgehensmodelle/themenbereiche/prinzipMethodeWerkzeug.html [accessed: 2018/02/10]

A definition that can be found in the German Wikipedia is considerably softer:

> Method (Ancient Greek: μέθοδος, methodos) literally means a pursuit of knowledge, investigation, mode of prosecuting such inquiry, or system. In recent centuries it more often means a prescribed process for completing a task. It may refer to: Scientific method, a series of steps, or collection of methods, taken to acquire knowledge[2]

Taking these two definitions as a criterion, it seems difficult to deny that QDA software provides functions that are not found in any methodological textbook. Take geolinks, for example, which connect data with locations or features for visualizing data, as discussed in this book. Functions such as this can be described as methods. The criteria of a systematic approach and clear procedural instructions are undoubtedly fulfilled, at least to a much greater extent than is the case with very well-known qualitative methods such as grounded theory or phenomenological analysis. Hence, from a methodological perspective, that is, from the point of view of the study of scientific methods, QDA software constitutes a method or—to put it more carefully—*may* constitute a method under certain circumstances. This cautious wording, which always takes into account and checks for potential "implementations deficits," is of course also appropriate in relation to other methods. The mere assertion that one "has worked according to grounded theory" does not ipso facto prove that a method has been used.

Let us look again at the toolbox metaphor. Is it inaccurate to say that researchers who adhere to different schools and employ different analysis strategies have successfully used the same QDA program? Certainly not, there is enough empirical evidence to demonstrate that this has been done—and yet this still does not prove the validity of the tool metaphor. Instead, QDA software may more accurately be described as containing many analytical capabilities that can be used in different methodologies, research styles, or specific analysis techniques, which themselves may be influenced by these capabilities to a greater or lesser extent. Additionally, CAQDAS has great potential for methodological innovation that goes beyond existing research styles and methods. In other words, QDA software possesses a certain surplus of methods, which calls on users to make use of the extended methodological possibilities: similar to the original Grimm fairy tale (Grimm & Grimm, 2016), in which the loaves of bread in Mother Holle's oven shout out to the passing girl "Oh, take me out! Take me out!," these technical opportunities challenge researchers to apply them and thereby expand on the established methods.

---

[2]https://en.wikipedia.org/wiki/Method [accessed: 2018/02/10]

References

Charmaz, K. (2014). *Constructing grounded theory* (2nd ed.). Thousand Oaks, CA: SAGE.

Corbin, J. M., & Strauss, A. L. (2015). *Basics of qualitative research: Techniques and procedures for developing grounded theory* (4th ed.). Thousand Oaks, CA: SAGE.

Fielding, N., & Lee, R. M. (1998). *Computer analysis and qualitative research*. Thousand Oaks, CA: SAGE.

Glaser, B. G. (1992). *Basics of grounded theory analysis: Emergence vs forcing* (2nd ed.). Mill Valley, CA: Sociology Press.

Glaser, B. G., & Strauss, A. L. (2009). *The discovery of grounded theory: Strategies for qualitative research* (4th ed.). New Brunswick: Aldine.

Grimm, J., & Grimm, W. (2016). *The original folk and fairy tales of the brothers grimm: The complete first edition (Reprint)*. Princeton, NJ: Princeton University Press.

Johnson, R. B., Onwuegbuzie, A. J., & Turner, L. A. (2007). Toward a definition of mixed methods research. *Journal of Mixed Methods Research, 1*(2), 112–133. https://doi.org/10.1177/1558689806298224.

Kelle, U., Prein, G., & Bird, K. (1995). *Computer-aided qualitative data analysis: Theory, methods and practice*. Thousand Oaks, CA: SAGE.

Reichertz, J. (2014). Die Konjunktur der qualitativen Sozialforschung und Konjunkturen innerhalb der qualitativen Sozialforschung. In G. Mey & K. Mruck (Eds.), *Qualitative Forschung* (pp. 87–102). Wiesbaden: Springer VS.

Reichertz, J. (2016). *Qualitative und interpretative Sozialforschung: Eine Einladung*. Wiesbaden: Springer VS.

Silver, C., & Lewins, A. (2014). *Using software in qualitative research: A step-by-step guide* (2nd ed.). Thousand Oaks, CA: SAGE.

Tesch, R. (1990). *Qualitative research: Analysis types and software tools*. New York, NY: Falmer Press.

Zhao, P., Li, P., Ross, K., & Dennis, B. (2016). Methodological tool or methodology? Beyond instrumentality and efficiency with qualitative data analysis software [49 paragraphs]. *Forum Qualitative Sozialforschung/Forum: Qualitative Social Research, 2*(17), Art. 16. https://doi.org/10.17169/FQS-17.2.2597.

Getting to Know the Interface of MAXQDA

2

After you have clarified your research question(s), created a plan for your project, and perhaps even collected your first set of data, it is time to familiarize yourself with the MAXQDA interface. When you open MAXQDA after launching the program, it may seem similar to opening a toolbox for the first time. You might try to make sense of how it is organized, look into the different compartments, and take a tool or two in hand. There are many different ways to explore the unknown. The software includes tools, menus, and options waiting to be discovered and mastered.

> **In This Chapter**
> - Start working with the software: define a user name and create project
> - Learn how your work is saved
> - Get to know the four-window interface
> - Navigate the program via the main menu and context menus
> - Use the toolbars in the four main windows
> - Have an overview of MAXQDA's basic terminology

MAXQDA's Start Dialog

Once you have launched MAXQDA, a start dialog will appear containing all the tools you need to create new projects or open existing ones. Additionally, this window provides direct access to various online guides to MAXQDA, such as the Getting Started Guide and several video tutorials, as well as to a number of sample projects (Fig. 2.1). You can also submit feedback to the development team from here. When launching the program for the first time, it is important to enter a user name in the field at the top left of the window or at least double-check the name suggested by MAXQDA. This is especially important if several people are working on the same project, because in MAXQDA a lot of performed actions are tagged

© Springer Nature Switzerland AG 2019
U. Kuckartz, S. Rädiker, *Analyzing Qualitative Data with MAXQDA*,
https://doi.org/10.1007/978-3-030-15671-8_2

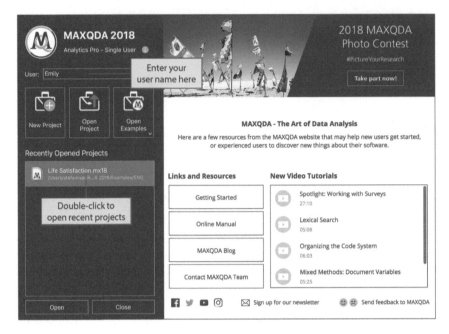

Fig. 2.1 MAXQDA's start dialog

with the respective user name. For this reason, it is best to avoid nicknames or fantasy names when choosing your user name and to use the same one across all devices. For projects with many collaborators who are to be granted different access rights, MAXQDA has a special user management system, which we describe in detail in Chap. 18.

MAXQDA works with *projects* in much the same way as Excel does with *workbooks*. Project files from MAXQDA 2018 always have the file extension . *mx18*; if the file extensions are hidden, you can recognize them by their file type "MAXQDA 2018 Project." (Almost) everything you import as data into MAXQDA is saved as part of your project—for example, transcripts of interviews or focus group discussions, documents, images, tables, and so on. Moreover, everything you create in the course of working with MAXQDA is also saved in the *project*, for example, your entire category system, your category descriptions, all your memos and notes, any links you add, as well as all the graphics and concept maps you create with the visualization tool MAXMaps.

Project files can be saved anywhere, but it is best to avoid opening projects stored in the cloud, on Dropbox, or similar, since unstable or slow network connections can then disrupt your work.

When it comes to saving project files, there is one key feature of MAXQDA which is so central to using the program that we have highlighted it in the following box:

> **Please Note**
> MAXQDA automatically saves everything you import into the program and everything you create with it. It is therefore not necessary to actively "save" your projects as you progress with your work.

In principle, the rule "one project = one file" applies to the storage of all your project data, which greatly simplifies data backup and transfer procedures. However, this rule does not apply to the often extremely large media files (a video file can quickly reach 1 gigabyte in size). For PDF files and images, you can specify the file size up to which you would like them to be saved in your project file. The default size is 5 megabytes, and this can be adjusted in MAXQDA's settings, which you can open via the gear symbol at the top right corner of the interface. You can find more detailed information on how to manage files which are not included in your project file, but stored externally, in Chap. 3.

Like all important data, MAXQDA project files should be backed up regularly. A simple method would be to create a copy of the project at the beginning of each working day and then add the current date to the file name. You can duplicate open projects via the main menu by selecting *Home > Save Project As.* Alternatively, you can create file copies using Windows Explorer or Mac Finder. MAXQDA also automatically creates backup copies: when a project is opened, the system checks when the last automatic backup took place and, if necessary, creates a project copy in the set backup folder. You can adjust the backup time interval and define a backup folder in MAXQDA's settings.

MAXQDA lets you open projects created with older MAXQDA versions. To do this, select the corresponding file type in the file dialog box, e.g., MX12 for project files from MAXQDA 12.

MAXQDA's User Interface

Once you have created your first project, you will at first see MAXQDA's distinctive interface—its four main windows will still be mostly empty at this point. At the top, you can see the *main menu* with several ribbon tabs which give you access to all the most important tools and functions in MAXQDA. The *Home* tab, for example, contains functions for opening projects, configuring the interface layout, or opening the logbook, in which you can record key insights and analysis steps just like in a research diary. The tabs of the additional modules MAXDictio and Stats are only visible if you have acquired the appropriate licenses. The view shown in Fig. 2.2 is identical on Mac and Windows, but unlike Windows, the Mac version of MAXQDA has an additional menu bar at the top of the screen. Since this menu contains the same options as the MAXQDA tabs, it is not necessarily needed, which is why you can easily switch to full screen mode on Mac and all the important functions will still be readily available. To maximize your working space, you can hide the main menu

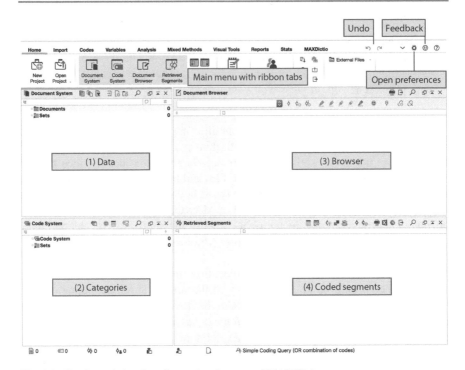

Fig. 2.2 The four-window interface and main menu of MAXQDA

(by clicking the arrow icon at the top right of the interface); clicking the tab names will reveal the menu again at any time.

The window at the top left of the figure (1) is called the "Document System" and will later contain all your data (sources) with which you can work. The second window (2), just below the first, is the "Code System," which will contain your category system. The third window (3) at the top right, the "Document Browser," is a working window in which documents can be viewed and edited. Here you can edit texts, code text passages or parts of images, add memos to texts, or link certain parts of documents with each other. Below this you will see the fourth window (4), the "Retrieved Segments." This is a results window in which coded segments are compiled in later stages of work.

These four windows form the basic structure of MAXQDA. You can change the arrangement of the windows (e.g., the relative window sizes), swap them (the two left windows on the right side), or arrange them in three columns instead of two. This can be done via the *Home* tab, which contains four icons for rearranging MAXQDA's main windows. The three-column view is very practical if you are working with a wide screen of an appropriate size.

On the right side of the top toolbar of each main window, there are three window control icons: ⊡ ⊼ ✕ . For example, you can remove a window from this arrangement to place it on a second monitor. It can also be expanded to its maximum size or closed. However, at least one of the four main windows will always remain open. The *Home* tab can be used to reopen windows that are not currently visible. Directly next to the control icons for adjusting the main windows, you will see *a magnifying glass* icon, which you can click to perform a local search within the respective window.

Below the main window, you will see the *status bar*, in which MAXQDA displays information about your current selections and currently active settings. If you move the mouse over an icon, its respective meaning will be displayed.

The MAXQDA interface can be displayed in numerous languages, including English, German, Spanish, Chinese, and Japanese. You can select your preferred language in MAXQDA's main settings, which you can access via the gear symbol in the top right corner of the interface.

The Context Menus and the Icons in the Main Windows

Context menus can be opened in each of the four main windows via a right mouse click. These menus provide all the functions relevant to the window in question. For example, all functions relating to managing your documents are available in the "Document System" window. These allow you to, for example, create (or delete) document groups and organize your documents in a logical manner. You can import documents of various types, start transcribing audio or video files, and much more. To open a context menu, right-click on the icon for which you want to view the relevant options. When you have just started working on a project and have not yet imported any data, the windows will initially be empty; hence the number of objects you can click this way will be very small. In the "Document System" window, you will only see two icons, for *Documents* and *Sets*. When you right-click on *Documents*, a thorough list of options for working with documents will appear, including import options. The same applies to the "Code System" window: here, too, only two icons will initially be visible. A right-click on *Code System* will display several options for working with codes (Fig. 2.3).

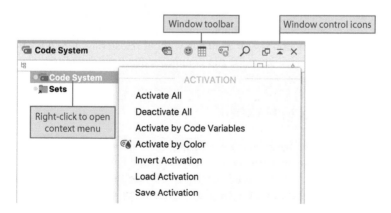

Fig. 2.3 Context menu in the "Code System" window

▶ **Tip** To right-click on a Mac computer, tap the trackpad with two fingers
simultaneously. For some devices, hold down the **Ctrl** or **control** key and
tap on the trackpad with one finger to right-click.

The header of each of the four main windows contains a row of icons that give
you easy access to tools related to the window in question. From here you can also
start a local search in the window and adjust the window's display settings. Additionally, the "Document Browser" and "Retrieved Segments" windows contain an
icon that allows you to export the contents of the window in various formats.

The Undo Function

Almost all the actions you can perform in MAXQDA, from importing a document,
to creating and deleting a category, to modifying a memo, can be undone. To do this,
there is an icon (a backward arrow) at the top right of the MAXQDA interface. With
the icon next to it (a forward arrow), you can restore an action that has been undone.

The Help Functions

At the top right of the MAXQDA menu bar, there is a question mark icon which
gives you access to MAXQDA's numerous help options. Clicking the question mark
will open a menu with links to MAXQDA's online help manual, the MAXQDA
Getting Started Guide, and online video tutorials. The online help manual contains
comprehensive information on the content and technical aspects of MAXQDA's
individual functions and is well-suited, for example, to looking up the setting options
of specific tools. It is also especially helpful that many MAXQDA dialog boxes
include a small info icon. Clicking this icon opens context-specific online help at the
corresponding location. The help menu also contains a list of available keyboard
shortcuts, which can make the program even quicker and easier to use.

If you need further support beyond that available on the MAXQDA website or via
the help menu, you may wish to access the MAXQDA user forum. You can register
for the forum online and post public questions (www.maxqda.com/en/support/
forum/). A search function is also available without registering, through which you
can find all the questions, answers, and comments that have already been posted.

Important Terms in MAXQDA

Before we explore the basic functions of MAXQDA in the chapters that follow, we
would like to take this opportunity to briefly explain the most important and, above
all, most frequently used terms in MAXQDA. While the names and terms in the
software are largely based on the standard terminology used in methods literature,

there are nevertheless certain MAXQDA-specific terms. Being familiar with these will prove very helpful when learning how to use the software. Over the next chapters, these terms will then be explained in greater detail in their respective contexts; you can easily leaf back to this chapter at a later stage to gain an overview of this "vocabulary."

Projects are the work and data storage units of MAXQDA. They contain all the data you import (texts, PDFs, images, etc.) or create (categories, coded segments, memos, comments, concept maps, etc.) during your analysis.

Documents are your project's data. Documents can contain different types of data such as interview texts, PDF documents, images, field notes, videos, and much more (see Table 1.1). The "Document System" window gives you access to the data contained within a project.

Document groups let you group documents together in the "Document System." These are comparable to folders on a computer. Usually data is grouped by type (e.g., interviews, focus groups, observations) or by content criteria (e.g., hospital A, B, and C or teachers, children, and parents).

Document sets let you group documents according to any criteria and allow for additional groupings of your data. Document sets are temporary in nature, that is, they can be deleted without deleting their corresponding documents. A document can belong to any number of document sets simultaneously and can also be removed from a document set without further consequences.

Codes are a key analysis tool. They enable you, among other things, to systematize and assign meaning to your data material. They can be assigned to text segments, image segments, or video clips. In MAXQDA all forms of categories are called codes; which underlying category is behind a given code is up to the researcher. The only exception to this rule is MAXDictio, the tool for word-based analysis and quantitative content analysis: here MAXQDA uses the term "category."

Code sets are the counterpart of document sets. They allow you to compile codes and are also temporary in nature, i.e. they can be deleted without deleting the corresponding codes. A code can belong to multiple code sets and be removed from a code set; it will nonetheless remain in the "Code System."

Code System or **code tree** refers to a project's complete set of categories and subcategories, which can be organize hierarchically in MAXQDA's "Code System" window.

Coding is the process of assigning a category (a code) to a currently selected section or part of data material.

Coded segments are the sections or parts of the data to which a code has been assigned.

Coding Query refers to the compilation of coded segments, e.g., all the coded segments on a given a topic.

Memos contain researchers' notes. They can be used to formulate and record assumptions and hypotheses about relationships or important findings in the data material. Code memos can also contain descriptions and instructions about the use of categories.

Comments always refer to specific coded segments and are shorter than memos. They can be used to make suggestions or identify contradictions in the data and can also be useful for category building and teamwork.

Document variables contain standardized information regarding each case, e.g., the level of education and the age of an interviewee.

Links enable you to connect a point or section in your data material to another point in the material, a website, a file, or a geolocation.

Overviews contain table lists of analysis information. There are overviews available for coded segments, memos, document variables, links, and other elements of analysis. Overviews make it easier to keep track of the substantial amounts of data that accumulate over the course of an analysis project.

Setting Up a Project and Importing Data

3

The development of MAXQDA was based on the research process in the social sciences. This means that the logic behind the analysis of qualitative data and mixed methods data can be directly applied to working with the software. It also means that there is no need to learn new terminology and that the software offers a high degree of flexibility. You can therefore collect new data, differentiate or integrate new categories, or reverse previously assigned codes at any time. Despite all this flexibility, however, it is still worthwhile thinking about the planning of a MAXQDA project, your analysis units (cases) and the optimal preparation of your data.

In This Chapter

- Planning a MAXQDA project and defining the organization of the relevant data: cases and analysis units, document groups, variables, etc
- Preparing your data: texts, PDF documents, pictures, videos and tables
- Importing data into the software
- Exploring the "Document Browser": using tabs, editing texts
- Managing your "Document System"
- Creating new texts in MAXQDA
- Documenting your analysis work: the logbook and project memos

What Should You Think About in Advance?

All research begins with a research question, whether it is very precise or somewhat vague. Even if you are not doing research but want to analyze the minutes of meetings of a given institution, company or association, etc., the question still arises as to how this data should be analyzed and how it should be prepared and organized.

© Springer Nature Switzerland AG 2019
U. Kuckartz, S. Rädiker, *Analyzing Qualitative Data with MAXQDA*,
https://doi.org/10.1007/978-3-030-15671-8_3

In this section we have compiled several relevant and frequently posed questions and answers regarding the organization of data in MAXQDA, which need to be clarified before beginning any analyses.

What Do You Define as a Case?
This is probably the most important question in data management. Since almost all MAXQDA analysis functions allow the inclusion, exclusion and comparison of individual documents, it is generally best to use the simple principle of "Each case in a separate document". For example, if each interview to be analyzed exists as a separate document, it is easy to compare interviews using MAXQDA and group them together for analysis, whereas it would significantly limit the analysis if several interviews were combined in one document. This principle of "one case = one document" is also supported by the fact that MAXQDA enables you to link exactly one qualitative document with exactly one set of quantitative data. In this way, the socio-demographic data of the interviewee can be entered for each interview, for example, or the membership figures and fields of activity can be recorded for individual annual reports of NGOs.

Responses to open-ended questions of a survey are often presented together with the relevant quantitative data in a data matrix, i.e. in a single table document. We recommend creating a separate document for each case inside your MAXQDA project to make full use of MAXQDA's analysis capabilities when analyzing open questions and also to be able to analyze qualitative coding results with statistics software later. MAXQDA can do this automatically when importing survey results, and this is described in detail in Chap. 16.

Analyses that track changes over periods of time are special in this regard. If a qualitative longitudinal study has been carried out with repeated interviews, video recordings or observations, it is usually helpful to create separate documents at each point in time this data was collected. This makes it easier to trace the development of a case during analysis.

How Should You Organize Your Documents?
If you have collected five interviews, you do not need to worry too much about organizing your project. But only a few more are enough to raise the question of how they should be grouped and systematized. MAXQDA is very flexible in this respect and allows you to use *document groups* and *document sets* to create different organizational structures for your data material. The division of the cases into different groups is often obvious and can be taken up directly from the research design. For example, cases can be classified according to survey time periods, surveyed groups (parents, teachers, students), professional status, organizational structure or also according to data types (interviews, focus groups, Twitter data). If the research question already entails the comparison of two or more groups, this should be reflected in your document groups in MAXQDA.

Although it is helpful to clarify this grouping of documents in advance, the arrangement can easily be adjusted later, i.e. you do not lock yourself into any system you set up during the import.

What Additional Quantitative Information Is Available?
As previously mentioned, MAXQDA allows you to assign a set of quantitative data to each document, for example, to record the age and professional status of interviewees. This additional quantitative information for individual documents is the key to MAXQDA's numerous mixed method functions, such as the use of "Joint Displays" (Guetterman, Creswell, & Kuckartz, 2015). When conducting a mixed methods study, it is also useful to clarify what qualitative data and what quantitative data is available and at what levels and at which point this data should be integrated: at the end of the research project when contrasting results or already during the analysis (Kuckartz, 2017).

What Should You Consider When It Comes to Transcriptions and Audio/Video Recordings?
MAXQDA enables you to assign an audio or video file to every transcript and to connect both through timestamps. Clicking on a timestamp in the transcript will instantly play that part of the original recording. If you have completed transcripts available, you might consider whether such links are necessary for further analysis and whether the relevant audio and video files need to be accessed from within your MAXQDA project.

If you want to transcribe recordings using MAXQDA, you should certainly ask yourself, among other things, what type of transcription method you want to use. Do you need to transcribe everything word for word, or is a partial and/or summarized transcription sufficient to answer the research questions? You can find more information about transcribing with MAXQDA in Chap. 4.

Should All Your Data be Stored in One Project or in Several?
Usually it is a good idea to save all the data of a research project in a single MAXQDA project. This facilitates easy access to your data and allows for cross-over analyses that involve different data collection methods and different sets of material. However, when it comes to teamwork it is often helpful to work on smaller subprojects that can be merged into one project later, since these subprojects will have smaller file sizes and offer a clearer overview of the work. We have provided further relevant information about teamwork in Chap. 18.

Preparing Data

Of course, researchers are generally quite eager to start analyzing their data as quickly as possible, but it is always best to carefully prepare your data for computer-assisted analysis in advance. This can usually be done rather quickly and will save subsequent—and usually difficult—reworking later.

Anonymization is a particularly important step in the preparation of research data. Depending on how sensitive the data is, who will be working on the MAXQDA project, whether the project will be passed on to third parties later or even made publicly accessible, varying degrees of anonymization will be necessary. Standard procedures can be used to this end: by using "Search" and "Replace" in your word processing program, the names of respondents and other people in the transcripts can be replaced with pseudonyms or abbreviations. Other people, places, professional positions and other information which could be identifying can be replaced by more general terms like {sister}, {city}, {managing director} etc., though it should be noted that potentially significant contextual information can be lost in this process. Since it is advisable to carry out the later exploration of the data with computer assistance in MAXQDA (cf. Chap. 5), you can limit the pre-anonymization of texts to the simple and automatable steps and manage the anonymization of further identifying information in MAXQDA at a later stage; texts can be edited even after importing them into the software. In any case, it is important to create an anonymization list (usually kept outside the MAXQDA project) showing which names and information have been replaced by which anonymized data.

In contrast to text data, PDF documents generally permit only very limited processing and are difficult to render anonymous, which fortunately is rarely necessary. However, in the event that a PDF document must be made anonymous, text content can be adapted, and elements removed using the "Adobe Acrobat" program. If you need to make extensive changes to a PDF document, it may be better to extract the entire text with the help of a software tool and save it as a normal text file.

Images can also only be anonymized to a limited extent. Using image editing tools, people and other critical areas can be blacked out or masked, but relevant interpretive data can be lost in this process. With audio and video files there is even less likelihood of being able to anonymize the recordings without losing too much relevant information. In this case you will more likely need to think about securing safe storage locations during the project and finding appropriate ways to present the data in publications.

▶ **Tip** MAXQDA also offers the option in the *Home* ribbon tab of saving project copies in which selected text passages are automatically anonymized by xxx. The prerequisite is that the relevant text passages are coded as described in Chap. 6.

Preparing Text Documents
In addition to anonymization, other aspects of text data should be checked and processed. Whether you are working with interview transcripts, research notes or other text data, a font type and size that is easy to read on screen should be selected. We also recommend setting a line spacing of 1.1–1.5. Although texts can be corrected later in MAXQDA, the texts should first be run through a spell checker, so that you do not have to worry about avoidable typing errors during later analysis and can fully concentrate on the actual data. For interview transcripts, it is also wise to ensure a uniform spelling of the interviewer's and interviewees' names to be able

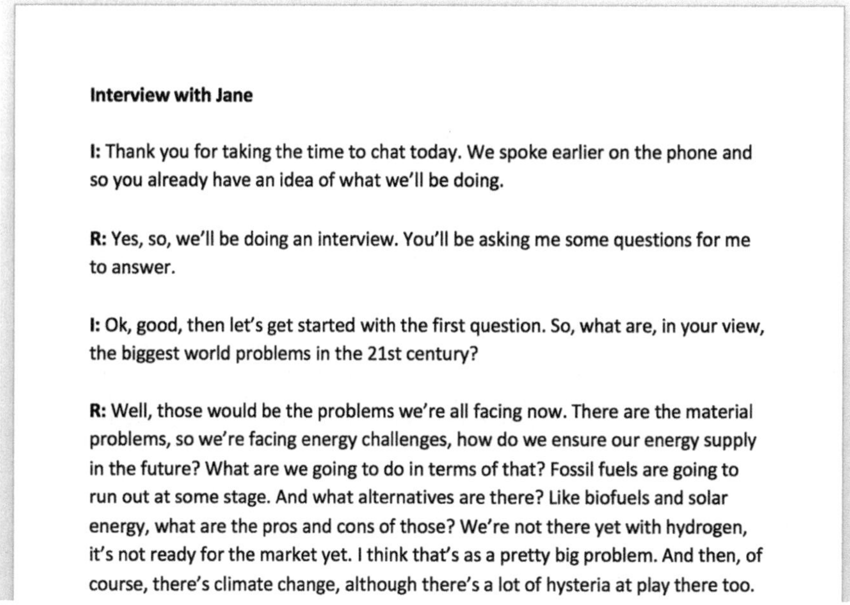

Interview with Jane

I: Thank you for taking the time to chat today. We spoke earlier on the phone and so you already have an idea of what we'll be doing.

R: Yes, so, we'll be doing an interview. You'll be asking me some questions for me to answer.

I: Ok, good, then let's get started with the first question. So, what are, in your view, the biggest world problems in the 21st century?

R: Well, those would be the problems we're all facing now. There are the material problems, so we're facing energy challenges, how do we ensure our energy supply in the future? What are we going to do in terms of that? Fossil fuels are going to run out at some stage. And what alternatives are there? Like biofuels and solar energy, what are the pros and cons of those? We're not there yet with hydrogen, it's not ready for the market yet. I think that's as a pretty big problem. And then, of course, there's climate change, although there's a lot of hysteria at play there too.

Fig. 3.1 Prepared interview text in Word

to easily distinguish their contributions later for automated searches and analyses. For a well-prepared interview text, see Fig. 3.1:

- The first line contains the name of the interviewee for easy identification of the text.
- Each contribution has its own paragraph and a blank line is inserted between each contribution for better differentiation.
- All contributions of the interviewer are introduced by the abbreviation "I:", of the interviewee by "R:"; of course, more meaningful names, pseudonyms or abbreviations for the interviewees can also be used.

Figure 3.2 depicts the interview transcript directly after importing it into MAXQDA. During the import, the formatting of the font and paragraph are retained. The contents of headers and footers, footnotes and endnotes, page numbers and comments whose texts appear in bubbles on the margins in word processing programs are not imported. In the image you can also see that MAXQDA includes a column with the paragraph numbers in the left margin. All non-empty paragraphs are consecutively numbered, which can be used as references when quoting from interview transcripts. It is important to emphasize that the paragraph numbers are not inserted directly into the text but are numbered only in the MAXQDA display. If a paragraph is added to or deleted from an imported text in MAXQDA, this numbering also changes.

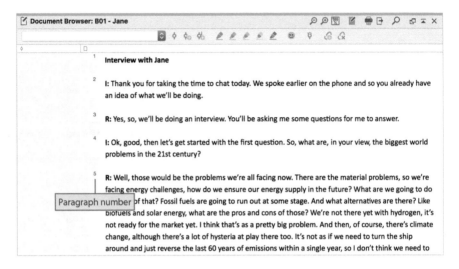

Fig. 3.2 Imported interview transcript in MAXQDA

> ▶ **Tip** For some methods and research styles it is necessary to be able to
> quote the data material line by line. In these cases, paragraph numbering
> is not sufficient. After switching on the Edit Mode (see below), right-click
> to select the function **Convert to line numbered text** and specify a
> maximum line length in characters. MAXQDA then automatically inserts
> paragraphs breaks at the end of each line so that the result is numbered
> to the exact line. Depending on the screen width and desired level of
> detail, a line width of 60–100 characters is recommended.

When importing texts into MAXQDA, color settings are not transferred because they would be overwritten in MAXQDA when working with the highlighter tool and other text marking functions. Images and graphics contained in the text are imported by default, but you should make sure that these are not multiple 20-megapixel photos (importing images directly is better suited for this) and that their resolutions are reduced in advance for display on screen.

When working in MAXQDA, it is impractical to work with very long tables in one text. If you are dealing with a transcript that was stored entirely in a single table, it is better to split it up before importing it and make the speaker changes identifiable, as shown in Figs. 3.1 and 3.2. In Microsoft Word, this can easily be done using the "Convert to Text" function in the "Layout" tab.

It is important to note that you can also transcribe directly in MAXQDA, which we describe in detail in Chap. 4. In this case, you can set the font formatting in MAXQDA in advance and usually anonymize the data as you enter it.

There are also special notes for the preparation of focus group transcripts, which can be read in detail in Chap. 15.

Preparing PDF Documents

Since PDF documents are standardized files that cannot be edited, there are usually no or only few precautions to be taken when importing them into MAXQDA. PDF files can contain both text and images that can be selected or highlighted. If you want to analyze a scanned book, you should check in a PDF reader whether the text can already be selected. If this is not the case, programs such as Adobe Acrobat can perform optical character recognition (abbreviated to "OCR") to convert the images into editable text. Adobe Acrobat can also be used to reduce the size of a PDF file to optimize storage.

If you are only interested in the pure text without its layout, you can save a PDF file in TXT format using the free Adobe Reader and import this file into MAXQDA after. Alternatively, the steps "(1) Select all in PDF", "(2) Copy to clipboard" and then "(3) Paste clipboard contents into Word or MAXQDA" can achieve quite good results, even retaining most of the font and formatting.

Preparing Images

Images require very little preparation for later analysis. Before importing them, the quality of the images should briefly be checked. This can be automatically improved in many programs by clicking "Optimize".

If several hundred images are to be analyzed, it is also wise to keep an eye on your available memory. Due to the multitude of image formats and resolutions, and continual technical improvements, it is difficult to give concrete figures at this stage. As a rough guideline, however, you can expect a JPG image taken with a modern smartphone to measure around 4000×3000 pixels, take up approx. 2–3 megabytes of memory space and have sufficient quality even on high-resolution retina or 4K monitors. The more you are interested in any details and the greater the need to zoom in, the more pixels the images should contain.

Preparing Tables

If you have data in a table form and want to preserve this format for analysis in MAXQDA, please note the following: the table will be copied one-to-one into your MAXQDA project where it can be sorted alphabetically, in ascending or descending order, according to each individual column. If you reset this sort order, the table will be reset to the sort order it originally had when you imported it, so you should ensure that the table is organized in meaningful way before importing it.

Table documents can also be used in MAXQDA to perform paraphrasing, as suggested by Mayring (2014). Since MAXQDA does not let you subsequently add columns or rows to an imported table, you should add enough extra columns next to the text before importing to allow for this paraphrasing process. Notwithstanding this, however, the *Analysis > Paraphrases* function, which we describe in Chap. 11, is better suited to paraphrasing.

Preparing Audio and Video Data

MAXQDA can play most standard audio and video formats, so preparation is rarely necessary. Only when MAXQDA indicates that the given format cannot be played, or if your file has a very rare format, should it be converted into a standard format before importing it, e.g. with free applications like XMediaRecode for Windows or with Apple's own QuickTime for Mac. The MP4 format with the H.264 codec is recommended for videos and the MP3 or M4A format for audio files. On Windows, the WMV and WMA formats are also suitable, but these cannot be played on a Mac, which can make teamwork difficult.

Importing Text Files

Once you have created a new project in MAXQDA as described in Chap. 2, you can begin importing your prepared data. After selecting the function *Import > Documents*, a file dialog will open in which you can select all the files that MAXQDA can handle. Here you can click on individual files or select several files while holding down the *Ctrl* (Windows) or *command* ⌘ key (Mac). Figure 3.3 shows how three imported texts appear at the top of the MAXQDA "Document System" window after they have been imported. Documents in MAXQDA are automatically labelled with their file names, which is why it makes sense to assign meaningful, unique and uniformly structured names to your text files before importing them. Of course, you can always rename these documents after importing them into MAXQDA, e.g. by simply right-clicking on the name in the "Document System".

Texts are saved directly to your MAXQDA project when you import them—and they will no longer be linked to the original files. If a text is modified in MAXQDA, this has no effect on the original text and vice versa. If you send the project file by e-mail, it will include all your imported texts.

The word "Sets", which you can see at the bottom of Fig. 3.3, has the following meaning: compilations of any number of documents can be saved in so-called *document sets*. A document set contains a short-cut link to each document listed within it, there is no duplication of data. There can be any number of links in each set and any document can be linked to any number of different sets. Sets facilitate quick groupings of documents for a variety of analytic purposes. Document sets are particularly useful for group comparisons in later stages of analysis, which we describe in detail in Chap. 12.

Fig. 3.3 The "Document System" window after importing three text files

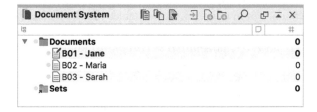

Viewing and Editing Texts Using the "Document Browser"

The fastest way to open a document is to double-click on its name in the "Document System". The document will then be opened and displayed in the "Document Browser" window. The pencil symbol in the document icon in front of the document name, as well as the document name in the title bar of the "Document Browser", indicate which document is currently open. By right-clicking on a document in the "Document System", you can open a context menu, as shown in Fig. 3.4, which will offer you further options as to how to open it. Documents can be opened in a new tab, for example, which is convenient for quickly switching between documents (Fig. 3.5), or they can be displayed in a second "Document Browser" so that two documents can be viewed simultaneously.

Further down in the context menu you can also assign colors to a document. This is useful, for example, to keep track of your progress, for example documents marked in red are currently in the process of being analyzed while for documents marked in green, the first analysis has already been completed.

As in all MAXQDA's four main windows, you will see a toolbar along the top edge of the "Document Browser" (Fig. 3.6).

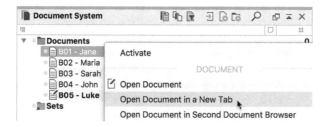

Fig. 3.4 Document context menu in the "Document System"

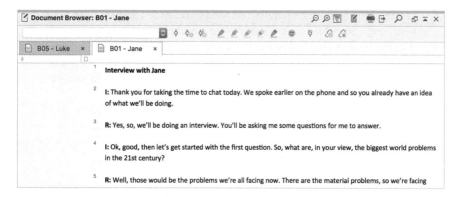

Fig. 3.5 The "Document Browser" with two open texts in two tabs

Fig. 3.6 Toolbar in the "Document Browser"

Among other things, this toolbar contains icons for expanding and reducing the window as well as for editing, printing and exporting the document:

Edit mode on/off—Once you have opened a document you normally can't change it, since it would be quite inconvenient if a document you want to analyze were accidentally changed by an inadvertent keystroke. Hence, to be able to edit a document and correct typing errors, for example, you must first activate the Edit Mode by clicking on the Edit icon. To protect a text document from unintended editing, open *Properties* in the document's context menu and select the *Read-only* option. When the Edit Mode is switched on, the global undo function of MAXQDA is disabled. This means that changes made before or while the Edit Mode is switched on cannot be undone. Text changes in the Edit Mode can be undone using the icon in the Edit Mode toolbar, but only while this mode remains switched on.

Print document—A text document can be printed with the paragraph numbers assigned by MAXQDA (and other later analysis details such as the coding stripe at the edge of the text)—on paper or in a PDF file, which can be integrated into the appendix of a research paper.

Export document—The opened text can be saved to any location as a Word or Excel file. You can choose whether the paragraph numbers assigned by MAXQDA are also to be exported, which is very helpful for documentation purposes. The exported file can also serve as an attachment to a publication.

▶ **Tip** Beyond importing texts you can also create them in MAXQDA via the *Create Document* option in the *Import* ribbon tab. The newly created document is opened directly in Edit Mode and here you can enter your new text. Sometimes you get better results when importing text documents on a Mac, particularly when you want to preserve the original formatting, if you create a new document in this way and copy the content of the original text document in your word processing program and paste it into the new document in MAXQDA via the clipboard.

Managing Documents and Document Groups Within the "Document System"

Documents can be organized and systematized with the help of so-called *document groups*: right-click on the word "Documents" in the top row of your "Document System" to open a context menu and select the entry *New Document Group*. These

Fig. 3.7 The "Document
System" with document
groups

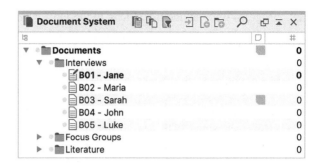

groups are only available at the uppermost level; document groups cannot be contained or created within other document groups. Document groups are mainly useful as a visual grouping to facilitate locating a particular document during analysis.

Documents can be moved back and forth between document groups via drag and drop, and you can select multiple documents by holding down the *Alt* key (Windows) or the *option* ⌥ key (Mac). You can save yourself this quite time-consuming moving work by using the import function available in a document group's context menu. The imported files will then be imported directly to the selected group. The same applies when the target document group is highlighted in blue as in Fig. 3.7 and you import your documents via the main menu.

Document sets, as mentioned above, can be reorganized as needed, without having to continually reorder individual documents. This means you will not be locked into your original grouping of documents when it comes to later analyses.

Importing PDF Documents, Images, and Tables

PDF documents, images and Excel spreadsheets can be imported using the same functions as text documents, e.g. via the previously mentioned ***Import > Documents*** option in the main menu. In the "Document System", different document types can be distinguished by their own document icons, and in the "Document Browser", special functions are available for individual document types (Fig. 3.8):

⊡ PDF documents—For quick navigation, there are some icons displayed in the "Document Browser" toolbar with which you can scroll page by page, jump to the beginning or end, or jump to bookmarks within the document. You can also adjust the zoom to suit the page width or the entire page.

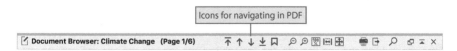

Fig. 3.8 The toolbar in the "Document Browser" for PDF documents

📷 Images—With an additional icon in the toolbar, images can be rotated by 90° and the display can also be adjusted to suit the window width.

🖿 Excel table—When importing Excel tables, only the plain text is copied, and the columns and rows are numbered consecutively. After switching on the Edit Mode, you can edit the text in single cells.

MAXQDA generally adheres to the principle of "All your data in a single project file". However, since PDF documents and images can be very large and could therefore result in very large and unwieldy project files, you have the option of not embedding PDF documents and images into the project file itself, but instead saving them externally in a user-defined folder. Only references to the externally stored documents will then be stored in the project file.

Managing Externally Stored Files
This of course raises the question of how externally stored documents can be managed from within MAXQDA and synchronized across several computers, especially when working in teams. By default, PDF documents and images larger than 5 megabytes are copied to the folder for external files and not embedded into the project file. In these cases, MAXQDA will warn you that the file in question will not be embedded when you import it. Both the folder for external files (also called the "Externals Folder" for short) and the size limit for embedded files can be changed in MAXQDA's settings. You can access the settings via the gear symbol in the upper right-hand corner of the interface. If the threshold value is 0 megabytes, all PDF files and images will be saved in the folder for external files and not embedded into the project file (Fig. 3.9).

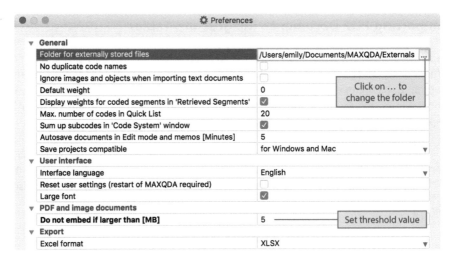

Fig. 3.9 Options for embedding and storing external files

The folder for external files should always be stored on a (preferably fast) local drive so that the loading time when opening a document is as quick as possible. While we do not recommend opening project files directly from Drobox or similarly synchronized cloud folders, it is still technically possible to select a synchronized folder as your folder for the external files—which you may wish to do if you are working in a team or on different computers.

For files that you want to save externally, you should pay special attention to their file names before importing them. After they have been imported they may not be renamed in the folder for externally stored files, otherwise the link will be lost. Of course, the document names in MAXQDA can be customized, but this has no effect on the link or the name of the externally saved file.

There are two different strategies for working with PDF documents and images, depending on what is technically feasible. First, you can integrate all documents into the project file. This is useful if the data volume is manageable and the project file can be easily sent and saved between team members despite its size. Second, you can save all your files externally so that you have a small project file that is easy to back up and exchange, which, for example, is useful if there are going to be no additions to the externally stored files, so that once they have been copied to all members of the team there is no need to share them again.

Importing and Playing Audio and Video

Audio and video files are never stored in a MAXQDA project file due to their potential size. In the "Document System" they are not listed as independent documents but are always assigned to a text document in which a complete or partial transcript of the media file can be stored. Text documents with associated media files are indicated by a corresponding icon in the "Document System": a musical note for audio files and a film camera for video files (Fig. 3.10).

Audio and video files can be added to a project like other files via *Import > Documents*. A new text document is created for each imported file and the media file is assigned to the newly created document. In addition, the media file is always automatically copied to the folder for external files.

You can also assign a media file to an existing text document. To do this, right-click on the document in the "Document System" and select *Properties*. In the dialog window that opens, you can add (or change) the link to a media file. Alternatively, you can create a link by right-clicking on the document and selecting *Link Audio/ Video File*.

Fig. 3.10 Audio/video file in the "Document System"; opening a video file in the "Document Browser"

Fig. 3.11 Multimedia browser for displaying video files and audio tracks

To play an audio or video file, open the corresponding text document and click on the icon with the note or video camera at the far left of the toolbar of "Document Browser" window (Fig. 3.10). This will open the so-called "Multimedia Browser", which can be used to play back and analyze the media file (Fig. 3.11). A wave form of the audio track is displayed in the "Multimedia Browser" to make navigating the file easier. Preview thumbnail images can also be created for videos for better navigation. The process can take several minutes, depending on the length and type of video.

When importing or opening a media file for the first time, MAXQDA creates a file with the extension .dat in the folder for externally saved files. This file has the same name as the media file and contains its audio track and—if they have been created—any preview images. If you are working in a team or want to edit the same project file on several computers with MAXQDA, we recommend copying these .dat files to the external files folder on all computers, as this will save time when loading the audio track and the preview images on the other computers.

Please Note

MAXQDA always searches for externally saved audio, videos, PDF files and images in a specified order when opening a document. First it tries to open the file from the original location. If the file no longer exists in this location, the system searches in the folder for external files. If the file cannot be opened from here, MAXQDA will look in the folder where the open project is saved.

Importing Web Pages

Company websites, newspaper articles and blog articles are typical examples of web pages the form and content of which can be qualitatively analyzed. To import web pages into MAXQDA, the MAXQDA Web Collector is a free extension for the Chrome browser. The easiest way to install the extension is to search the internet for "MAXQDA Web Collector Chrome" to access the Chrome Web Store, then click **Add**. Once you have installed the extension, a small MAXQDA icon will appear in the upper right corner of your browser. Click this icon to prepare the web page opened in Chrome to import into MAXQDA. The Web Collector will open and give you a choice between two options (Fig. 3.12):

- Web Page—saves the website including all graphics and retaining the layout.
- Simplified Web Page—reduces the presentation of the website to its text and the individual images contained in the text, similar to the read mode for articles on mobile phones. This function can only be selected if the current page can be viewed in a reduced format.

In the Web Collector, you can assign a name and write a memo to the page for when it is included as a document in MAXQDA. In this way you can make a note of important information for the research process, such as why the page was selected or how you found it. Click **Collect** to download the website. The Web Collector will then create a separate file, with the extension .mxml, for each downloaded website in your chosen Downloads folder.

Go to **Web Collector Data** in the **Import** ribbon tab of MAXQDA's main menu to import the downloaded files. An options dialog box will appear in which all of the web pages in the chosen folder are listed and in which different formats can be selected for the import (Fig. 3.13). Simplified websites are usually imported as text

Fig. 3.12 MAXQDA Web Collector in the Chrome browser

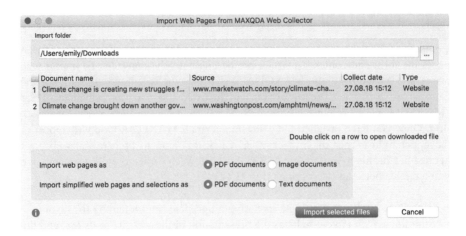

Fig. 3.13 Dialog box for importing web pages into MAXQDA

documents. Whole web pages, on the other hand, are usually imported as PDF documents, because in this case the layout is retained for analysis and the text on the web page can be coded and searched.

If a web page is already saved in an HTML format, it can also be imported directly (without using the Web Collector) via ***Import > Documents***. MAXQDA then creates a new text document. However, this can lead to changes in the layout, which is why this form of import is usually only suitable for text-oriented analyses.

Recording Meta-Information in Memos

Memos are very powerful analysis tools in MAXQDA. They allow you to record your own notes, comments and thoughts at any time and attach them to almost any part of the data material, similar to the yellow Post-it® note that are used with paper documents. Once you have made your project preparations and imported your data, it is helpful to record a summary of your methodological procedure in a so-called *project memo* (Fig. 3.14): "Which research questions are being pursued", "What data was collected when and within what type of research design?" This meta-information about your research is an effective way of providing quick and easy access to relevant details about your project to team members, assistants and later reviewers. Storing this meta-information in your project file is also advisable for documentation and archiving purposes, which can prove particularly useful should you go back to an old file a few years later.

To create a new memo for your overall project, right-click on the top row of the "Document System" (the row with the word "Documents") and select ***Memo*** in the context menu. A memo input dialog box as shown in Fig. 3.14 will open. In the upper area you can enter a title for your memo and select a memo type by clicking on one of the 11 yellow icons that defines how the memo will be displayed on

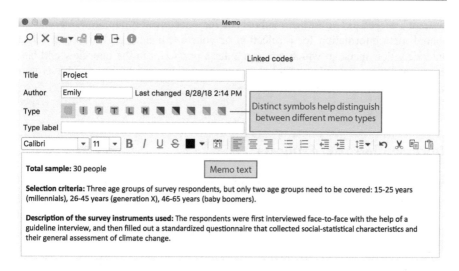

Fig. 3.14 A memo with information about a research project

MAXQDA's interface. You can enter and format the actual content of the memo in the lower area of the dialog box. Using the clipboard, texts and even graphics and tables can be copied and pasted directly into the memo. Even for memos there is no extra save button; MAXQDA creates the memo immediately and when you close the input dialog box all the changes you have made will be saved. In addition, your memos are automatically saved within your project file every 5 minutes by default. This time interval for automatic saving can be adjusted in MAXQDA's settings and also applies to texts opened in Edit Mode.

Memos are displayed as yellow notes on the MAXQDA interface and can be opened by simply double-clicking on their yellow icon. Figure 3.15 displays the project memo icon within the so-called memo column at the top of the "Document

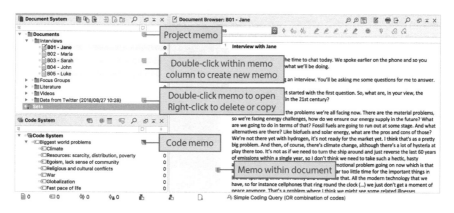

Fig. 3.15 Direct access to memos on MAXQDA's user interface

System", as well as two further memos: one for a document group, in which you can record meta-information for a selection of your documents; and a second for an interview document, in which you can enter a postscript to the interview and later case summaries. A preview of the memo content is displayed when you hover your cursor over a memo icon.

Documenting Your Progress

When you are getting started on a research project and full of enthusiasm, it may seem like a nuisance to record every decision, every milestone and every path taken in the analysis process in a research diary. But then when it comes to writing the methods chapter for a publication, it will quickly become clear just how valuable this stage-by-stage documentation over the course of your project can be—and how much work you can save yourself by avoiding the need to jog your memory for the details of those stages in your research process. One of the characteristics of a good empirical study is clear documentation that presents the research process in a transparent and comprehensible manner. How was the data collected and how was it anonymized? Which analytical procedure was chosen for which purpose and why? MAXQDA does some of this documentation work for you: when importing documents, the import date and user name under which the import was performed are noted in the project file. Both details appear in a tooltip when you hover your cursor over a document name. Newly created memos and the codes described later in this book are also annotated with an author name and date.

MAXQDA provides a so-called *logbook* for writing a research diary, which can be accessed in the *Start* tab of the main menu. As with memos, you can note any text here; clicking on the first icon with the calendar creates a new date entry, which can be very useful for documenting the course of your project over time (Fig. 3.16).

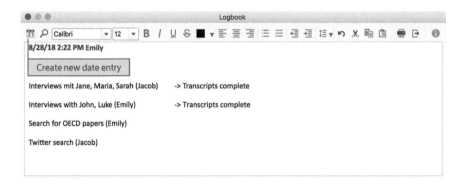

Fig. 3.16 Using the logbook as a research diary

References

Guetterman, T., Creswell, J. W., & Kuckartz, U. (2015). Using joint displays and MAXQDA software to represent the results of mixed methods research. In M. T. McCrudden, G. J. Schraw, & C. W. Buckendahl (Eds.), *Use of visual displays in research and testing: Coding, interpreting, and reporting data*. Charlotte, NC: Information Age Publishing.

Kuckartz, U. (2017). Datenanalyse in der Mixed-Methods-Forschung: Strategien der Integration von qualitativen und quantitativen Daten und Ergebnissen. *KZfSS Kölner Zeitschrift für Soziologie und Sozialpsychologie, 69*(S2), 157–183. https://doi.org/10.1007/S11577-017-0456-Z.

Mayring, P. (2014). *Qualitative content analysis: Theoretical foundation, basic procedures and software solution*. Klagenfurt. Retrieved from http://nbn-resolving.de/urn:nbn:de:0168-ssoar-395173

Transcribing Audio and Video Recordings

4

Many researchers dearly wish there was a software that could automatically transcribe recorded interviews. Well, unfortunately, there is still no reliable way of doing this, so in most cases you have to transcribe audio recordings of interviews or focus groups in the traditional way. MAXDQA's Transcription Mode makes this work a great deal easier, but, despite this valuable support, transcribing still takes a lot of time and effort. You will be rewarded, however, by the fact that you can play the original sound at any time and that you can quickly jump to interesting points in the recording via timestamps. As for video recordings, transcriptions may not be absolutely necessary in every case or can be limited to only specific parts of the material.

In This Chapter
- Setting appropriate transcription rules
- Selecting effective transcription settings and starting the transcription process
- Writing partial transcriptions of media files
- Setting and managing timestamps to link transcripts to recordings
- Importing transcripts with timestamps
- Checking completed transcripts

No Transcription Without Rules

In today's research environment, interviews and focus groups are usually recorded with an audio recorder or a smartphone. The recording should be transcribed as soon as possible after the interview so that any potential unintelligible passages can be more easily completed through memories of the spoken words. It depends on the objective of the analysis how detailed and exact the transcription needs to be and

© Springer Nature Switzerland AG 2019
U. Kuckartz, S. Rädiker, *Analyzing Qualitative Data with MAXQDA*,
https://doi.org/10.1007/978-3-030-15671-8_4

which rules should be followed. There are numerous transcription systems (Dresing & Pehl, 2015; Hepburn & Bolden, 2017; Kuckartz, 2014) which differ, among other things, in how particular verbal and nonverbal elements are taken into account in the transcription process. Transcriptions are time-consuming and can therefore also be a cost factor, so it is important to consider what level of accuracy is truly necessary in order to answer your research questions. In most cases, relatively simple transcription systems are sufficient. We defined a set of simple and easy-to-learn transcription rules as part of a previous evaluation project. These software-independent rules are—as supplemented by our own experiences in the meantime and further recommendations by Dresing and Pehl (2015)—listed here:

1. Each speech contribution is transcribed as a separate paragraph. To increase readability, after the paragraph, a blank line is added.
2. Paragraphs for interviewer(s) or moderator(s) are introduced by "I:" or "M:", those for the interviewee(s) by unique abbreviations, e.g., "R:". Numbers are added to the abbreviations ("M1:", "M2:", "R1:", "R2:", etc.) to distinguish between several people in a recording. As an alternative to abbreviations, names or pseudonyms can be used. Labels for speakers are written in bold for better recognition.
3. Speech is transcribed verbatim, i.e., not phonetically or in summary form. Dialects are not transcribed but translated as accurately as possible into the standard form, e.g., standard English.
4. Language and punctuation are standardized slightly where necessary, i.e. to approximate written language. For example, from "He's gonna write a book" to "He is going to write a book." The word order, definite and indefinite articles, etc. are retained even if they contain errors.
5. Clear, longer pauses are indicated by ellipsis points in brackets (. . .). Depending on the length of the pause in seconds, one, two, or three points are used; for longer pauses, a number (in digits) corresponding to the duration in seconds.
6. Intentionally stressed words are underlined.
7. Very loud speech is indicated by writing in capital letters.
8. Affirmative or agreeing utterances made by interviewers (mhm, aha, etc.) are not transcribed so long as they do not interrupt the flow of speech of the interviewee.
9. Short interjections made by the other person, such as "Yes" or "No," are included in brackets in the speech without starting a new paragraph.
10. External interruptions or interferences are noted in double brackets stating the cause, e.g., (cell phone rings).
11. Vocal utterances made by both the interviewee and the interviewer are noted in simple brackets, e.g., (laughs), (groans), or similar.
12. For videos: nonverbal actions are placed in simple brackets, such as (opens the window), (turns away), or similar.
13. Incomprehensible words and sections are identified by (unclear).
14. All information that would allow an interviewee to be identified is to be rendered anonymous.

> **I:** And you're meeting up just now at the end (**R:** Yes, exactly.) or have you been meeting up for a while.
>
> **R:** Well, during the practice sessions we often had lunch together and did other things but yes, we've only met up for this at the end.
>
> **I:** Right, right. What grade are you expecting in your exam?
>
> **R:** You mean as a final grade? (…) I guess probably around a B+ or A-. I mean I'm pretty confident I'll get through it (laughs). So old papers are going around and when I look at them I think, yeah, they're definitely doable. And even just the mock exam took a lot of the anxiety around it out of it for me.

Fig. 4.1 Excerpt from a transcript of an interview

An interview transcribed according to these rules may then look similar to Fig. 4.1. For research papers, the rules used should be documented in the methods section or appendix.

In addition, you might want to consider that you can also transcribe in summary form. In this case, you would not transcribe an interview verbatim but rather summarize the points of interest in longer passages in your own words. This approach can be used if only the content of what is said is of interest and not the wording, and this of course needs to be justified accordingly.

Transcribing Audio Files: Interviews and Focus Groups

To transcribe an audio file, you must first import it into your MAXQDA project, as described in Chap. 3. Once you have imported it, you will see a new text document with a musical note symbol in the "Document System," labeled with the same name as the imported audio file. This is the document in which you will enter your transcription. To start transcribing, right-click on this document in the "Document System" and select **Transcribe Audio File**. MAXQDA will then switch the display to Transcription Mode, where the audio file is visualized in the "Multimedia Browser" and the transcript in the "Document Browser" directly below it (Fig. 4.2). A transcription settings dialog window will also be displayed each time you launch the Transcription Mode. This window can be closed when it is not required; you can reopen it at any time via an icon in the "Multimedia Browser" when the Transcription Mode is active.

The rewind interval and several transcription-supporting functions can be configured in the settings window. The rewind interval can be set between 0 and 10 seconds, so that this set number of seconds is rewound each time playback is restarted. Usually an interval of 2–3 seconds is a good setting, the optimal value being dependent on the rate of speech, the intelligibility of the recording, and the level of detail required in the transcription. The "Timestamp on enter" setting should always be checked, since this automatically generates a timestamp and inserts a blank line each time you press the enter key in the "Document Browser" (see Rule

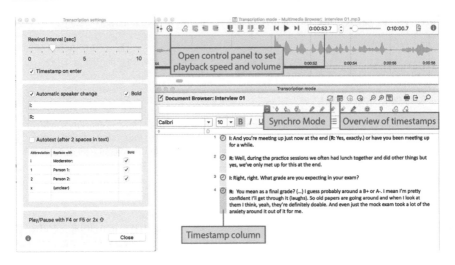

Fig. 4.2 MAXQDA's transcription mode

1 above). The advantage of this is that a section of speech can be played at any time during the analysis by clicking on the corresponding timestamp. Timestamps are used to link the transcript to the audio file such that any part of the original recording can be accessed at any time. Each transcript contains at least one timestamp, set automatically by MAXQDA at the position 0:00:00, which cannot be deleted. Timestamps are displayed in the "Document Browser" as clock icons in a separate column to the left of the transcript (Fig. 4.2). If you hover your cursor over one of these icons, the corresponding time will appear in the tooltip. Clicking on the icon plays the audio file at this point, so that later when you are working with the transcript, you can use the original sound to further interpret and evaluate what was said.

Automatic speaker changes can be switched on when transcribing individual interviews to save yourself typing work. Each time you press the enter key, the next paragraph will start alternately inserting "I:" and "R:", or other freely definable abbreviations for the interviewer and interviewee, optionally in bold (see Rule 2 above). For group discussions, however, you can use the ***Autotext*** option, which means that abbreviations followed by two spaces are automatically replaced by freely definable texts. For each person participating in a group discussion, you can define an appropriate abbreviation, e.g., an i for the moderator, an a for person A, b for person B, and so on. The inclusion of pauses in speech can also be made easier with the autotext option, e.g., by using the 1 for (.) and the 2 for (..).

After all the necessary settings have been made, you can start transcribing. The easiest way to control the audio file and transcription is to use different keys:

- The ***F4*** or ***F5*** keys start playback at the current position—with the rewind interval as set earlier. Press again to pause playback. (The keys ***F4*** and ***F5*** work identically; it doesn't matter which key you use.)

- The same can be done by pressing the **Ctrl** key (Windows) or the **Shift** ⇧ key (Mac) twice, so that hands can always remain in their original position when typing with ten fingers.
- **F6** inserts a new timestamp at the current playback position in the transcript. These manually added timestamps can be used to indicate hard-to-understand, or potentially misinterpretable transcriptions, or other places to be flagged. MAXQDA makes sure that no chronologically erroneous timestamps are added. You can therefore only set another timestamp between two existing timestamps if the current playback position is between the time positions of those two existing timestamps. The current playback area between the last and the next timestamp is highlighted in blue for easier orientation in the timestamp bar.
- **F12** *fast-forwards 5 seconds,* ⇧+**F12** *rewinds 5 seconds, so that you can quickly jump back to unclear sections or find the spot you are looking for more easily.*

The current position in the audio file can always be seen in the "Multimedia Browser." Here you can also jump to a required playback position by using the slider or by directly entering a time.

▶   **Please Note** On a Mac, function keys **F1** through **F12** are usually assigned system-specific functions. To use them for transcription in MAXQDA, press and hold the **fn** key at the same time. Since this can be very cumbersome, you may want to open the system settings and select the setting **Use F1, F2, etc. as standard function keys** in the "Keyboard" menu. Then it will no longer be necessary to press and hold the **fn** key. On some Windows computers, the function keys are also assigned to system functions. In this case, it may be helpful to conduct an internet search as to how the function keys on your computer can be used without holding the **fn** key.

If it turns out during the transcription that the recorded people are speaking very quickly, you can reduce the playback speed. To do this, click on the **control panel** icon in the "Multimedia Browser" (first icon on the left, Fig. 4.2) to open a control window for the volume and playback speed. These settings are also available for playing back when the Transcription Mode is switched off. MAXQDA supports some foot pedals for easier and faster transcription. A list of supported models can be found in the online manual.

To end the transcription, close the "Multimedia Browser" window by clicking on the corresponding icon at the top of the window. MAXQDA then automatically docks the "Document Browser" window with the transcript into its previous position.

▶   **Tip** To continue with your transcription having closed it, simply right-click on the document and select **Transcribe Audio File** again.

Transcribing Video Files

In principle, video files can be transcribed in exactly the same way as described in the previous section for audio files. Right-click on the video document in the "Document System," select the *Transcribe Video File* option to activate the Transcription Mode, and adjust your settings for the transcription, if necessary. MAXQDA will display the video images in a window above the waveform visualization of the audio track so you can choose whether to type a description of the images, a verbatim transcription of the speech, or a combination of both.

Occasionally in the case of video files (and sometimes also audio files), only selected parts need to be transcribed, for example, because parts of the recording are irrelevant to the research question or because only particular interaction sequences need to be transcribed and analyzed in detail. For partial transcriptions, you can play the recording by pressing the *F4* or *F5* key until you reach the point that you want to transcribe; if you already know which point this is, you can of course jump directly to it. Then start the transcription as described above for audio files and continue until the relevant part is over. To keep an overview of the material the whole video covers, it can be helpful to describe the non-transcribed areas, at least in a few keywords, set in brackets in the transcript. If necessary, also type the respective start and end times into the text (Fig. 4.3). Either way, a timestamp should be set at the beginning of each transcribed section, which can be done by pressing the *F6* key.

If, while viewing a video in the "Multimedia Browser," you happen to come across a sequence that you would like to transcribe, MAXQDA includes a function for starting transcriptions of selected video clips immediately. To do this, highlight a selection of the video with your cursor in the "Multimedia Browser," right-click on it, and select *Transcribe* in the context menu. MAXQA then positions the video at beginning of your selection, switches on the Transcription Mode—if not yet active—jumps to the appropriate position in the existing transcript, and inserts a timestamp there. To help orient you, this timestamp will also be entered as text into your transcript in the form #H:MM:SS-m#. You can then press *F4* once, *F5* once, or the *Ctrl* key (Windows) or the *Shift* ⇧ key (Mac) twice in a row to start transcribing immediately.

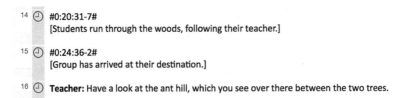

14 🕐 #0:20:31-7#
        [Students run through the woods, following their teacher.]

15 🕐 #0:24:36-2#
        [Group has arrived at their destination.]

16 🕐 **Teacher:** Have a look at the ant hill, which you see over there between the two trees.

Fig. 4.3 Video transcript with omissions in brackets

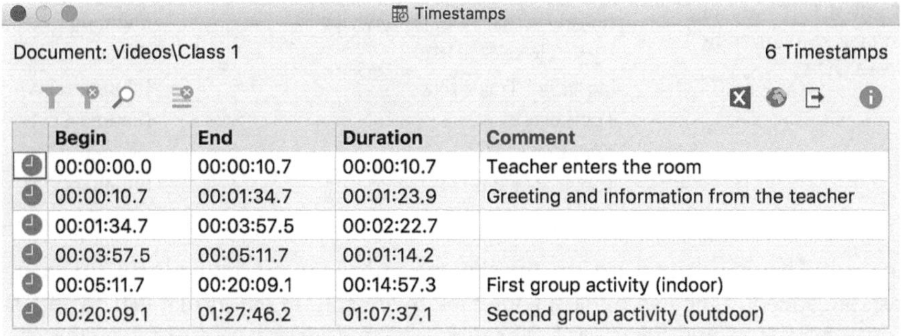

Begin	End	Duration	Comment
00:00:00.0	00:00:10.7	00:00:10.7	Teacher enters the room
00:00:10.7	00:01:34.7	00:01:23.9	Greeting and information from the teacher
00:01:34.7	00:03:57.5	00:02:22.7	
00:03:57.5	00:05:11.7	00:01:14.2	
00:05:11.7	00:20:09.1	00:14:57.3	First group activity (indoor)
00:20:09.1	01:27:46.2	01:07:37.1	Second group activity (outdoor)

Document: Videos\Class 1 — 6 Timestamps

Fig. 4.4 Overview of Timestamps with comments as an instrument for structuring the transcript

The Overview of Timestamps

As previously mentioned, timestamps are a helpful instrument for linking transcriptions to the original audio or video recordings. MAXQDA also lets you add a comment to each timestamp, in which you can describe the corresponding section of the recording in a few words. In this way, timestamps can help provide a structure to the content of your transcriptions, a tool for partial transcriptions that should not be underestimated. You can add or edit a comment at any time by right-clicking on the timestamp icon. If you hover your cursor over a timestamp, the tooltip that appears will not just show the corresponding time position, but also the comment.

The Overview of Timestamps lists all the times and respective durations of each section (up to the next timestamp) as well as all the comments that have been assigned to these timestamps (Fig. 4.4). You can open the overview by clicking on the icon with the same name in the "Document Browser." This icon appears as soon as an audio or video file is assigned to a text. You can write, edit, and delete comments in the overview, and it is interactive too: double-clicking a row will play the corresponding recorded section, while positioning the text in the "Document Browser" at the same corresponding position in the transcript.

Importing Existing Transcriptions with Timestamps

MAXQDA's transcription functions are perfectly suited for common standard of transcriptions, like the one proposed in Kuckartz (2014, p. 126). Quite often research teams will turn to external service providers to transcribe their data material, who themselves work with specialized programs like Express Scribe, F4, InqScribe, or Transcribe. These programs usually generate transcripts in RTF format, which then need to be imported into MAXQDA together with their corresponding audio or video file. The transcripts usually already contain timestamps entered directly into

Table 4.1 Timestamp formats recognized by MAXQDA	easytranscript, f4 & f5transcript	#hh:mm:ss-x#
	HyperTRANSCRIBE	[hh:mm:ss.xxx]
	Inqscribe, Transcriva	[hh:mm:ss.xx]
	Transana	(h:mm:ss.xx)
	Transcribe	[hh:mm:ss]
	Transcriber Pro	hh:mm:ss

the text. The timestamps used by the abovementioned transcription tools, for example, are added to the end of each paragraph by default, in the format #HH:MM:SS-m#, where H stands for hour, M for minute, S for second, and m for tenths of a second.

To import a transcript of this kind, select *Import > Transcripts with Timestamps*, then select one or more transcripts in the file dialog that appears. If MAXQDA recognizes a timestamp format in the selected document, it will ask you for a corresponding media file to assign to the document and copy to the folder for external files. When you import it into MAXQDA, the existing timestamps will be removed from the document and displayed as timestamp icons next to the text in the "Document Browser." You can also import a transcript with timestamps using all the standard import options in MAXQDA, for example, via *Import > Documents*, or by dragging and dropping the document from a folder into your "Document System." MAXQDA automatically checks all text documents to see if they contain timestamps.

MAXQDA automatically recognizes the timestamps used by the transcription programs listed in Table 4.1. If you want to import transcripts from other programs, the timestamp format in these transcripts may need to be adapted. This can be done using, for example, the advanced search and replace functions in word processing programs.

Checking a Transcript

Once you have completed your own transcription or imported an existing transcript, it is usually a good idea to check that the transcription matches the original recording. If necessary, you can increase the playback speed for this process and use MAXQDA's so-called Sync Mode, where the section in the transcript being played is indicated with a color-highlighted background in the "Document Browser." The exact procedure for checking transcripts is explained in Box 4.1.

Box 4.1: Checking a Transcript

- Open the transcript in the "Document Browser," e.g., by double-clicking its name in the "Document System."
- Activate the Sync Mode in the "Document Browser" by clicking on the ⬢ icon with the same name.
- If it is not already visible, open the "Multimedia Browser" by clicking on the icon with the same name in the "Document Browser." Position the "Multimedia Browser" so that you can see the transcript at the same time.
- Go to the beginning of the audio or video file and start playback.
- If people are not speaking quickly, you can increase the playback speed to hear the transcript faster. To do this, open the *control panel* via the 🔅 icon on the far left of the "Multimedia Browser" toolbar.
- If you find an error in the transcript, pause playback by pressing the *F4* or *F5* key or by pressing the *Ctrl* key (Windows) or the *Shift* ⇧ key (Mac) twice. Alternatively, you can skip back 5 seconds to replay the moment in question using the key combination ⇧+*F12*.
- To correct a section of the transcript, switch on the Edit Mode by clicking on the corresponding icon in the "Document Browser," and make the necessary changes to the text. Then switch off the Edit Mode, because the Sync Mode will not work when the Edit Mode is active.

For the Sync Mode to work, several timestamps need to have been assigned to the transcript. If your transcript does not contain any timestamps, except for the very first (MAXQDA generates this one automatically, starting at 0:00:00), there is no need to activate the Sync Mode. In this case simply make sure that you set the playback speed at a reasonable rate.

References

Dresing, T., & Pehl, T. (2015). *Manual (on) transcription: Transcription conventions, software guides and practical hints for qualitative researchers* (3rd ed.). Marburg: Dr. Dresing & Pehl GmbH.

Hepburn, A., & Bolden, G. (2017). *Transcribing for social research*. Thousand Oaks, CA: SAGE.

Kuckartz, U. (2014). *Qualitative text analysis: A guide to methods, practice & using software*. Los Angeles: SAGE.

Exploring the Data

5

Qualitative data analysis is a fascinating and rewarding process that challenges researchers to properly engage with their material and explore it in great detail. The software will not do this for you, but it does provide a number of tools to support you in your explorative work. You can make notes and comments, record questions and ideas, highlight anything that seems important, and search for words or word combinations in texts using lexical search functions. At first, working with digitized texts may seem much like working with a physical reference book. But digital tools are far more powerful, because text passages can be linked to each other, for example, as well as to other documents, websites, images, or geographical locations. In this first phase of your analysis, you will not only get to know your material, but you will also begin to build a large network of connections, comments, ideas, and hypotheses. You can begin to explore images and video recordings, too—a task that is certainly very different from exploring textual data. Video data is multidimensional, appeals to different senses, and can affect the viewer much more potently than texts can.

In This Chapter
- Get to know the memo function
- Writing, editing, and assigning memos
- Organizing and exporting memos
- Highlighting interesting and unusual text passages
- Performing lexical searches in texts and exporting the results
- Creating word clouds and using word stop lists
- Creating links and using this function as cross-linking tool
- Paraphrasing texts

© Springer Nature Switzerland AG 2019
U. Kuckartz, S. Rädiker, *Analyzing Qualitative Data with MAXQDA*,
https://doi.org/10.1007/978-3-030-15671-8_5

Exploring Your Data and Making Notes in Memos

From a technical point of view, you can start analyzing the data as soon as you have collected your first material and imported it into the software. However, the way you work will strongly depend on your chosen methodology. It may be that researchers applying the grounded theory method (Charmaz, 2014; Glaser & Strauss, 2009; Strauss & Corbin, 1990) will start their analysis as soon as the first sample of data has been collected and then proceed with further data collection based on these initial results. On the other hand, if you are working with a predetermined qualitative sampling plan, it may be more effective to first collect the data as comprehensively as possible and then start the analysis process in the subsequent phase. Another important factor, which should not be underestimated when it comes to determining how the data analysis phase should be approached, is how the project's researchers are accustomed to working, and this includes their computer competency. While some prefer to work with paper first, highlighting text passages and making annotations in the margins, others prefer to work exclusively with computers from the very beginning. Moreover, there are countless hybrid approaches between these two poles, none of which can be described as right or wrong, better or worse.

MAXQDA offers various tools for this stage of research data exploration without the need for systematic data coding. *Memos* are a very important tool in this regard. These are text notes that can be assigned to various elements in MAXQDA. *Paraphrases* are another helpful tool. These let you briefly summarize texts, in much the same way as you would write the subject headers for messages. You can also *color-code* particularly interesting text passages, just as you would highlight important passages in a reference book.

Memos can be assigned to various elements in MAXQDA, namely:

- Documents
- Document groups and sets
- Codes
- Points in documents as well as audio and video recordings

Additional forms of memo are the "project memo" (see Chap. 3), which can be used to describe the entire project, and "free memos," memos that are not assigned to any specific element in MAXQDA. MAXQDA visually displays memos where they are assigned; they look similar to Post-it® note.

Memos can fulfill a variety of functions in analyses. Particularly for methodologies in the social sciences, working with memos is very common. Indeed, memos play a particularly important role in the grounded theory methodology, as originally developed by Glaser and Strauss (Glaser & Strauss, 2009; Strauss & Corbin, 1990). Grounded theory distinguishes between a range of memo types that each have specific tasks in the research process, such as theory memos and code memos. Memos are fundamentally distinct from primary data: while primary data is normally granted the status of a document, i.e., it is the subject of analysis and should

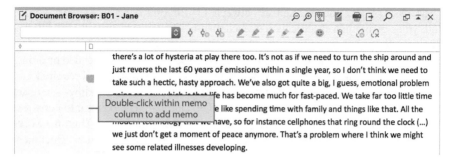

Fig. 5.1 Creating in-document memos

not be significantly changed, memos are products of the researchers themselves and can be edited at any time. Memos can be expanded on, modified, and integrated.

In the exploratory stage of work, "in-document memos" are most commonly used. Comments, ideas, questions, and hypotheses are directly assigned to specific points in the data material. In MAXQDA, the "Document Browser," in which texts, PDFs, and images are displayed, features a separate column to the left of the data for in-document memos. If you move your cursor to this column, a double-click will let you add a note here (Fig. 5.1). But by highlighting a text segment and using the context menu, you can assign the memo to a very specific bit of data.

The memo input dialog box (Fig. 5.2) has the same structure for all MAXQDA memo types. At the top you can enter a title for the memo; this should be unique and meaningful enough so that you can easily identify it later in a complete list of your memos.

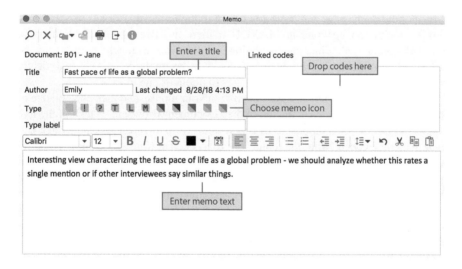

Fig. 5.2 The memo input dialog box

MAXQDA lets you distinguish between 11 different types of memos. To this end, you can assign a specific icon to each memo. The icons featuring the symbols ! (highly relevant), ? (questions regarding the material, preparations for further data collection), T (theory), M (methods), and L (language) do bear an intended meaning. However, they can equally be assigned with user-defined meanings if required.

The actual text of the memo is entered in the lower part of the window—there are also various options for formatting the text. The clipboard can be used to copy text from the memo or to insert text, e.g., quotations from the source text. This also works by dragging and dropping a text passage into this field from the "Document Browser."

Any memo can be displayed simply by pointing at it with the mouse cursor, without any need to click, even in the middle of a coding procedure. Double-click on the displayed memo icon to reopen a memo and modify it as required, for example, to connect a memo to a thematic code later in the analytic process. A table listing of memos is available under *Reports > Overview of Memos*; this gives you quick access to individual memos or memo types (for further details see Chap. 9).

Highlighting Text Passages with Assorted Colors

You may not have thought about possible analysis categories yet, or even what your analysis process will look like exactly—you may nevertheless want to highlight passages in a text or make note of observations, hypotheses, and further ideas. Almost everyone can relate to the impulse to pick up a highlighter and mark significant points when reading a reference book. If you want to write something down yourself and there is not enough space in the book margin, you might stick a Post-it® note on the page and write down your thoughts and questions this way. Very similar things can be done in MAXQDA: there are five virtual highlighters in assorted colors (red, blue, green, yellow, and violet) with which texts can be *color-coded*. With these highlighters you could, for example, color-code analytically significant passages in yellow and passages to quote or cite in red.

First, select the relevant passage of text with your mouse, and then click on one of the five color icons located at the top of the "Document Browser." Which of the five colors you use for what purpose is of course entirely up to you. The text passage will then be color-coded with the color of your choice (Fig. 5.3). In contrast to highlighting text passages in books, however, MAXQDA makes it very easy to find these color-coded passages later. With a book, you might be leafing through pages for a long time before you find the underlined passage you were looking for, whereas in MAXQDA you can easily retrieve any color-coded segments in the same way as thematically coded segments. Color-coded text passages can also be combined and processed further for both single and multiple texts. This is described in detail in Chap. 9.

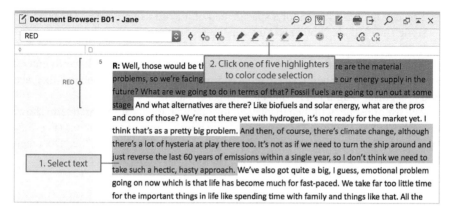

Fig. 5.3 Highlighting a text with the "color coding" function

Searching in Texts with Lexical Search

The exploratory stage of your analysis also involves being able to search for specific words or word combinations in the documents. MAXQDA allows you to search locally in all four main windows, that is, your search will be focused on the window within which you opened the search function. You can search for document names in the "Document System" and for the occurrence of words in the "Document Browser." In the toolbars, which are displayed at the top of each window, there is an icon of a magnifying glass. Click on the magnifying glass and then enter the term you are looking for. The frequency with which the term appears in the window will be displayed; you can move from hit to hit with the up and down keys on your keyboard.

Far more powerful than the local search, however, is MAXQDA's *lexical search* function, which you can access in the *Analysis* ribbon tab—or alternatively via the shortcut keys *Ctrl+⇧+F* (Windows) and *⌘+⇧+F* (Mac). The *lexical search* function not only allows you to search in the open document but also in multiple documents simultaneously. In Fig. 5.4 you can see the lexical search dialog box. In the example pictured, the search terms "climate" and "energy" are being searched for in all documents.

Any number of search terms can be entered. By default, searches are conducted using the OR logic, i.e., if *one* of the terms in the list of search terms is found, this counts as a hit. Alternatively, the AND combination can be used to search for simultaneous occurrences of words in the document or within a set number of paragraphs. Search terms can contain the placeholder characters * and ?:

- If you enter the character ? for a single character, e.g., m?st, MAXQDA will find "mast," "most," and "must."
- The character * denotes any given string of characters, e.g., MAXQDA will find "cold" and "chilled" for c*d.
- A specific beginning of a word can be found with <(...). The character string <(inter) therefore finds "interest" and "internal," but not "winter."

- You can likewise search for a specific end of a word using (...)>. The character string (im)> finds "him" and "interim," but not "time."

If the option ***Include words from lemma list*** is checked, the search words entered are also searched for their respective word forms. The search term "begin" then also finds "begins," "beginning," "began," "begun," etc.

The list of results will then display all the hits with the located search term shown in capital letters within a short segment showing its immediate context (Fig. 5.5). When you click on a hit, the corresponding document is opened in the "Document Browser" at that precise location so that you can explore its full context.

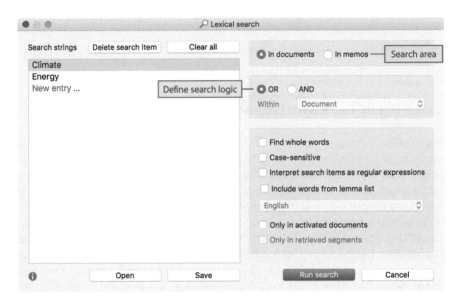

Fig. 5.4 "Lexical search" dialog box with several options

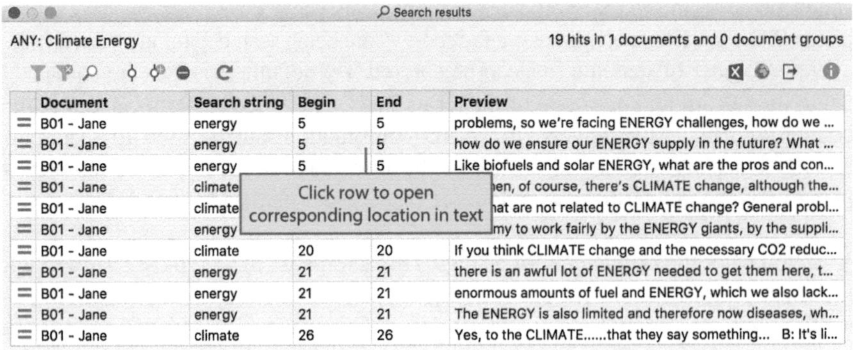

Fig. 5.5 Lexical search results window

Another useful feature for exploring your data is the option that allows you to select a word or text passage in the "Document Browser" and search for further occurrences of this text in the same or other documents. To do this, select the text and choose the option ***Search for Highlighted Text*** in the context menu.

Word Clouds: Visualizing the Most Frequently Used Words

Word clouds have become a very common means of visualizing the words contained in a given source. A typical representation is an alphabetical list of the most common words, whereby particularly frequent words are displayed with a larger font size. Different colors are often used, too. In fact, there are many different ways of displaying word clouds, in general. Why create a word cloud? Word clouds can provide a quick overview of the most common terms in a text. When they are displayed visually, such overviews are far more accessible than a table with a list of words and their frequency. Initial assumptions and hypotheses can be inferred from word clouds, especially if—as in the case of Twitter data, for example—a great deal of data is being analyzed. You can create a word cloud for a single document or for document groups or document sets by right-clicking on an entry in the "Document System" window and choosing ***Word Cloud***. Alternatively, one can request a word cloud for different documents via ***Visual Tools > Word Cloud***.

Figure 5.6 depicts a word cloud of a three-page interview from an online newspaper with the 50 most common words. Words such as "the," "a," "and," and "in" are the most common words that are not suited to identifying text content. Words such as "landscape," "nature," and "hikers" are more significant. One could reasonably assume that this interview is about walking in the country.

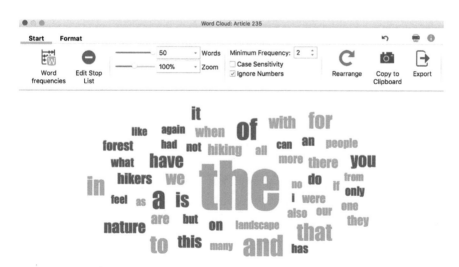

Fig. 5.6 Word cloud with the most common terms in a text

Word	Word length	Frequency	%	Rank	Documents	Documents %
the	3	137		1	1	100.00
and	3	51		2	1	100.00
a	1	49	2.23	3	1	100.00
of	2	49	2.23	3	1	100.00
in	2	43	1.95	5	1	100.00
to	2	40	1.82	6	1	100.00
that	4	38	1.73	7	1	100.00
for	3	33	1.50	8	1	100.00
is	2	30	1.36	9	1	100.00
have	4	27	1.23	10	1	100.00
you	3	27	1.23	10	1	100.00
we		25	1.14	12	1	100.00
it		24	1.09	13	1	100.00
nature		21	0.95	14	1	100.00
this	4	20	0.91	15	1	100.00
with	4	20	0.91	15	1	100.00

Fig. 5.7 List of word frequencies with selection of excluded words

If you switch to the list of word frequencies, you can transfer all unwanted words to a stop list (Fig. 5.7). To do this, double-click the column in front of the word in question. All words marked in this way will no longer be taken into account in the word cloud.

A list of the most common words which has been cleaned up in this way results in a much clearer picture (Fig. 5.8). It is now apparent that this text is about hiking and related topics such as views, landscapes, travel, hiking trails, water, and the wilderness.

Fig. 5.8 Word cloud after applying the stop list

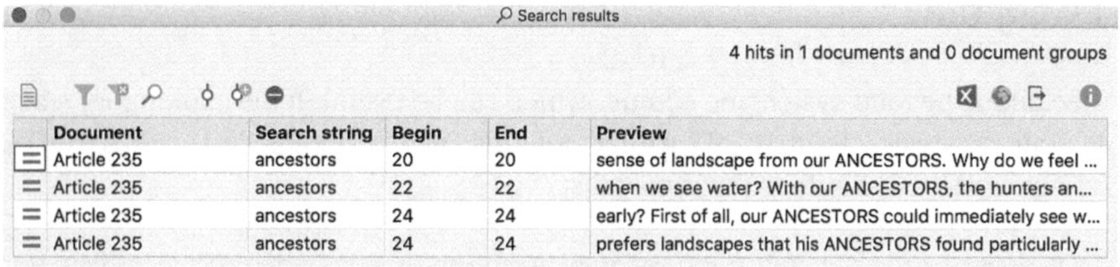

Search results

4 hits in 1 documents and 0 document groups

Document	Search string	Begin	End	Preview
Article 235	ancestors	20	20	sense of landscape from our ANCESTORS. Why do we feel ...
Article 235	ancestors	22	22	when we see water? With our ANCESTORS, the hunters an...
Article 235	ancestors	24	24	early? First of all, our ANCESTORS could immediately see w...
Article 235	ancestors	24	24	prefers landscapes that his ANCESTORS found particularly ...

Fig. 5.9 List of locations where the clicked word was found

The word “ancestors” also seems to refer to historical topics. All MAXQDA word clouds are interactive: clicking on a word, here on “ancestors”, lists all occurrences of the word as a “keyword in context.” These clearly show that all four passages found in the interview text do, in fact, address such topics (Fig. 5.9). To read the context of a reference in question, simply click on that row.

Exploring Video Files

The first steps of video analyses involve familiarizing yourself with the video data, which in this case means watching the videos in a focused manner, occasionally jumping back and watching scenes of interest several times. Exploring video data is more difficult and, above all, more time-consuming than exploring text data. Fast and informative tools like the word cloud or word frequency analyses are unfortunately not available for videos. That is, of course, unless the video recording is transcribed (see Chap. 4). In this case, all previously discussed methods of text exploration can also be carried out on the video transcripts. In most cases, however, transcriptions are dispensed with for video data (unlike audio data), for example, in the analysis of classroom research, where video data plays an essential role. This is not only because the transcription is time-consuming and costly but because video recordings contain so much information, which even the most detailed transcription system cannot hope to capture. Think of the scene from the film “Casablanca,” in which the lead actor says the famous line “Here’s looking at you, kid.” How reductive would an analysis of this scene be, if it focused only on the transcript?

Exploring video and text data is naturally quite different, but two of the tools MAXQDA offers to help with this exploration are the same:

- Memos: You can make notes of ideas and comments in the form of memos. This pauses the video and assigns a memo to the current playback position. Memos are inserted at the top of the audio track. As always, you can choose between different memo types, the icons of which will be displayed. If you hover your cursor over a memo, the title and the beginning of the memo will be shown in the tooltip.
- Color codes: Interesting sequences can be highlighted in color. To do this, however, the corresponding markers for the start and end of the clip must first be set in the video –for further details see Chap. 7.

Linking Data

A technique beyond systematic coding, which can be useful in the exploratory stage of your analysis, is that of setting internal and external links. MAXQDA distinguishes between four types of links:

1. *Document links*—a link between two locations in a text, image, or video. For example, two statements made by a respondent could therefore be linked to each other in order to compare them. Or two people may have made statements about the same facts and you want to be able to easily jump from one statement to the other.
2. *External links*—a link between a location in a text or image you are analyzing and a file outside your current MAXQDA project. For example, to an image, document, sound, or video recording stored on your hard disk.
3. *Web links*—a link between a location in a text or image you are analyzing and an internet page. Clicking on that part of the text or image opens the corresponding web page in your default internet browser.
4. *Geolinks*—a link between a location in a text or image and a geographic location in the world using GPS coordinates. This geolocation is then displayed in Google Earth or other available geodata viewer.

Links can be set (and if necessary deleted) in the "Document Browser" (for texts, PDFs, images) or "Multimedia Browser" (for audio and video data); the four different types of links are represented by different symbols in the Overview of Links which is available in the ribbon tab **Reports** or in context menus in the "Document System."

Linking Two Locations in a Document

In the exploratory stage of your analysis, document links—the first type, with which two locations in your documents can be connected—play a particularly important role. Document links are internal links; they only connect points or sections within a MAXQDA project. These links have the same function, and can be used in the same way, as hyperlinks on websites. They connect two points: an anchor point and a target point. As soon as you click on the anchor point of an existing link, the corresponding target point will be opened, or, alternatively, by pointing at an anchor link, you will see the target link data displayed in a tooltip panel. In MAXQDA, these links are two-way, i.e., they not only lead somewhere but also back again. Clicking on the target point jumps back to the anchor point (Fig. 5.10). Box 5.1 explains in detail how to create document links. Document links can be used to link points or sections in and across all types of data in MAXQDA, i.e., texts, images, and PDFs, as well as audio and video files.

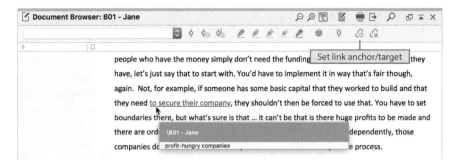

Fig. 5.10 Document link with a tooltip preview of the link target

---

Box 5.1: Creating Document Links
- Select an anchor point in the "Document Browser" with your mouse, and then select the *Insert Document Link* option from the context menu (shortcuts: *Ctrl+L* on Windows and ⌘ + *L* on Mac), or click on the *Set link anchor/target* icon in the coding toolbar in the "Document Browser." The location you selected will now be displayed differently. In text documents the text will appear underlined in blue, and in images and PDF documents, you will see a blue frame.
- Then select the target point for your document link. First scroll to your desired location in the same document, or, if you want to create a link to a separate document, open that document and scroll to the relevant location there. Select your target point with the mouse, just as you did with the anchor point.
- Click on the *Set link anchor/target* icon again to complete the link; these locations will now be linked to each other.
- If you decide not to set the link after the first step, you can remove the anchor point of the link by clicking on the *Remove start of link* icon.

To create a document link in a video, open the video in the "Multimedia Browser," select a section of the video, and then select *Insert Document Link* in the context menu.

When linking text passages from two documents, it can also be very helpful to open the second document in an additional "Document Browser," so that both documents can be placed next to each other.

The Overview of Links, which is available for individual documents, document groups, and entire projects via the context menu in the "Document System," makes it easier to find links again later. In this overview, document links appear twice, with their anchor and target points, while external links, web links, and geolinks appear only once in the list. The list is interactive: double-click a link to open the corresponding target.

Paraphrasing Texts

MAXQDA enables you to write paraphrases for text passages. This technique is particularly useful at the beginning of the data analysis, because this stage is all about getting to know your material and understanding what has been written or said. The term "paraphrase" is derived from the Greek for para- (expressing modification) + "tell." Accordingly, to paraphrase means expressing the meaning of something (written or spoken) using different words. However, in this case, paraphrasing is used in a rather more specific sense than simply rewriting something. The text should be *accurately* paraphrased in that the semantic meaning of the original text should be reflected in your paraphrased version. In other words, your paraphrasing should not change, augment, or subtract from the meaning of the original.

Paraphrasing can be used in many different ways to analyze research data. But there are three main tasks that take precedence: first, paraphrasing can be a useful technique for creating categories for your material (Kuckartz, 2014; Mayring, 2014). Second, paraphrasing forces you to be accurate, which can be a valuable aid in interpreting data. In this sense, paraphrasing can be a means of properly understanding your material. This is reflected in the fact that the technique is also used in the development of surveys. In the pre-test phase, it is important to ensure that the questions asked in a survey are "accurately comprehensible" to respondents. They are therefore asked to reproduce the question in their own words, so that a review of the "correct" understanding can take place. Third, paraphrasing can be useful if the core statements of a text need to be summarized relatively quickly and without coding. For example, if a journalist wants to summarize the most important statements of a press release or a political scientist wants to summarize the central statements of a party platform. Qualitative content analyses also frequently involve paraphrasing the available material as an initial stage of analysis.

To paraphrase a text or PDF document in MAXQDA, first activate Paraphrase Mode in the ***Analysis*** ribbon tab by clicking on the ***Paraphrases*** icon (Fig. 5.11). Now the "Document Browser" will respond differently to normal: as soon as you select a section of the document with your mouse and release the mouse button, a window will appear in which you can paraphrase the selected passage.

Paraphrases can contain a maximum of 255 characters including spaces, which is the equivalent of about three to four lines in this book. The text you have written is then displayed to the right of the original text in the paraphrase column (Fig. 5.12).

Fig. 5.11 Active Paraphrase Mode in the "Analysis" tab

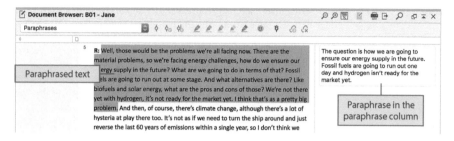

Fig. 5.12 Paraphrases as shown in the paraphrase column

The original passage which you have paraphrased is highlighted in green by default, so you can immediately see which text sections you have already covered. In the "Code System" window, you will also see a new "Paraphrases" code, with which the paraphrased text passage is coded. This means that you can use all the usual functions that apply to codes and coded segments for this "paraphrase code" too. For example, you can compile all paraphrased text sections of a document in the "Retrieved Segments" window (see Chap. 9 "Working with Coded Segments and Memos").

Any number of paraphrases can be generated for a text. However, new paraphrases cannot overlap with existing paraphrases. If you try to create a new paraphrase within a green marked text section, no window will appear for entering another paraphrase. Paraphrase texts can be edited and deleted: double-clicking on a paraphrase opens it for editing; clicking on the red cross in the paraphrase box deletes it.

You can deactivate the Paraphrase Mode in the same way you activate it, namely, by clicking on the **Paraphrases** icon in the **Analysis** tab. The paraphrase column next to the text will also be closed. This column can also be displayed again later without activating the Paraphrase Mode. Simply select the corresponding option in the "Document Browser" context menu; you can also adjust the width of the paraphrase column here.

Paraphrasing is not just an excellent entry point into the data material of new fields of research; it is also a useful training tool for teams in terms of handling material with care and making sure you have a consensus in your understanding of key statements.

References

Charmaz, K. (2014). *Constructing grounded theory* (2nd ed.). Thousand Oaks, CA: SAGE.
Glaser, B. G., & Strauss, A. L. (2009). *The discovery of grounded theory: Strategies for qualitative research* (4th ed.). New Brunswick: Aldine.
Kuckartz, U. (2014). *Qualitative text analysis: A guide to methods, practice and using software.* Thousand Oaks, CA: Sage.

Mayring, P. (2014). *Qualitative content analysis: Theoretical foundation, basic procedures and software solution.* Klagenfurt. Retrieved from http://nbnresolving.de/urn:nbn:de:0168-ssoar-395173

Strauss, A. L., & Corbin, J. M. (1990). *Basics of qualitative research: Grounded theory procedures and techniques.* Newbury Park, CA: Sage Publications.

Coding Text and PDF Files

6

How do I code my data or parts of my data, for example, text passages or parts of images? This chapter deals with the basics of coding. Working with categories (codes) and coding parts of your material is not only one of the oldest qualitative data analysis techniques; it is probably still the most widely used. In the past, this was done by laboriously cutting out clippings of text with scissors and pasting them onto index cards and adding a keyword. QDA software lets you do all this far more quickly and efficiently. The specific coding procedure will vary considerably between the different methods and research styles. So, for example, you would proceed rather differently in the context of a grounded theory approach than you would in that of a qualitative content analysis or discourse analysis. QDA software does not restrict you to a certain method—in fact it facilitates a wide range of coding processes.

In This Chapter
- Understanding the coding process
- Creating codes in MAXQDA and defining code properties
- Organizing and sorting your codes
- Exploring coding techniques in MAXQDA
- Writing a comment on a coded segment
- Working with the Overview of Coded Segments
- Learning how to work with MAXQDA's overviews in general
- Exploring a variety of options for automatic coding

© Springer Nature Switzerland AG 2019
U. Kuckartz, S. Rädiker, *Analyzing Qualitative Data with MAXQDA*,
https://doi.org/10.1007/978-3-030-15671-8_6

About Codes and Categories

Working with categories in the context of qualitative data analysis fulfills numerous functions, ranging from naming, describing, and explaining data to systematizing, organizing, and summarizing them. Hence, in the qualitative content analysis tradition, for example, the categories are used for structuring the content, for generating types, and for the assessment (evaluation) of statements (Kuckartz, 2014). In research projects following a grounded theory approach, categories take on an important role in the development of theories (Charmaz, 2014; Corbin & Strauss, 2015). Categories often consist of a simple word ("Recycling") or a combination of a few words ("Individual environmental behavior in the area of mobility"). Longer word combinations or statements are much rarer.

As the two examples above suggest, categories can be defined and differentiated according to a multitude of characteristics, including their breadth of content, their level of abstraction, and how closely they are based on the empirical material. Moreover, the context of their development and theoretical framing, as well as their applicability and organizational effectiveness regarding the analyzed data, are all important criteria for differentiating categories. The characteristics and functions of categories can be used to differentiate between several prominent types of categories, including:

- *Factual categories* denote easily identifiable facts in the data, for example, if someone is a member of a given political party or not.
- *Content-based or thematic categories* usually serve to structure the content. You can imagine them as a "road sign," which points out a thematic area or topic in a text.
- *Analytical categories* are the result of an intensive examination of the data and reflect a higher degree of abstraction than "in vivo categories," which are formed using original terms present in the data (e.g., words used by research participants).
- *Evaluative categories* primarily assume an evaluative function. They often form an ordinal scale. For example, a low, medium, or high sense of responsibility.
- Categories in the form of *emoticons and symbols* play a special role. In fact, they were first made systematically applicable for the analysis of qualitative data by MAXQDA. They can be used to work with symbol-like categories without using textual language, that is, as we know it from communicating via SMS and WhatsApp, where symbols can express text-free sentiments, emotions, or objects of everyday life.

Until now we have only mentioned "categories," but very often the terms "codes" and "concepts" can also be found in literature on category-based analysis of qualitative data. This can easily lead to confusion, as these terms are sometimes used to mean different things and sometimes used synonymously. For example, in research projects that follow the grounded theory approach, so-called "concepts" (sometimes used synonymously with "codes") are used at the beginning of the analysis process, while the development of categories—and, above all, a "main category"—represents the primary objective of this analysis (Corbin & Strauss, 2015). In his textbook on coding qualitative data, Saldaña (2015, p. 12) draws a different conceptual path, at least linguistically: in his introductory chart, codes develop across categories to concepts and theories.

In MAXQDA itself, you will not encounter the confusion regarding the terms mentioned above, since the interface almost exclusively uses the word "code." This does not mean, however, that MAXQDA locks researchers into using one particular meaning—the opposite is the case. Whether researchers treat a MAXQDA code as a code in the narrow sense or rather as a concept is entirely up to them. It therefore remains an important task for researchers to use their categories in an analytically thought-out manner. This is all the more important given that the use of QDA software like MAXQDA makes coding so fast and simple that it can be tempting to see the coding process merely as a technical chore and not as an analytical process. To ensure a good research process, however, it is essential to be clear about the function and interpretation of each specific MAXQDA code within your analysis methodology. (To avoid confusion, we will use the terms "code" and "category" synonymously in this book.)

What Does "Coding" Actually Mean?

In simple terms, "coding" means that a selected part of the data is assigned to a code—or vice versa: a code is assigned to a data segment. Hence, when responses to an interview question about the world's biggest problems are assigned with the thematic code "world problems," this process is called "coding." It is important to know that the coded part of the data is called a *coded segment* in MAXQDA; coded video segments are also referred to as *clips*.

Generally, there are two different coding procedures. *Following a deductive, concept-driven approach*, codes can be developed before viewing the data, and the phenomena discovered there can then be classified and assigned accordingly. This is also referred to as "tagging." *Following an inductive, data-driven approach*, codes can be regarded as condensed descriptions of the phenomena discovered in the data. In the context of coding data, a distinction should always be made between two basic activities: the *creation of categories* and the *application of categories*.

Saldaña (2015, pp. 6–7) refers to "coding filters" and an "analytic lens" when working with codes in order to illustrate that, in category-based analysis, researchers essentially look at their data through the "lens" of codes. Indeed, the formation and selection of categories along with the totality of all categories in the shape of a coherent category system is of vital importance to the analysis process, which is why we will address this topic in detail in Chap. 8.

Creating New Codes and Building a Coding Frame

Open Coding of Texts

Open coding is a data-driven coding procedure in which, as a rule, no categories have been defined in advance of analyzing the available data and discovered phenomena and facts are coded with new codes that are closely related to the material. This approach can be implemented very easily in MAXQDA: open a text in the "Document Browser," select a section of text to be coded, and then choose the function *Code with New Code* in the context menu (Fig. 6.1). A dialog box for defining new codes will open, in the topline of which you can enter a code name (Fig. 6.2). The newly created code is inserted at the top of your "Code System" window, and a corresponding stripe will appear along the edge of the text to indicate the coded section.

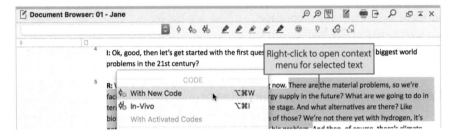

Fig. 6.1 Open coding in the "Document Browser": create a new code and assign it to the selected segment

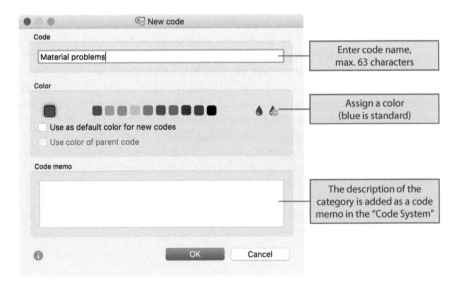

Fig. 6.2 New code dialog box

Adding a New Code Directly to the "Code System"

New codes can be added to the "Code System" directly at any time, without being immediately assigned to a text passage as they are when following the open coding approach. In the "Code System" window, you can manage a hierarchical code system with codes and subcodes on several sublevels. Right-click on the topline containing the word "Code System," and select the option **New Code** from the context menu to create new categories at the top level. If you follow the same procedure after clicking on an existing code, a subcategory will be added to this code, called a *subcode* in MAXQDA. In both cases, the same dialog box will appear for defining new codes (Fig. 6.2).

When you create a new code, you can also assign it with a color of your choice. This color has analytical value in several respects and should be considered carefully. On the one hand, it serves to differentiate between different categories (or types of categories), which in turn allows for the use of many of MAXQDA's visual analysis tools. On the other hand, it makes it easier to recognize where different codes have been assigned to texts in the "Document Browser," since each individual code assignment can be made visible, in color, both next to the text and within the text itself.

Once you have created a new code, you can add a description of the category, if required. This description can contain a definition and rules for its use or give information about the background of the code's development. The description is stored as a so-called *code memo* in the "Code System," as a yellow memo icon directly next to the code, and can be accessed and changed at any time by double-clicking on it. Of course, both the code name and its color can also be modified at any time throughout the analysis.

Adjusting the Order and Sorting of Codes

Especially in the initial stages of the research process, adjusting the sequence and hierarchical structure of codes is part of the daily routine of working with a coding frame. Individual codes need to be moved and sorted, others need to be given a new parent code. Technically, MAXQDA allows you to build a code system with up to ten hierarchical levels and any number of codes. As far as the content of the data is concerned, however, it very rarely makes sense, in practice, to exhaust all the available levels and define several hundred codes.

In MAXQDA, codes on the highest level are called *top-level codes* and sometimes *main codes*. A given code, e.g., "Sense of responsibility," with three subcategories "low," "medium," and "high" can also be referred to as a *parent code* according to its hierarchical position, while its subcategories are referred to as *subcodes*. If you move a code with the mouse and drop it on another code, the moved code will become a subcode of the target code, but if you drop it just below another code, the moved code will be placed at the same level as the code above (sometimes called a "sibling" of the target code). In this way you can move whole groups of codes to a different position in your code system.

Sorting codes within a hierarchy level can also be done by moving individual codes with the mouse. By right-clicking on a parent code and selecting **Sort**

Subcodes, you can find functions to automatically sort its subcodes alphabetically or by their number of coded segments.

Coding Text

If you want to code a text with codes that have already been created in MAXQDA, the typical coding process is always carried out in two simple steps. For the first step, the segment to be coded is selected with the mouse. Technically speaking, the smallest unit for assigning a code to a text is a character, but in most cases, you will probably choose at least one word as the smallest unit for coding. For the second step, there are two possibilities: either you drag the selected segment onto a code with the mouse and drop it there or you drag a code onto the selected segment. You can see the coding process in Fig. 6.3: a text passage at the beginning of paragraph 5 has been selected and then dragged onto the code "Biggest world problems." To the right of the code, the number representing how many times the code has been assigned will have increased by one. Next to the text, exactly at the same level as the coded segment, a coding stripe with the code name visually indicates that the text has been coded with a specific code.

▶   **Tip** To code an entire paragraph without selecting it first, you can drag a
      code onto a paragraph number next to the text.

Figure 6.3 shows a comfortable setting of the MAXQDA interface for coding: the space for the "Document Browser" was enlarged by switching off the "Retrieved Segments" window. The width of the column for coding stripes can be adjusted by clicking between the column headers and moving your mouse, so that even long code names are easier to read. If you prefer to see your coding stripes to the right of the text, you can click on the column header with the mouse and place it on the right side.

When it comes to coding, you will sooner or later be faced with the question of which document to start with. In many cases, it makes sense to avoid a text that is already known to be a special case, such as a particularly detailed interview or a very

Fig 6.3 Coding text by dragging and dropping with the mouse

short interview with a noncooperative interview partner. Instead, it is better to start with the less conspicuous and easy-to-understand texts in order to be able to test and sharpen the code system on the basis of this data. However, once your code system has proven itself for some of these "simple" texts and has been further developed based on this material, it is recommended that you add some of the more "divergent" texts as soon as possible in order to increase the variance of the data. If this only happens after three quarters of the coding work has been completed and it only then turns out that the coding frame should have been fundamentally changed in several places, this would be very annoying since all the previous material would have to be looked through yet again.

Very often you will not have divided the text into coding units prior to coding it; instead, you will work with the text as it is or as it was written. For this reason, the question automatically arises how much to code, i.e., how large each of the individual coded segments should be. This can vary depending on the approach of research chosen and the category type in question. In language analyses that focus on the use of verbs or the use of metaphors, for example, the coded segments will naturally be smaller than for thematic analyses, which initially work with broad thematic categories. In thematic analyses, "broad-brush coding" is often used at the beginning, during which all text passages are first assigned to broad categories, e.g., all passages in which an interviewee has spoken about his or her purchase decisions. The second step then involves coding individual sections of these large segments more precisely, for example, by using subcodes developed empirically based on the material. Alternatively, it is also possible to consistently code everything that seems pertinent to the research question with a single code. As distinct from large-scale "macro-coding," which is often used to code interviews for the first time with the interview questions as the guide, there is also "micro-coding" approach. This is done line by line or word by word with great attention to detail.

No matter how you proceed, it has proven itself worthwhile to set up coding rules. A very common coding rule, for example, is that units of meaning—at least one sentence—are coded so that coded segments are still understandable outside of their context. The interviewer's question should only be coded if it is necessary to understand the answer.

More Techniques for Coding

In addition to the coding options we have already outlined, MAXQDA offers you numerous other ways to assign text passages to categories and vice versa.

Coding with the Coding Toolbar in "Document Browser"

The coding toolbar in the "Document Browser" is particularly useful for the coding process. Its individual coding functions are explained in Fig. 6.4.

You can find the so-called *Quick List* for codes at the left of the toolbar. It is updated with every coding step you make, always displaying the code last used or last clicked, and it can be expanded to select a recently used code. Coding with the

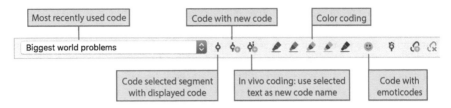

Fig. 6.4 The coding toolbar in the "Document Browser"

help of the Quick List is particularly suited to cases in which a text needs to be worked through with respect to one selected code, e.g., to define your coding units or to identify all the parts relevant to a particular research question. The text passages of interest can be selected and coded one after the other with a click on the icon to the right of the Quick List. There are several locations in MAXQDA where the Quick List with the most recent codes can be used to select a code.

The ***Code with New Code*** option corresponds to the coding technique described above in the context of open coding. A new code is created for and directly assigned to a selected text passage. *In vivo codes* are usually codes whose names are taken directly from the original material, terms usually mentioned by the interviewees themselves (Corbin & Strauss, 2015). To create this kind of code in MAXQDA, select a particularly salient word that is suitable as a code name (it can also be several words), and click on the ***Code in vivo*** icon in the toolbar. The selected text is then inserted as a new code at the very top of the "Code System," and the text passage is assigned to the new code.

MAXQDA enables you to work with emoticons and symbols, the idea behind it being the trans-verbal coding of data material. Instead of assigning a language-based, textual code to a phenomenon or piece of information, it is coded with a so-called *emoticode*. For example, smileys can be used to code emotional expressions in interviews or the auto-ethnographic perceptions of researchers when reviewing data; ghost symbols serve as reminders for sections that allow interviewees to be identified and must later be rendered anonymous for reports and publications; references to nature can be symbolized by trees and city references through high-rise buildings. To work with emoticodes, you must first open the emoticode window (Fig. 6.5) by clicking on the smiley icon in the coding bar. To code a text, simply select a text passage and click on the emoticode of your choice. The emoticode icon will then appear in the "Code System" for this newly created code, instead of the normal code symbol. Each symbol is additionally assigned a predefined yet customizable code description. Once an emoticode is listed in the "Code System" window, you can continue working with the code even when the emoticode window is closed, because you can now use it just like any other code.

The coding toolbar in the "Document Browser" also contains the five icons already introduced in Chap. 5 for color coding texts—especially for explorative purposes—as if with a highlighter (Fig. 6.4). When one of the highlighters is used for the first time, a new color code with its own symbol is created in the "Code System," and each selection counts as a coded segment.

Fig. 6.5 The emoticode window

Coding with the Code Favorites Window

Code Favorites are particularly useful if you want to work through data material with respect to fewer selected codes, often in the context of a "macro or broad-brush coding" approach described above. You can open the Code Favorites window via *Codes > Code Favorites* and then proceed to drag and drop codes from the "Code System" into the window (Fig. 6.6). Alternatively, the *Add Code to Code Favorites* option is also available in each code's context menu. Once you have selected the codes you want to work with, you can start working on the text: select relevant passages and code them by clicking on one of your Code Favorites. Alternatively, you can drag and drop passages onto these or vice versa, that is, drag and drop the codes onto the relevant passage.

Coding with User-Defined Shortcuts

For many of the coding techniques described above, MAXQDA provides fixed keyboard shortcuts that you can see both in the context menus and when hovering your cursor over an icon in the coding toolbar in the "Document Browser." You can

Fig. 6.6 The list of code favorites

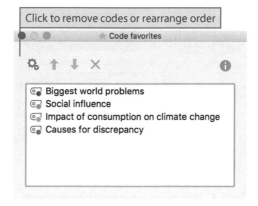

also freely define shortcuts for up to nine individual codes. The ***Codes > Keyboard Shortcuts for Codes*** function opens a window in which you can drag and drop individual codes onto one of several keyboard shortcuts—from ***Ctrl+1*** to ***Ctrl+9*** (Windows) or ⌘ + *1* to ⌘ + *9* (Mac)—and thereby assign them. For example, you could assign a shortcut to the code "Interesting passages" and then quickly code any text segment that seems significant but does not directly concern the research question at hand, or for which there is no specific code yet, without having to first search for the "Interesting passages" code in the potentially quite long code system. If you code with keyboard shortcuts, you can even hide all the MAXQDA windows except the "Document Browser" and view the document in full screen size.

The Display of Codes in the "Document Browser"

No matter which coding technique you choose, each code is displayed in the "Document Browser" next to the text as a coding stripe, with the color of the stripe corresponding to the respective code color. As soon as a segment contains many codes assigned to it in a dense space, you may want to hide individual coding information and limit the display of the coding stripes to only selected ones. For this, MAXQDA has an options dialog box, which appears when you right-click in the grey area where the coding stripes are displayed (Fig. 6.7).

In the window you can restrict the display of the coding stripes by their color or their author, which can be helpful, for example, if you want to concentrate on a certain topic. In addition, the option ***Color-coded text*** lets you display all your coded

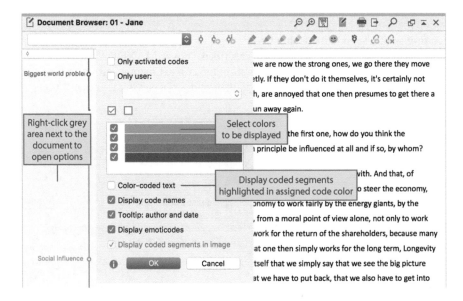

Fig. 6.7 Options dialog box for setting the display of encodings

text passages as highlighted in their respective code color, which is useful for making these coded passages visible within the text. Only the codes currently visible as coding stripes are taken into account, and a mixed color is displayed for overlapping codes.

Working with Coded Segments: Comment, Weight, and Delete

The coding functions in MAXQDA are very flexible and allow you to make changes to code assignments you have made already in a variety of ways. For example, a coded segment can be made shorter or longer by marking the text passage with new segment boundaries and reassigning the same code to the passage. MAXQDA will then automatically adapt the boundaries of the existing coded segment, since MAXQDA works according to the rule "the same code may only be assigned once per segment" (of course any number of different codes can be assigned per segment, and the coded segments of different codes can overlap as desired).

Further editing functions for coded segments are available in the context menu for a coding stripe. The menu appears once you right-click on the coding stripe and contains options for commenting, weighting, and deleting the selected coded segment (Fig. 6.8).

Adding Comments to Coded Segments

Unlike memos within a document, comments for coded segments are not only attached to a specific text segment but are also permanently linked to that specific assignment of a code. Code comments can take on a variety of tasks in the research process: they are the ideal place for short summaries of the coded content, and they can reference themselves ("uncertain code assignment, check again later") or can be used to make notes for team members ("I wouldn't assign this code here"). To write a comment, select *Edit comment* from the context menu of a coding stripe (Fig. 6.8). In the comment dialog box, you can then enter up to 255 characters, which corresponds to approximately three to four lines of text in this book.

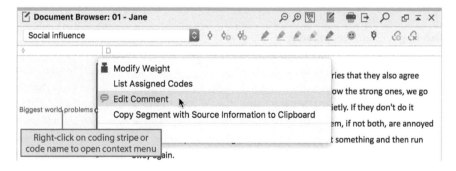

Fig. 6.8 The context menu for the coding stripe

As soon as you enter your comment, the coding stripe will show the following: the circle in the middle of the stripe is now filled in with the coding stripe's color. If you hover your cursor over the coding stripe, the comment will be displayed in the tooltip that appears.

▶   **Tip** You can edit a comment quickly by double-clicking on the coding stripe or code name in the "Document Browser."

Weight Scores

MAXQDA allows you to assign a weight score—a relevance score—to each coded segment. Supposing an analysis is about finding specific text passages that are typical of a certain way of reasoning or of a certain theoretical concept, then codes are generally used as "sign posts." In other words, they are sign posts that point out relevant text passages for a particular category.

MAXQDA's weighting function can then be used to determine the degree to which a coded segment expresses what is meant by the category. MAXQDA offers the option of assigning a weight score on a scale from 0 to 100. These weight scores can also be described as "fuzzy variables," because they allow for uncertainty and are not intended to be assigned using exact values with a corresponding reliability—in some cases and for some analysis techniques, however, this may well be necessary. Code weights can also be used to perform numerous other analysis tasks:

- Team members can record the status of a code assignment in the terms of this weight, e.g., a 50 can be defined for the status "Only coded by one person, not yet double-checked" and a 100 for "Checked by project leaders."
- Code assignments that you are unsure of can be assigned a special weight so that you can easily find and check them later.
- In the case of multiple mentions of the same information in the text, the first occurrence can be assigned a different weight than those that follow.

Each newly coded segment is assigned the currently set default weight, which is between 0 and 100. The default value is 0 and can be changed at any time using MAXQDA's main preferences or by clicking on the weight icon in the status bar at the bottom of the screen.

Deleting a Code Assignment

As already described, any assignments of code you have made can be undone using the ***Undo code*** symbol in the coding toolbar. This is particularly useful for the most recent code assignments, but it is often more practical to be able to delete one of these assignments in their actual location. To do this, right-click on the coding stripe: the context menu then gives you the option of deleting this code assignment (Fig. 6.8).

Overview of Coded Segments: Keeping Track of Your Coding

During the coding process, you will undoubtedly want to keep track of your coded segments. For example, you may want to check back on which text passages have been assigned a particular code or you may want to compile the coded segments within a selected text and go through them again. The coding stripes at the edge of the text provide a continuous overview of how a document has been coded. To work with these coding stripes, it is helpful to widen the coding stripe column next to the text so that even long code names are clearly visible. If you hover your cursor over a coding stripe, the full name of a code will be displayed. Clicking on the stripe automatically also selects the corresponding code in the code system so that you can easily open the code memo and read its description.

MAXQDA provides numerous table overviews of the data generated during the course of a project, including an overview of your coded segments. Double-clicking on a code opens the so-called Overview of Coded Segments, which contains all the segments to which this code was assigned (Fig. 6.9). If the code clicked on has subcategories and these were collapsed, these are also integrated into the overview.

The Overview of Coded Segments is divided into two parts. In the lower part of the window, you will see as many rows as there are coded segments for this code. The coded segment clicked on is displayed in the upper window area. Like all MAXQDA overviews, this table is interactive. Clicking on a coded segment here (i.e., a row in the table) highlights the source document and the assigned code in blue in their respective system windows and also jumps to the coded text in the "Document Browser" where you can see it in context. The window header lists the total number of coded segments and the numbers of documents and document groups, respectively, within which they are contained. The toolbar also provides functions for filtering, searching, further processing, and exporting. The various columns of the overview provide further information on the details of the individual coded segments: *Document group* and *Document name* indicate the origin of the coded

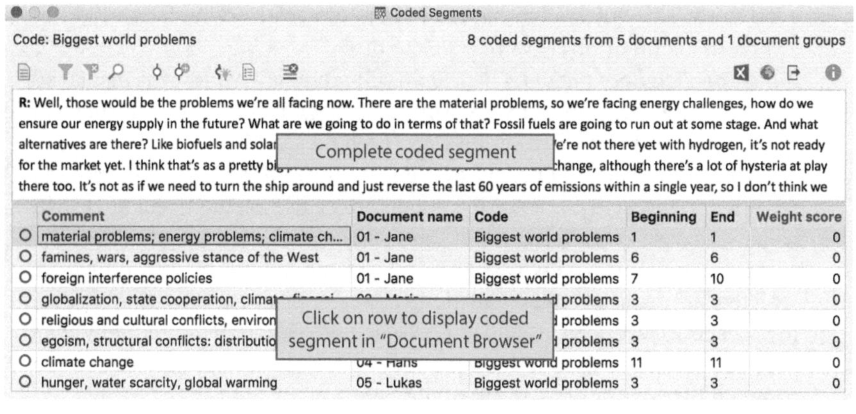

Fig. 6.9 All the coded segments in the table view of the Overview of Coded Segments

segment, and *Beginning* and *End* contain the paragraph numbers where the coded segment begins and ends. How you can manage and adjust table overviews in MAXQDA is described in detail in Box 6.1.

The contents of any column with a blue heading can be changed in MAXQDA's overviews. For example, you can enter a weight score for a coded segment directly into the *Weight score* column of the Overview of Coded Segments. In the *Comment* column, you can enter a short text, which can be used very effectively for defining or differentiating categories: for each coded segment, a comment in the form of a summary or abstract of the text material can be entered—existing formulations can be reused and adapted—which is supported by the auto-complete function in MAXQDA overview tables. In this way, you can formulate potential subcategories next to the material and gain a good overview of the contents of a category.

You can open the Overview of Coded Segments in many places and contexts in MAXQDA, including from the context menu of a document in the "Document System." From here, the overview will list all the coded segments within the selected document.

Box 6.1: Managing Table Overviews in MAXQDA

In MAXQDA, table overviews are available in many places, in which you can compile coded segments, memos, and other data. These overviews can all be managed very similarly:

- *Sort columns:* Click on a column header to sort the table according to this column; another click reverses the sort order.
- *Arrange columns:* The individual columns can be arranged horizontally as you like by clicking and dragging the column header.
- *Show/hide columns:* Right-click on a column header, and choose the **Select Columns** option to determine which individual columns to hide or show.
- *Filter rows:* If you select the **Set Filter** function in the context menu of a column header, a dialog box will open in which you can set filter conditions. The filter icons in the header of the overview allow you to switch filters on or off as well as delete them.
- *Adjust the height of the preview window:* If a preview window is displayed in the upper area of the overview, you can change its height by clicking and moving the horizontal divider between each area of the dialog box.
- *Export overview*: The content of the table can be exported using the icons in the upper right-hand corner of the dialog box. Click on the Excel or HTML icons to create a temporary file, and open it directly in your device's standard programs for displaying Excel files or web pages. If no rows are selected in green, all rows will be exported, otherwise only the selected rows. The export icon provides additional export formats for individual overviews, such as the RTF format for Word, and you can also specify the name and location of the exported file here.

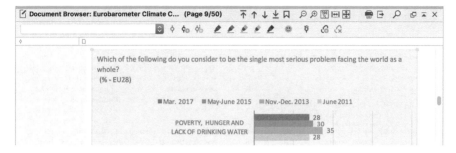

Fig. 6.10 Selected area in a PDF document

Coding PDF Documents

Coding PDF documents involves the same procedure as coding text documents: select a text passage then drag and drop it onto a code. All other coding techniques described above can also be applied to texts in PDF documents. Since PDF files were originally designed for a uniform print layout on different output devices, they do not contain any information about paragraphs or line numbers. In the Overview of Coded Segments, the PDF page number and character position are therefore displayed as the beginning and end of a coded segment instead of the paragraph number.

Often it is not only the pure text that is of interest in PDF documents but also the graphics and images contained in the PDF or even the areas of a web page that can be imported as a PDF file. Even in documents where the content has not been converted to text by automatic character recognition, as described in Chap. 3, you may want to code selected areas within the text. To code by area in this way, first draw a frame in the PDF document with your mouse (Fig. 6.10), and then drag the selected area onto a code. The Overview of Coded Segments will list the PDF page number and the coordinates of the frame points in the coded segment's area column.

Autocoding Search Results

In Chap. 5, we described how the lexical search functions of MAXQDA can be used effectively to explore qualitative data material. The result of this search process is a table list of search hits as shown in Fig. 6.11.

This exploration of your data material can be linked effectively with the coding process, as MAXQDA enables you to automatically code search hits and thereby record your explorative results in the form of codes and store them for further analysis later. Automatic coding allows several hundreds of code assignments to be generated in one go, which is why this technology is also suitable where qualitative data has been collected in large quantities. But even with more manageable data volumes, automatic coding can still be useful since

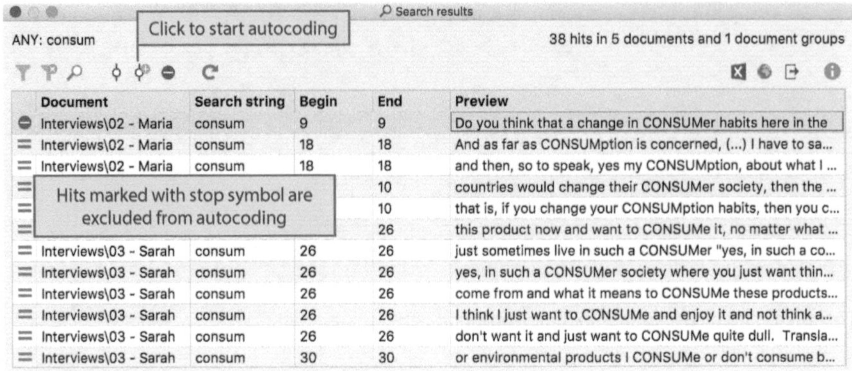

Document	Search string	Begin	End	Preview
⊖ Interviews\02 - Maria	consum	9	9	Do you think that a change in CONSUMer habits here in the
═ Interviews\02 - Maria	consum	18	18	And as far as CONSUMption is concerned, (...) I have to sa...
═ Interviews\02 - Maria	consum	18	18	and then, so to speak, yes my CONSUMption, about what I ...
═			10	countries would change their CONSUMer society, then the ...
═			10	that is, if you change your CONSUMption habits, then you c...
═			26	this product now and want to CONSUMe it, no matter what ...
═ Interviews\03 - Sarah	consum	26	26	just sometimes live in such a CONSUMer "yes, in such a co...
═ Interviews\03 - Sarah	consum	26	26	yes, in such a CONSUMer society where you just want thin...
═ Interviews\03 - Sarah	consum	26	26	come from and what it means to CONSUMe these products...
═ Interviews\03 - Sarah	consum	26	26	I think I just want to CONSUMe and enjoy it and not think a...
═ Interviews\03 - Sarah	consum	26	26	don't want it and just want to CONSUMe quite dull. Transla...
═ Interviews\03 - Sarah	consum	30	30	or environmental products I CONSUMe or don't consume b...

Callouts in figure: "Click to start autocoding" — "Hits marked with stop symbol are excluded from autocoding" — "38 hits in 5 documents and 1 document groups" — "ANY: consum" — "Search results"

Fig. 6.11 Automatically code search hits with a new code

the usual procedure consists of searching for words of interest in the data and then looking up the contexts in which they occur. For example, when analyzing interviews with students at a statistics seminar, Kuckartz, Dresing, Rädiker, & Stefer (2008) searched for the word "nervous" in the statements of the interviewees, autocoded the references, and analyzed them in their context. This example is also a good illustration of the problems of the automated process: both "very nervous about the exam" and "not nervous at all about the exam" were found and coded following this procedure, which is why it is necessary to check the individual coded segments with respect to their actual meaning and content. Furthermore, no synonyms were found for the word nervous, only those that were explicitly searched for.

How do you carry out automatic coding in practice? First, conduct a simple or complex lexical search in all or selected documents via the *Analysis* ribbon tab. To automatically assign the resulting search hits to a code, two alternative icons are available at the top of the search hit window: one for autocoding these hits with an existing code and one for autocoding them with a new code. When you select the function *Autocode search results with new code*, a window for defining a new code will appear, followed by an options dialog box for determining the extent of the search hit's context you want to code. As a rule, it is best to set the context to "sentence," because coding the search term alone is usually only analytically useful if you are interested in the frequency of words in selected documents, and the MAXDictio extension module provides significantly more convenient functions for this.

You can also restrict the autocoding to selected search hits by excluding any uninteresting or irrelevant hits. To do this, you need to go through each hit one after the other and double-click in the first column of each row containing a hit you don't want to include so that a stop symbol appears there. Alternatively, you can select one or more rows and then click the stop icon in the toolbar.

▶ **Please Note** Automatic coding with the same code does not change any existing code assignments, where these are found, in order to avoid overwriting previous, potentially time-intensive manual coding work. However, since it usually makes sense to code your search hits with a new code, from which they then can be distributed to other codes, this problem rarely arises.

References

Charmaz, K. (2014). *Constructing grounded theory* (2nd ed.). Thousand Oaks, CA: SAGE.

Corbin, J. M., & Strauss, A. L. (2015). *Basics of qualitative research: Techniques and procedures for developing grounded theory* (4th ed.). Thousand Oaks, CA: SAGE.

Kuckartz, U. (2014). *Qualitative text analysis: A guide to methods, practice & using software.* Thousand Oaks, CA: SAGE.

Kuckartz, U., Dresing, T., Rädiker, S., & Stefer, C. (2008). *Qualitative Evaluation: Der Einstieg in die Praxis* (2nd ed.). Wiesbaden: VS Verlag für Sozialwissenschaften.

Saldaña, J. (2015). *The coding manual for qualitative researchers* (3rd ed.). Thousand Oaks, CA: SAGE.

Coding Video Data, Audio Data, and Images

7

The tremendous technical progress made in recent years means that we can now take amazingly high-quality photos and video recordings with commercially available smartphones. And this, in turn, has opened up new opportunities for empirical research and the areas of field research and educational research in particular. Now virtually all researchers can produce high-quality video recordings in the field—at no cost. Consequently, there has also been a steadily growing need to be able to analyze this type of data material scientifically and to treat it in a similar methodological manner to interview or focus groups. As a method of data collection, video has of course led to great progress, especially for research into nonverbal behavior. In contrast to previous logging of observations, it is now possible to watch scenes repeatedly and have them coded by several people at different times, which significantly improves the quality of the analysis. In addition to working with videos, this chapter will also cover how to code and analyze still images, such as photos and screenshots of web pages.

> **In This Chapter**
> - Getting to know the key characteristics of video analysis
> - Answering the question, "Start coding immediately or transcribe first?"
> - Using the "Multimedia Browser" in MAXQDA
> - Direct coding of videos and adding memos and links
> - Exporting still images for publications and inserting them as new image documents
> - Customizing the display of images and coding image sections

© Springer Nature Switzerland AG 2019
U. Kuckartz, S. Rädiker, *Analyzing Qualitative Data with MAXQDA*,
https://doi.org/10.1007/978-3-030-15671-8_7

Characteristics of Video Analysis

Video data can be analyzed in a wide variety of ways. In sports and movement science, for example, it is important to study movement sequences very precisely (and very slowly) and, in the case of competitive sport, to improve them. You might have taken a skiing course, for instance, in which your skiing was filmed and then watched back with the whole group—sometimes in slow motion. Perhaps you were rather impressed with your skiing style, then again, perhaps not so much. "Video analysis" is also an innovative field in the area of "artificial intelligence," where the aim is to automatically recognize temporal and spatial events, for example, objects, movements, and situations. This plays a key role in the surveillance of public space. In the social and educational sciences, video technology has been used in research for several decades, especially to record interactions and learning situations in classroom research. The analysis technique used often involves coding the material, whereby the methods—not dissimilar to those used for the analysis of texts—differ according to whether they tend to be more content-analytical and category-based (z. Rose, 2000) or more oriented toward interpretation and hermeneutic analysis (e.g., Knoblauch, Soeffner, Raab, & Schnettler, 2012).

Coding Video Data Directly or Transcribing First?

When working with videos, the question arises whether you should first transcribe them as you would for audio recordings (Heath, Hindmarsh, & Luff, 2010) or whether you should begin coding them immediately. At first, it may seem tempting to skip the transcription process and start coding the video straight away. Transcription involves a lot of work, and it can feel like a rather tedious exercise with little of the exciting "research adventure" to it. On the other hand, experience suggests that in the case of interviews, for example, it is much easier to find your way around written data. You can search for words or specific topics in the transcript, meaning that sections of text that take several minutes to relate verbally can be coded very quickly. In individual cases, therefore, it is worth considering whether the written form is preferable. You are most likely to forgo transcribing a video if you are primarily interested in interactions, paraverbal communication, body language, and the like. The more the spoken language plays a role in the analysis, the more advisable it is for the video data to be written down or at least partially written down. It should also be noted that any transcription automatically involves a loss of information and constitutes an interpretation of the data. This should be clear in the case of video data where the wealth of information captured goes far beyond any text version. While it is not unusual in audio recordings—for example, for open question style interviews or focus group discussions—to continue working only with the transcript and not the original recording, for most video recordings the images are also analyzed and at least partially coded in addition to the text. MAXQDA allows you to work with a combination of text and images in your analysis work, so it is certainly possible to directly code some parts of a video and then transcribe and code the transcript of other parts.

Coding Video Data in the "Multimedia Browser"

As described in Chap. 3, video files are not displayed and played back in the "Document Browser" like other documents, but in the separate "Multimedia Browser" (Fig. 7.1). The video is played in the upper window of the browser. Directly below, there is a toolbar that contains all the playback functions as well as tools for coding it.

All the important steps for coding and working with videos can be performed using the icons in the toolbar or by using their corresponding keyboard shortcuts:

- To play and pause the video, use the *Play/Pause* icon or the *F4* or *F5* keys, or, with the "Multimedia Browser" currently in focus, press the *Space bar*. In addition, pressing the *Ctrl* key twice (Windows) or *Shift* ⇧ key (Mac) also starts and pauses playback.
- The blue vertical stripe at the bottom of the window displays the current playback position, and the corresponding time is shown in the toolbar. The slider in the toolbar is useful for navigating quickly in a long video. Use the fast-forward and rewind icons or the *F12* and ⇧+*F12* keys to jump forward and backward in 5-second increments for navigating to nearby scenes.
- Preview images below the toolbar will help you navigate within a video file that contains different scenes (they are less helpful in the case of an interview because they all look very similar). These images can be displayed or hidden using the second icon from the left. The first time they are displayed, you can determine the time interval between them as well as their size.
- In the *control panel*, which you can access via the first icon on the far left, the volume can be reduced for loud recordings and increased for quiet recordings, and you can also adjust the playback speed here.

▶   **Please Note** On a Mac, function keys *F1* through *F12* are usually assigned system-specific functions. To use them for transcription in MAXQDA, press and hold the *fn* key at the same time. Since this can be very cumbersome, you may want to open the system settings and select the setting *Use F1, F2 etc. as standard function keys* in the "Keyboard" menu. Then it will no longer be necessary to press and hold the *fn* key. On some Windows computers, the function keys are also assigned to system functions. In this case, it may be helpful to conduct an Internet search as to how the function keys on your computer can be used without holding the *fn* key.

Fig. 7.1 The "Multimedia Browser" for working with video files

In the lower area of the "Multimedia Browser," the audio track is displayed as a waveform parallel to the video timeline. The higher the volume at a point in the video, the higher the peaks in the waveform. The waveform will predominantly help you navigate through individual scenes, since there are little gaps or dips in it for pauses in speech. The four icons in the top right corner of the waveform window control how much of the video timeline is displayed, i.e., the visible time span in the window. A short time range is suitable for detailed analyses and for coding short scenes, while zooming out is useful for working with longer video sequences.

The procedure for coding parts of a video file in MAXQDA corresponds to the procedure for coding texts: select a segment of the video (Box 7.1) and assign an existing or a new code to it. A selected video segment is often referred to as a "clip."

Box 7.1: Selecting a Clip in the "Multimedia Browser"
- Start the playback of the video recording, e.g., by pressing the *F4* key, and stop it exactly at the point from which you want to assign a code.
- Then click the ***Start of clip selection*** icon or press the *F7* key.
- Now restart playback and stop at the end of sequence you want to code. Click the ***End of clip selection*** icon or the *F8* key.
- The borders of the clip can be easily changed by moving the boundaries of the blue frame in the waveform display, or the time indicator directly beneath these boundaries, with your mouse (Fig. 7.2). When you click on a clip boundary, you can use the arrow keys ← and → on the keyboard to adjust the clip to within a tenth of a second.
- To check your selected clip, you can play it by clicking on the blue area or pressing the *F9* key.

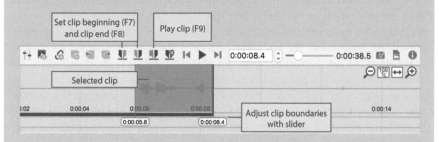

You can also select a clip in the waveform itself by drawing a horizontal area across it, keeping your left mouse button pressed down. The peaks and troughs in the audio track's waveform and the video images that accompany your mouse movement will help you navigate through the video.

Your selection can then be coded in MAXQDA as usual, e.g., by dragging and dropping the selection onto a code. When you right-click on the selection, three alternative coding options will appear in the context menu: (1) code with a new code, (2) code with "the most recently used code," and (3) code with activated codes. You can also use the predefined keyboard shortcuts, such as *Alt+W*

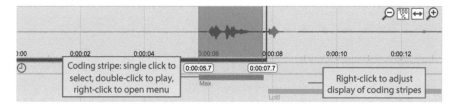

Fig. 7.2 Coding stripes in the "Multimedia Browser"

(Windows) or ⌥ + ⌘ + *W* (Mac), for assigning a new code, as well as your own user-defined keyboard shortcuts, to code within the "Multimedia Browser."

How Codes Are Displayed in the "Multimedia Browser"

Assigned codes are indicated by coding stripes below the timeline; the code name is always displayed below its stripe. In addition, the audio track is highlighted with the corresponding color of the code in the corresponding time range. If several assigned codes overlap in the video, a mixed color is displayed in the waveform. Clicking on the coding stripe once will select the corresponding time range in the waveform; a double-click plays the clip. Right-click on the coding stripe to see further options for adding a weight or code comment to the clip or deleting the assignment of the code to this section of the video.

Just as the display of the coding stripes can be configured in the "Document Browser," you can also specify which code assignments you want visually displayed in the "Multimedia Browser." To do this, right-click in the area in which the coding stripes are displayed. In the dialog box that opens, you can restrict the display of assigned codes by color or according to the user who assigned them. The option *Fixate code favorites at the top* will display the coding stripes of the codes listed under *Codes* > *Code Favorites* at the top of the "Multimedia Browser," each in its own row. This option is particularly suited to working with codes intended to break down and structure a video or to identify different camera settings. The assigned codes then facilitate easy navigation through the video and can be used for correlation analyses that track questions such as "Which interactions take place in which teaching phase?".

Attaching Memos to Video Files and Linking Video Clips

Memos can perform a variety of functions in video analyses. They can be used to identify relevant points or sequences in the video, to make notes of interpretations of selected scenes, and they can also be used to structure the video material. To assign a memo to the current playback position (Fig. 7.3), click the *New memo* icon in the "Multimedia Browser" toolbar or, alternatively, use the *Alt+⇧+M* (Windows) or ⌥+⇧+*M* (Mac) shortcut keys. If you right-click a point in the audio track, a memo is added at that position. The memo can be moved up and

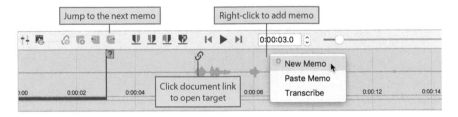

Fig. 7.3 Add a new memo to the playback position

down as well as to the right and left by dragging and dropping it with the mouse. As you move the memo, the video image will run along with it, so you can place it exactly where you want it. If you have used memos to structure the material, the icons *Next memo (F3)* and *Previous memo (⇧+F3)* in the "Multimedia Browser" toolbar will help you to navigate within the video file.

In MAXQDA, document links can be used to connect two places of the data material to each other and to jump quickly from one location to another (you can find further details on working with document links in Chap. 5). These locations may be in the same document or in different documents. You can also set document links in videos open in the "Multimedia Browser," which either lead to another place in the same video, a separate video or—as will almost certainly be the case more often—to a section of text. Suppose you watched some video sequences with students studying to be teachers and then transcribed their discussions about the videos. You can then use a document link to connect a student's statement in the transcript about a particular event to that scene in the video. To do this, select a location in the transcript, right-click on this selection, and choose the entry *Insert Document Link*. This will set a link anchor at that location. Then, in the second step, select a clip in the video and follow the same procedure: right-click on the selection and choose the same entry in the context menu to set the target of the link. Alternatively, you can also link two locations using the *Set link anchor/target* icon, which is available in both the "Multimedia Browser" and the "Document Browser."

Creating Still Images and Integrating Them in Publications

Videos can only be added to research reports to a limited extent; this is often prohibited not only by data protection regulations but also by practical concerns. These days you can certainly make videos or excerpts of videos available online and reference their respective web page in reports. However, only limited reference can be made to such external links in publications. For this reason, still images are frequently used to illustrate the results of video analyses. MAXQDA lets you copy a currently displayed video image to your clipboard and then paste it directly into a publication. To do this, click the *Copy video image to clipboard* icon in the "Multimedia Browser" menu. Additionally, the function *Insert video image as a document in "Document System"* inserts the currently displayed image at the top of your document list. From here you can analyze this image further, for example, by coding and commenting on parts of it. The options MAXQDA offers for coding images are described in detail in section "Coding and Analyzing Images".

Coding Audio Data in the "Multimedia Browser"

Audio data is coded in the same way as video data. Simply open the audio file in the "Multimedia Browser" and you will have all the tools you need to code it, annotate it with memos, and link points in the recording to each other or other places in your data, at your disposal. The only difference to analyzing video data is, of course, that there are no still images or preview thumbnails available. Accordingly, the coding and analysis of audio data has a completely different objective to that of video data analysis. Transcriptions, including partial transcriptions of recordings, usually play a far greater role in the analysis of audio data. The analysis of the audio track itself is particularly useful if you want to go beyond the analysis of its content and consider, for example, an interview respondent's speech or whether they are nervous or not. The transcription and the relevant points in the audio recording can then be connected using document links or timestamps.

Coding and Analyzing Images

MAXQDA not only lets you analyze still images from videos, but as described in Chap. 3, you can also import numerous image formats. In the case of very large image files, these can be stored outside MAXQDA projects to keep the size of your project to a minimum. Images that need to be analyzed can come from a variety of sources, such as the photo documentation for evaluations. With the help of the MAXQDA Web Collector, an extension for the browser "Chrome," you can also compile web pages and then import them into MAXQDA as images (see Chap. 3). The entire website is displayed as one long image so that usability analyses of the website design can be carried out. Even photographs taken during a field study (e.g., with MAXApp, a free app for data collection) can be imported into MAXQDA as image documents.

As soon as you open an image in the "Document Browser," several icons will appear in the toolbar to adjust the view settings (Fig. 7.4): you can zoom in or out and rotate the image display clockwise. To code images, you can draw frames with your mouse, which can then be coded like text segments, e.g., by dragging and dropping the segment onto a code. The same procedure can be used to code graphics and images in PDF files.

Right-click in the gray area to the left of the image, and a dialog box will appear in which you can adjust how the coding stripes are displayed in the "Document Browser." By selecting the option *Display coded segments in image*, the coded areas are framed in the color of their codes and lightly colored as shown in Fig. 7.4. As with texts, the coded segments of different codes may overlap. As for overlapping segments of the same code, the MAXQDA logic must be respected that the same code can only be assigned once to the same segment. This rule applies to images in the sense that areas assigned with the same code may overlap, but a segment coded with code "A" can never completely surround another segment coded with the same code. Assuming that three people can be seen directly next to each other in a picture, it is not a problem if one code is applied to the three individual segments that are drawn, one for each person, whose areas slightly overlap. However, as soon as you select an area in the picture that includes all three people and the coded segments of them, and assign the same code to this area,

Fig. 7.4 Coded image in the "Document Browser"

then MAXQDA will replace the three individual segments with one all-encompassing coded segment.

When searching for coded segments (see Chap. 9 for details), images are treated exactly like other documents: the coded parts of the image are displayed in the "Retrieved Segments" window, and clicking on the source information highlights the corresponding segment in the "Document Browser." Memos can also be attached to coded image segments in the "Document Browser." They are displayed, as with memos for texts, to the left of the image (Fig. 7.4). If you want to perform a detailed analysis of one section of an image, first select the relevant section, right-click on it, and then choose the option *Insert as New Document*. The section will be added as a new image document at the top of your "Document System" and can be analyzed as a separate "case."

References

Heath, C., Hindmarsh, J., & Luff, P. (2010). *Video in qualitative research*. Thousand Oaks, CA: SAGE.

Knoblauch, H., Soeffner, H.-G., Raab, J., & Schnettler, B. (Eds.). (2012). *Video analysis: Methodology and methods: Qualitative audiovisual data analysis in sociology* (3rd ed.). Frankfurt am Main: Lang.

Rose, D. (2000). Analysis of moving images. In M. W. Bauer & G. Gaskell (Eds.), *Qualitative researching with text, image and sound* (pp. 247–262). Thousand Oaks, CA: SAGE.

Building a Coding Frame

8

The longer and more intensively you work with your data, the more codes are likely to be generated and the more coding is carried out. This chapter deals with different types of category systems and different ways of arriving at a coding frame that is optimally suited for analysis. The two opposing poles of category formation are usually referred to as deductive and inductive category formation. In the former case, the categories are concept-based, i.e., defined before the actual analysis of the empirical data starts. In the second case, the categories are developed based on the empirical data. Inductive, data-based category building is very effectively supported in MAXQDA by the "Creative Coding" function. When working with categories, the code definitions play a very important role; they are used to record what a code means and when exactly it is assigned. Because categories play such a central role in many analysis methods, one should take sufficient time over the construction of the category system.

> **In This Chapter**
> - Learning about different types of coding frames
> - Organizing hierarchical coding frames
> - Getting to know the procedure for deductive category formation
> - Developing categories based on data, forming inductive categories
> - Creating code definitions and a codebook
> - Working with the "Creative Coding" function
> - Rethinking and structuring your coding frame

© Springer Nature Switzerland AG 2019
U. Kuckartz, S. Rädiker, *Analyzing Qualitative Data with MAXQDA*,
https://doi.org/10.1007/978-3-030-15671-8_8

Different Types of Coding Frames

Codes can have very different forms, as described in Chap. 6; sometimes they consist of a single word or abbreviation and sometimes of several words or even a complete set of statements. Codes can be simple labels or names for complex constructs. Codes can be very concrete and very general or exhibit varying degrees of abstraction. Depending on the nature of the codes and their various functions, working with codes can also be very different. When coding, especially when working with the open coding technique, the number of codes can swiftly become confusing, which raises the question of how to organize them. The entirety of all these codes is also referred to as a "coding frame," "category system," or "code system." The code system can be designed in three different ways: as a linear list, as a hierarchical structure, or as a network.

A linear list is the simplest structure; here all codes are on one level and are lined up in a list, like this:

- Environmental attitudes
- Environmental knowledge
- Environmental behavior
- Level of personal concern
- Personal CO_2 balance
- Membership in an environmental protection organization
- Greenpeace member
- Energy saving
- Mobility behavior
- Consumption patterns
- Avoiding packaging
- Knowledge about nature, animals, and plants

Such *linear lists* quickly become unmanageable and offer few possibilities for creating a structure. To create an order beyond merely sorting the codes alphabetically, you can often make things easier by defining appropriate word combinations for subordinate codes, such as "Environmental behavior, energy saving," and "Environmental behavior, mobility," or by working with abbreviations for the parent code, e.g., "Enb_energy saving," "Enb_mobility," etc. Designing a code system like this is better than a simple linear list, but such a structure is still very limited in its possibilities.

A *hierarchical code system*, as supported by MAXQDA, is much more flexible. This consists of top-level codes and multiple levels of subcategories. In general, (almost) any number of levels can be provided for such code systems, but in practice two to four levels are usually sufficient. Figure 8.1 shows such a hierarchical code system in the typical MAXQDA representation. In this code system, two main categories (top-level codes) are defined, namely, "Biggest world problems" and "Social influence." Both codes have subcodes: the first main category "Biggest world problems" has the subcodes "Climate," "Resources: scarcity, distribution,

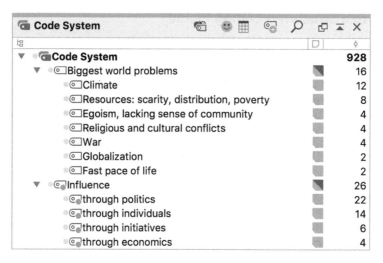

Fig. 8.1 Hierarchical category system with two levels in MAXQDA

poverty," and five more. A memo symbol is displayed to the right of each code. A double-click on this symbol opens the code memo, i.e., a detailed description of the respective code.

With such hierarchical category systems, you can gain a much better overview, for example, by hiding the sublevels. However, it is also important to note that the hierarchical structure is particularly useful for search processes and complex queries. For example, MAXQDA can compile all the text passages in which there is an overlap of certain top-level codes. Here, all the conceivable overlaps of subcodes can be examined, for instance, the simultaneous occurrence of "Biggest world problems > Climate" and "Influence > through economics." In a linear list, searching for subcodes that overlap with the subcodes of another top-level code would involve immense effort.

The structure as a *code network* is the third option for structuring a category system. In general, a network structure consists of a set of elements (nodes) that are linked to each other via connections (edges). The difference to a hierarchical structure is that there are no restrictions on these connections, whereas in a hierarchical structure, a subcode cannot be a subcode of several other parent codes at the same time.

MAXQDA can also be used to create category systems with a network structure, but not in the "Code System" window, where you can only set up and manage linear lists and hierarchical code systems. Network structures can be created with the help of the visualization tool MAXMaps. In the coding phase, you can code directly with this network (see Chap. 17).

Paths to a Structured Coding Frame

When working with MAXQDA, you will inevitably ask yourself the crucial question: "So, what about these categories, then?" More specifically, you may ask, "How do I even come up with my categories?", "How many categories do I need for my analysis?" or "Which steps do I need to take to form my categories?"

How exactly to proceed when forming your categories depends first and foremost on the research question, the objective of your research, and the previous knowledge you have about the subject area of your research. The stronger the orientation to a theory, the more extensive the previous knowledge; the more specific the questions and the more precise any potentially already existing hypotheses, the better it is to form categories before the analysis of the collected data. This type of category formation is also called *concept-driven category formation* or *deductive category formation*. The decisive factor here is that a meaningful structure for the content of the data has already been established before it is coded. This can be a theory or a hypothesis but also an interview guide or an existing structure in the given field of research. Sometimes deductive category formation is ascribed the attribute of "theory-oriented." However, this is not necessarily the case: concept-driven category building can be theory-oriented but does not have to be.

The counterpart to this approach is the *data-driven* or *inductive category formation*, in which the categories are formed directly on the basis of the data. The category system usually emerges as a hierarchical system in an iterative process that runs through several cycles. In methodological literature, the pairing of the terms inductive versus deductive category formation has become established in general usage, although the use of these terms which originate from philosophy to describe the practical procedure of category formation is by no means optimal. Like Schreier (2012, pp. 84–87), we prefer the more appropriate terms *concept-driven* for deductive and *data-driven* for inductive strategies of category formation (Schreier, 2012, pp. 84–87).

Creating Concept-Driven Categories (Deductive Category Formation)

How does the concept-driven formation of categories work? As described above, the starting point is an extensive structuring of the research questions that already exist before the coding phase. Frequently, such structuring has already determined the interview guidelines used to collect the data. A simple example is that before MAXQDA workshops we always send the participants an e-mail and ask them to answer some questions like the following:

1. Why are you attending the workshop? What are your goals, what do you want to learn?
2. Have you already gained experience with MAXQDA (or any other QDA software)? Please briefly describe your level of experience.

3. What kind of qualitative data do you want to analyze?
4. Here you can list up to five more questions that you would like to discuss during the workshop:

The following categories can easily be derived from these four questions:

- Goal of participation
- Experience with MAXQDA
- Type of data to be analyzed
- Questions to discuss in the workshop

The first step of the analysis is to code the corresponding text passages of the answers of the participants with these four codes. This first deductive step is followed by a second inductive step. For example, the "questions for the workshop" mentioned by the participants will be grouped and, in view of the design of the planned workshop, combined into question blocks. These blocks are then created in MAXQDA's "Code System" as subcodes of the top-level code "Questions to discuss in the workshop."

In a comprehensive guide, the definition of categories may be more complicated, but the principle is the same, namely, to derive categories for the analysis from the questions in the guide, which have already determined the structure of the data collected. It is very helpful to keep your own research questions in mind and to construct the categories in such a way that a suitable structure for the research report can be developed later. Of course, the analysis of data in qualitative research should have an open character, but foresight in planning is always useful.

Another option for concept-driven category formation—as an alternative to deriving the categories from the interview guide—is the formation of categories based on a specific theory or the current state of research. The former is rather rare in practice, but there are both good examples and good arguments in favor of this approach (C. Hopf, 2016). If the aim of research is to examine a theory or, as in the case of Hopf, the question of whether a certain theory (here the theory of attachment) can explain phenomena (here right-wing radical thinking), then it is only logical to derive the analysis categories from this theory.

It may also make sense to make the current state of research the basis of category formation. Kuckartz (2016, pp. 67–72) reports on the development of a coding frame on the topic of quality of life, in which the following categories were deductively formed in a rather elaborate group procedure based on the state of research:

- Work and occupation (also includes labor market and career opportunities)
- Education (also includes educational opportunities)
- Political freedom in the sense of participation and political participation
- Health
- Individual freedom in the sense of self-determination, self-realization, and free choice of lifestyle
- Culture (also includes cultural and leisure activities)

- Standard of living and wealth
- Security (in regard to war, civil war, crime, personal assaults, but also from personal poverty)
- Social inclusion
- Environment, nature, sustainability
- Work-life balance, time prosperity

These 11 categories cover all those areas that are relevant to quality of life according to the current state of research. The process of developing this category system made it clear to our group of researchers that the claim of consistency and reliability cannot be made when designing a category system. In contrast to what the term may suggest, such deductive categorization is also a constructive process in which researchers act on the basis of their previous knowledge and their specific views. An attempt at reaching a consensus here would be just as misguided as an attempt to have different working groups within a quantitative research framework constructs the same questionnaire with the same questions. However it is done, the category system must be formed in such a way that the categories are clearly defined and that the coders can use the categories in a reliable manner. The category definitions play a key role here. These are used to determine as precisely as possible when a particular category is to be applied.

Category Definitions and Code Memos
Working with categories is central to many projects; it requires a lot of brain work, a lot of time, and careful work. This is true for different methods and research styles but especially for projects that work according to the grounded theory approach or the method of qualitative content analysis. In both cases, it is important to describe the meaning of a category as clearly as possible, for example, by writing an appropriate memo. The grounded theory calls this a *code memo* (Charmaz, 2006, pp. 72–85; Glaser & Strauss, 2009), while in qualitative content analysis, *category definition* is the preferred term. At the beginning of a grounded theory analysis, a memo may only contain a few words or keywords and ideas. As the analysis progresses, code memos become more complex and sometimes take the form of highly differentiated theoretical thoughts on a specific key area of content.

The approach in grounded theory differs significantly from other methods such as qualitative content analysis. The latter is a more rule-based method in which it is particularly important to formulate category definitions as precisely as possible in the process of constructing the category system. Regardless of how the categories were developed, whether inductively based on the material or in advance without empirical data, each category should be defined precisely in a qualitative content analysis. The general structure displayed in Fig. 8.2 is recommended for a category definition.

Category definitions have a dual function: firstly, they document the framework of the analysis for the scientific community (and also for the reviewers of a publication), and, secondly, they form the basis of the coding guide used by the coders. This means that the better the definitions and the clearer the examples, the better the

Name of the category:	As concise a name as possible
Description of the category:	Description of the category, possibly with a theoretical linkage
Application of the category:	"Category x" is coded if the following aspects are present …
Examples of applications:	Quotations with reference (document, paragraph)
Further applications (optional):	The category is also assigned if … Quotations with reference (document, paragraph)
Differentiation from other categories (optional):	The category is not coded if…: …. in this case, "Category y" is used Quotations with reference (document, paragraph)

Fig. 8.2 General scheme for category definitions

coding and the higher the probability of achieving a good match between the coders will be.

MAXQDA also offers the option of compiling all categories and their definitions in a category manual, a so-called codebook, via the function **Reports > Codebook**. This is particularly important for masters' theses and dissertations, as it is an excellent way of documenting the rigor and accuracy with which work has been carried out. Figure 8.3 shows a code memo written in MAXQDA containing the name of the code, author and creation date, the code definition, and a "perfect example." This is the term used to describe text passages that are prototypical for the assignment of the code in question.

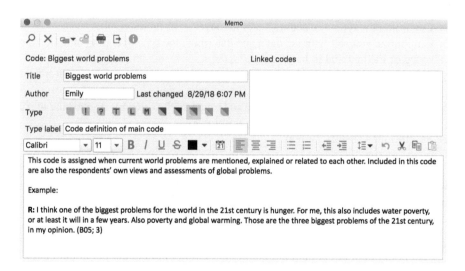

Fig. 8.3 Defining a code in a code memo

Creating Data-Driven Categories (Inductive Category Formation)

Typical for qualitative research is the formation of categories based directly on the data, which is called data-based or inductive category formation. Inductive does not mean, however, that the categories simply flow to you from the data, as it were, but it is an active process that is inconceivable without the active engagement, knowledge and understanding of the material, and linguistic competence of those involved in the category formation. Since the formation of categories thus depends on individual category-building competence and active engagement, it is difficult to postulate intersubjective agreement in the construction of a category system. If several people, alone or in groups, form categories based on the same data, the categories will be partly similar, partly even the same, but also partly different. Hence, any potential demand for inductive coding by several people or members of a team to result in the formation of the same categories cannot be met. It therefore also does not make sense to calculate coefficients of agreement or the intercoder reliability in general for purposes of category *formation*. Nevertheless, this does not mean that several people should not be involved in the categorization process. On the contrary, it is highly recommended that several people be involved in the process of category development. They should first develop category proposals independently of each other and then exchange ideas in order to fully exploit the group's creative potential.

The Process of Data-Driven Category Building

There are a number of approaches for data-based category building (z.B. Charmaz, 2006; Kuckartz, 2014; Mayring, 2014; Strauss & Corbin, 1990). A guideline for how to proceed in the research process can be found in Kuckartz (2014, pp. 58–60), where six phases of data-driven category formation are described for text data:

1. Determine the objective of category building on the basis of the research question.
2. Determine the type of categories and the level of abstraction.
3. Familiarize yourself with the data, and determine the type of coding unit, i.e., the scope of the material to be coded.
4. Process the texts sequentially, and create categories while working with a text, assigning either new categories or existing categories.
5. Group the formed codes, systematize and organize the category system, and make sure that the categories form a meaningful whole.
6. Set (fix) the category system.

At the outset of the data-driven category formation process, the "Code System" will still be empty, i.e., new codes must be generated. As the category-building process progresses, you will often combine these codes into more abstract codes or define new top-level codes and assign already generated codes to them.

Create a New Code While Working with a Text

If you want to create new codes during inductive coding of the data, the fastest way to do this is to press *Alt+W* (Windows) or ⌥ + ⌘ + W (Mac). Chapter 6 describes several alternative ways of creating new codes in addition to this key combination.

Assigning a Text Passage to an Existing Code

If codes that have already been defined in the "Code System" are to be assigned, this can be done quite conveniently by dragging and dropping the selected text onto the respective code or vice versa, the code onto the selected segment.

Merge Codes

If two codes have very similar meanings, which is not uncommon in open coding following the grounded theory method, it makes sense to merge the codes. Usually the code name will be adapted accordingly and replaced by a more general term. With inductive coding, there is automatically at least one coded text passage for each code; "empty codes" without assigned text passages do not exist here. Merging codes always takes place in the following three steps:

1. Right-click on the code to be merged ("Code A"), and select the option *Move Coded Segments from the context menu*.
2. Click on the code you want to merge Code A with, and select the option *Move Coded Segments from "Code A" from the context menu*. Now the coded segments are moved to this code, and the number 0 will be displayed next to the first selected code ("Code A"), i.e., there are no coded segments under this code anymore.
3. Now "Code A" can be deleted, and the code name of the target code can be changed if necessary.

Create a New Top-Level Category and Assign Existing Codes as Subcodes

New codes are always added to the "Code System" in the selected row, i.e., where the blue focus bar is located. If you want to create a new code at the top level, first click on the root of the "Code System," i.e., the row labeled "Code System." Next, click on the *New code* icon or select this option from the context menu. You can then enter the name of your new code, and, if desired, assign a color. You can also assign other existing codes as subcodes of this new code by dragging and dropping them onto the new code with your mouse.

Organizing Your "Code System"

The "Code System" can be sorted automatically or manually. The automatic settings sort the codes either alphabetically (in ascending or descending order) or by code frequency (in ascending or descending order). Manual sorting allows you to determine the sequence entirely as you wish. We recommend that you start sorting the codes from the top level downward. In case of a code system with many codes, it is a good idea to hide all the subcodes first. You can then move your codes back and forth with the mouse and arrange them as required. To do this, simply move the code to the relevant position while holding down the mouse button and drop it there. Note: if a code is dropped directly onto another code, it will become a subcode of that code.

Creative Coding: A Tool for the Visual Development of a Coding Frame

"Creative Coding" is an innovative visual tool for building a structured category system. Open coding can lead to a large number of codes that are difficult to manage and difficult to organize in the "Code System." "Creative Coding" supports the creation of a meaningful structure: you can sort and organize codes, define relationships between them, insert parent codes, and form a hierarchical structure of codes.

On a screen with a lot of space—at least if you use MAXQDA on a modern desktop computer—you can move the codes around and group them in a meaningful way. Codes that belong together in terms of content are placed close to each other, additional codes can be inserted, and codes can be renamed and assigned a color. In this way, you can create a suitable coding frame in a step-by-step manner.

"Creative Coding" involves three phases:

1. First, drag all the codes you want to organize from the code system onto the workspace. You can create a first, provisional order by manually placing thematically similar codes close to each other.
2. In the second phase, you can then thoroughly sort and group the codes, and, if necessary, create new top-level codes or subcodes. You can merge codes together or turn codes into the subcodes of others. Finally, you can also assign colors to codes or groups of codes.
3. In the third phase, the changes you have made are then transferred back and implemented in the existing code system. The complete coding frame you have generated can be exported as an image file, which you can later use for presentations (e.g., on a poster for a conference) and documentation.

In the following example, "Creative Coding" is used to set up a category system on the topic, "What do people personally think is important in life?"

Step #1: Start "Creative Coding" and Select Your Codes

- After you have started "Creative Coding" via **Codes > Creative Coding**, your code system will be displayed in the left window. In Fig. 8.4 this is a long list of codes inductively formed in the course of analyzing responses to the question "What do people personally think is important in life?"
- Drag and drop all the codes you want to sort into the workspace; if necessary, you can also remove them from the map by clicking on the corresponding icon.
- Once you have selected all the necessary codes, click the **Start Organizing Codes** icon in the upper left corner of the window to start the organization phase. The normal use of MAXQDA will then be paused until you stop the "Creative Coding" process.

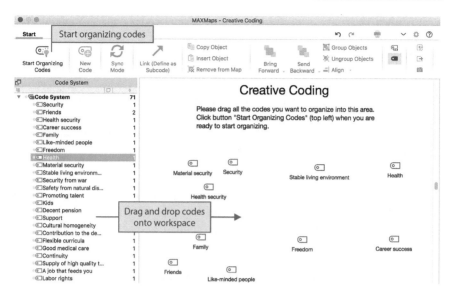

Fig. 8.4 Select codes for "Creative Coding"

Grouping and Organizing Codes

- When you start the organization phase, the code system will be hidden in the left window to maximize the workspace. At the same time, a color panel with all colors currently used in MAXQA will appear in the right margin.
- All codes can now be freely arranged and linked to each other with the mouse across the entire workspace. You can also select and move multiple codes at once by dragging a frame around them with the mouse and then repositioning the entire group.
- Relationships between codes are represented by arrows: if an arrow points to a code, it means that this code is a subcode of the other. "Code A" can be turned into a subcode of "Code B" as follows: click on the ***Link (Define as Subcode)*** icon to switch to Link Mode (Fig. 8.5). Then click on your desired top-level code and drag an arrow to the desired subcode while holding down the mouse button. To avoid circular relationships, any existing assignments of the subcode to other codes are automatically removed.
- By clicking the ***Link (Define as Subcode)*** icon again or by simply clicking on the workspace itself, you can return to the regular Selection Mode at any time.

Fig. 8.5 Important icons in the "Start" ribbon tab in Creative Coding

- It is often necessary or useful to combine several codes under a more abstract term. For this purpose, you can create new codes by clicking on the *New code* icon.
- To merge codes, be sure that Link Mode is switched off. Hold down the mouse button, and drag a code onto another code until "Merge Codes" is displayed on the mouse cursor. As soon as you release the mouse button, you will be asked if you want to merge the codes. If you click "Yes," the code you moved will disappear from the map, and its coded segments will be assigned to the target code when you complete the "Creative Coding" process.
- The color and appearance of codes can be changed quickly and easily. To change the color, select the respective code—you can select multiple codes by dragging a frame around the codes with your mouse. You can then either select a previously used color or define a new color in the color panel on the right side. The appearance of individual codes can also be configured by clicking on the respective code icon. In the window on the right side of the screen, you can then define the font size, icon size, and more. Changes can be undone step-by-step by clicking on the corresponding icon in the upper right-hand corner of the window.

Transferring the Generated Structure of the Codes Back into the Code System
None of the actions and changes you make while working with "Creative Coding" will have any effect on your "Code System" until you click *Quit Creative Coding*. At this point you must decide whether you want the new structure you have created to be transferred to your code system or not. If so, all the codes in the "Creative Coding" workspace will be inserted into the "Code System" according to their hierarchical position and sorted alphabetically, the changed colors of the codes will be adopted, and merged codes will be merged. At the same time, the "Creative Coding" workspace will be inserted into MAXMaps as a new map (see Chap. 17) and added to your list of maps for this project—this is very useful for documenting the development process of your coding frame.

Figure 8.6 shows the result of the grouping process: eight main categories were defined on the topic of "What is important in life?" including "Personal well-being," "Primary network," and "Secondary network." The codes created in the open coding phase, on which the main categories are based, are each linked to them by arrows. These do not necessarily have the function of subcategories for further analysis and further coding. In most cases they tend simply to be examples, and only during the next step are subcategories systematically formed for the eight main categories. Before doing so, however, it may make sense to code some more texts in order to test whether these eight categories can actually capture everything that is personally important in life for the research participants. Of course, new codes can also be created and arranged in a further iteration of the "Creative Coding" process during the course of the analysis.

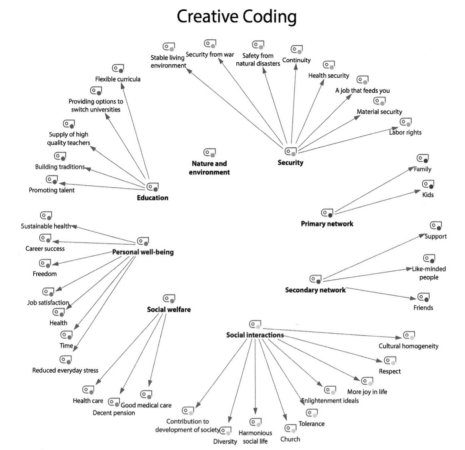

Fig. 8.6 "Creative Coding" at the end of the grouping process

Documenting the Evolution of the Coding Frame

In data-driven category formation, the category system develops in a step-by-step manner. It makes sense to document this development process and, for example, to record why categories were merged or why different categories were aligned with regard to their level of abstraction. This documentation helps to keep an overview of the development process and to be able to report on it in a comprehensible way later if required. This is also an important step as an audit trail in which the sequence of all actions in the analysis phase is recorded. An audit trail of this kind is an important quality criterion (not only) for qualitative research, as it makes the acquisition of new insights as well as the decision-making process during the analysis transparent.

MAXQDA offers various options for such documentation: firstly, an ongoing research diary can be kept in the logbook (to be found under **Home** > **Logbook**);

secondly, all relevant decisions can be recorded in free memos; and, thirdly, the status of the coding frame, as it is displayed in "Creative Coding" at certain points in time, can be saved as a "standard map" in MAXMaps.

Tips for Coding Frames

Finally, here are a few general hints and tips for designing coding frames:

- Do not define too many codes and keep the number of levels manageable. Codes are tools for analysis; in a toolbox with hundreds of tools, you wouldn't find some things when you need them.
- The number of categories should normally not exceed 20 top-level categories, and the number of subcategories per top-level category should not exceed 10.
- Usually, each code name should only exist once in the code system, because MAXQDA offers many possibilities to search for the common occurrences. Duplicate code names can therefore lead to unintended results. Only in exceptional cases should the same subcodes occur under different main categories, for example, in attitudes and behavioral research if attitudes and behavior are coded in different areas. Here, it makes sense to define the behavior areas as subcodes of the main categories "Attitudes" and "Behavior," for example, "Attitudes > Mobility" and "Behavior > Mobility."
- Always remember that the coding frame has the purpose of organizing the data and systematizing it with regard to the research question. It is not a rigid scheme; you should be open to changes and avoid seeing the code system as possessing the character of a code of law.

References

Charmaz, K. (2006). *Constructing grounded theory*. Thousand Oaks, CA: SAGE.

Glaser, B. G., & Strauss, A. L. (2009). *The discovery of grounded theory: Strategies for qualitative research* (4th ed.). New Brunswick: Aldine.

Hopf, C. (2016). In W. Hopf & U. Kuckartz (Eds.), *Schriften zu Methodologie und Methoden qualitativer Sozialforschung*. Wiesbaden: Springer VS.

Kuckartz, U. (2014). *Qualitative text analysis: A guide to methods, practice & using software*. Thousand Oaks, CA: SAGE.

Kuckartz, U. (2016). *Qualitative Inhaltsanalyse: Methoden, Praxis, Computerunterstützung* (3rd ed.). Weinheim: Beltz Juventa.

Mayring, P. (2014). *Qualitative content analysis: Theoretical foundation, basic procedures and software solution*. Klagenfurt. Retrieved from http://nbn-resolving.de/urn:nbn:de:0168-ssoar-395173

Schreier, M. (2012). *Qualitative content analysis in practice*. Thousand Oaks, CA: SAGE.

Strauss, A. L., & Corbin, J. M. (1990). *Basics of qualitative research: Grounded theory procedures and techniques*. Newbury Park, CA: Sage Publications.

Working with Coded Segments and Memos

9

How do I compile all the segments coded with the same category? How do I keep track of all the codes I have assigned? MAXQDA not only indicates within the texts, images, and videos themselves which codes have been assigned to them and where but can also compile a list of all the places that have been assigned with the same code. In contrast to earlier manual techniques, the surrounding context of each coded area is also immediately visible when working with the software. Moreover, codes are allowed to develop throughout the analysis process, and they can be changed, differentiated, or integrated into more abstract codes. MAXQDA lets you retrieve coded segments according to different criteria (e.g., those that overlap, those in close proximity to one other, etc.) and display or export them in several ways. The Smart Publisher is a tool that creates thematically structured reports in a finished layout. In conjunction with coding, many researchers also work with memos in which they write down notable observations, hypotheses, thoughts, code descriptions, and much more. But how do you keep track of dozens of memos and their valuable content?

In This Chapter
- Understanding the principle of activating documents and codes
- Displaying selected coded segments in the "Retrieved Segments" window
- Viewing the context of coded segments
- Understanding techniques for code differentiation and aggregation
- Exporting and processing coded segments
- Presenting the results of your coding work with the Smart Publisher
- Keeping track of memos

© Springer Nature Switzerland AG 2019
U. Kuckartz, S. Rädiker, *Analyzing Qualitative Data with MAXQDA*,
https://doi.org/10.1007/978-3-030-15671-8_9

Retrieving Coded Segments

Which text passages are assigned to the same category? Which segments were coded in a particular document? These are important questions that arise soon after you have coded the first few passages or sections in your data and want to keep track of them. To allow you to review and inspect your category contents and coded segments, MAXQDA lets you compile a selection of these segments in the "Retrieved Segments" window at any time. Remember: the "Retrieved Segments" window is the fourth main window in MAXQDA and can be opened and closed from the *Home* menu. The window has this name because it allows you to "retrieve" and compile coded segments in your data material. This process of retrieving and compiling coded segments is discussed in the methods literature under the term "Retrieval" and is also called a "Coding Query" in MAXQDA. The retrieval of coded segments is based on a simple principle:

1. In the "Document System," you select all documents from which you want to retrieve the coded segments.
2. In the "Code System," you select all the codes whose coded segments you want to include in this retrieval.

MAXQDA then lists all segments within the selected documents to which the selected codes were assigned in the "Retrieved Segments" window.

Selecting Documents and Codes by Activating Them
Documents and codes are selected in MAXQDA by "activating" them. There are several ways to activate a document:

- Right-click on a document name and select *Activate.*
- Hold down the *Ctrl* (Windows) or *command* ⌘ key (Mac) and click on a document.
- Click directly on the circle to the left of the document icon.

The result of activating a document is immediately visible in the "Document System." Activated documents are marked in red, and the circle next to the document icon changes to a red arrow (Fig. 9.1). You can also activate all the documents in a document group. To do this, simply follow one of the same procedures listed above at the document group level. To activate all the documents in a project, activate the top entry "Documents" in your "Document System" window.

A code is activated in the "Code System" in the same way as with documents:

- Right-click on a code and select the entry *Activate.*
- Hold down the *Ctrl* (Windows) or *command* ⌘ key (Mac) and click on a code.
- Click directly on the circle to the left of the code icon.

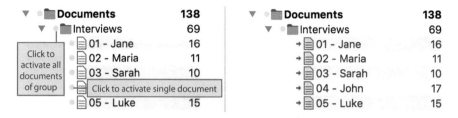

Fig. 9.1 Left: not activated. Right: activated documents in the "Document System"

Fig. 9.2 Left: not activated. Right: activated codes in the "Code System"

Figure 9.2 shows that this activation is also immediately visible in the "Code System," because an activated code is also marked in red. As indicated in the example, activating the code "Biggest world problems" selects all its subcodes at the same time.

▶ **Tip** To only activate a parent code without its subcodes, hold down the keys *Ctrl* and *Shift* ⇧ (Windows) or *command* ⌘ and *Shift* ⇧ (Mac) and then click on the code.

As soon as at least one document and at least one code are activated, MAXQDA compiles the corresponding coded segments in the "Retrieved Segments" window. Which segments are displayed depends on how you combine the activations of documents and codes:

Activated documents	Activated codes	Result in the "Retrieved Segments" window
All documents	One code	All coded segments of the activated code
One document	All codes	All coded segments of the activated document
One document	One code	All coded segments of the activated code in the activated document
All documents	Several codes	All the coded segments of the activated codes

In the "Retrieved Segments" window, all the coded segments are listed one below the other, with an info box to the left of each indicating from which document the segment originates. Figure 9.3 shows the first coded segments in the "Retrieved

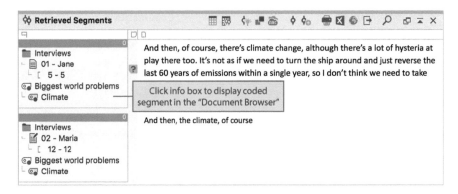

Fig. 9.3 Compiled list of coded segments in the "Retrieved Segments" window

Fig. 9.4 Status bar shows 5 activated documents, 1 activated code, and 12 coded segments

Segments" window for the code "Climate" from all the activated interviews. The info box next to the text reveals that the first coded segment comes from the interview with Jane at paragraph 5.

One of the great advantages of working with MAXQDA is that a simple click on the info box of a coded segment automatically opens its source document in the "Document Browser" and highlights the coded passage or section in the document. This makes it easy to jump from the coded segment to its origin at any time and to see its surrounding context. The info box not only displays the origin of the coded segment, but the number at the top right also tells you the weight assigned to it. Both segments shown in Fig. 9.3 have a weight of 0, which corresponds to the standard weight of MAXQDA. For more information on working with weights, see Chap. 6.

At the bottom of the window, there is a status bar with icons on the left-hand side that provide information on the number of codes that have been activated and compiled (Fig. 9.4).

If you assigned a memo to a document at a specific location, this memo will also be displayed in the "Retrieved Segments" window as soon as its location in the document appears there. In Fig. 9.3, you can see that on paragraph 5 of the interview with Jane, a memo was evidently assigned to the interview at a location that falls within a section coded with the code "climate." Memos are also interactive in the "Retrieved Segments" window: if you hover your cursor over the memo icon, a preview of the memo text will be displayed, and double-clicking on it opens the memo for viewing and editing.

Fig. 9.5 Resetting
activations using the icon in
the "Code System"

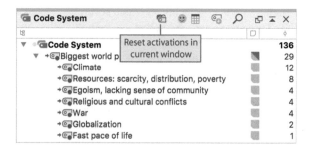

Deactivating Activated Documents and Codes

Once you have inspected the coded segments of one code and want to move on to the next code, do not simply activate the next code, because then the contents of both codes will be listed in the "Retrieved Segments" window. You also need to deactivate the first code. Deactivating codes—and documents—is done in the same way as activating them:

- Right-click on the code or document and select **Deactivate**. This is possible at all levels in the "Code System" and "Document System" and always includes any sublevels.
- Alternatively, you can click on a code or document while holding down the **Ctrl** (Windows) or **command** ⌘ key (Mac) or, without additionally pressing a key, simply click on the arrow to the left of the code or document icon.

Additionally, there is an icon on the far left in both the headers of the "Document System" and "Code System" windows that lets you reset all activations in the respective window at once (Fig. 9.5). The **Analysis** ribbon tab also contains a large icon for resetting all activations in both windows.

Scrolling Through Your Coded Segments in Table Overviews

In Chap. 6 we introduced the Overview of Coded Segments: by double-clicking on a code, you get a table list of all the locations assigned with this code. Clicking on a row in this list has the same effect as clicking on an info box in the "Retrieved Segments" window and displays the relevant segment in the "Document Browser." Using the arrow keys on your keyboard, you can then browse through code by code and, for example, review the coded text passages of interviews. A table view of this kind is also available for the "Retrieved Segments" window: click on the **Change to table view** icon ▦ in the window header to list the individual segments in a table format. In contrast to the Overview of Coded Segments, however, there is no additional window area in which a selected segment is displayed. This is also unnecessary, since the coded segments are displayed in the "Document Browser" when you click on a row.

Complex Coding Query: Analyzing How Your Codes Interact

The procedure described so far for compiling coded segments in the "Retrieved Segments" window refers exclusively to what could be described as a "simple" search for coded segments, in which several activated codes are linked with a logical OR. This means that the coded segments of all activated codes are displayed. For example, if you activate all documents and then the codes "Climate" and "Globalization," all the coded segments from both categories will be displayed in the "Retrieved Segments" window. Some segments may also be listed twice if both codes have been assigned to them.

MAXQDA allows you to perform not only simple coded segment searches but also complex searches in which several codes can be linked together. You can access this complex search via **Analysis > Complex Coding Query**, which will open a dialog box offering a total of nine different combination options:

- *Intersection:* searches for segments to which all of the selected codes have been assigned. This is particularly useful if segments have been assigned with several categories on different levels or dimensions. Let us assume that a project will examine the effects of increasing digitization on various professional groups. In guided interviews, text passages were coded with categories for various professional areas, technologies, and required competencies. The complex code search "Intersection" can now be used to search for text passages to which the codes for certain combinations of professional areas, technologies, and competencies have been assigned.
- *Intersection (Set):* like "Intersection," but not all the selected codes must be assigned to the coded segment simultaneously; it is sufficient if at least a freely definable minimum number of the selected codes intersect for this segment.
- *Overlapping:* like "Intersection," but instead of only retrieving the part of the segment where the selected codes intersect, this option retrieves the whole segment contained within the outer boundaries of all overlapping codes.
- *Only one code; Only this code:* lets you search for locations where one code has been assigned, but not other codes. These functions can be used, for example, to quality check the coding work. You could check, for instance, whether at least one new technology has been assigned for each professional area.
- *If inside; If outside:* in principle like "Intersection," only that the searched places must be completely inside or outside a segment assigned to a defined code. To clarify, a coded segment lies within another coded segment if its segment boundaries are not greater than those of the surrounding coded segment.
- *Followed by; Near:* lets you search for segments assigned with a particular code that are close to or follow a segment assigned to a different code. As maximum distances between them, you can specify *paragraphs* for texts, *rows* for tables, and *seconds* for videos.

The codes you want to combine in your search have to be entered in the areas "A" and "B" depending on the function you have selected, while in the "C" area, you can set options such as the distance between them (Chap. 13 provides further information on using the Complex Coding Query). MAXQDA always indicates in the dialog box how many segments meet your set conditions before you need to "run" it. When you start a coding query, the data segments found are listed in the "Retrieved Segments" window, with the selected function displayed in the status bar at the

Fig. 9.6 The status bar displays the selected function for your searches for coded segments

bottom of the screen (Fig. 9.6). This is important to note, because only when MAXQDA is set to "Simple Coding Query (the OR combination of codes)" does the activation of documents and codes enable the listing of results in the "Retrieved Segments" window, in the way described earlier in the chapter. To switch back to the Simple Coding Query after running a Complex Coding Query, select *Analysis > Reset Coding Query.*

Retrieving Coded Video Clips

Coded video clips are compiled in the "Retrieved Segments" window in the same way as text passages: activate all the documents with video files and all the codes you want taken into account, and MAXQDA will list the video clips found in the "Retrieved Segments" window. Once you have created preview images for a video in the "Multimedia Browser," the preview image closest to the beginning of the video clip is displayed in the "Retrieved Segments" window so that you can see the content of the video clip (Fig. 9.7). If no preview images have been created, only a corresponding icon will be displayed.

The info box with the source information displays the start and end times of a video clip, and clicking on this box plays the clip in the "Multimedia Browser."

▶ **Please Note** The transcript and video can only be activated together as a unit in the "Document System," i.e., both the coded segments from the transcript and the coded segments in the video are compiled in the "Retrieved Segments" for the activated codes.

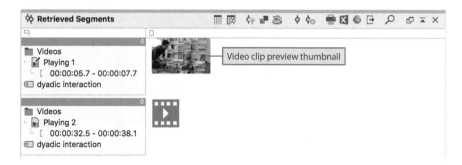

Fig. 9.7 Coded video clips in the "Retrieved Segments" window (one with and one without a preview thumbnail)

Differentiating Codes: Splitting Up Coded Segments into Different Codes

One of the most common activities when working with coded segments is to distribute the coded segments of a thematically broad code to its more concrete subcodes; in this case, we often say that the code has been "differentiated." Let us assume that you have carried out a rough coding process for several interviews with the code "Biggest world problems," in which you recorded all the text passages that broadly mention important global problems. As a second step, you might then want to distribute these coded segments into several subcategories using fine coding. How do you do this in MAXQDA? The procedure comprises three steps and is described in Box 9.1 for text segments (see also Fig. 9.8), where the focus is on the technical procedure and not on the formation of suitable categories, which we have already discussed in detail in Chap. 8. Another very convenient way to differentiate codes is described below in the section "Smart Coding Tool: Working Effectively with Codes and Coded Segments."

Box 9.1: Differentiating Codes into Subcodes
Preparation
    If you have already defined all or some subcodes a priori, you should first enter these into your "Code System."

Step 1: Compiling Coded Segments
- Activate all relevant documents and the code you want to differentiate. Be careful: if the code already has subcodes, only the code, and not the subcodes, should be activated so that no segments that are already assigned to the subcodes are included. MAXQDA compiles the segments coded with the activated code in the "Retrieved Segments" window.
- Alternatively, you can double-click on the code in the "Code System" to display the relevant segments in the Overview of Coded Segments table. Be careful: if the code already has subcodes, these must be expanded and visible, when double-clicking the code, so that only the coded segments of the parent code are listed.

Step 2: Read Coded Segments and Create Subcodes if Necessary
- Read the text of the first or next coded segment.
- If there is no suitable subcode for this segment yet, create a new subcode under the parent code.

Step 3: Move or Copy Code or Parts of the Code to Subcode
- If you want to move the complete segment into the subcode, drag its info box from the "Retrieved Segments" window, and drop it on the target code

(continued)

> **Box 9.1** (continued)
>
> in the "Code System" window. Hold down the **Ctrl** key (Windows) or the **option** ⌥ key (Mac) if you do not want to move the code, but copy it (e.g., to assign the code to several subcodes).
>
> - If you only want to assign part of the coded segment to a subcode, mark the relevant parts of the text passage in the "Retrieved Segments" window, and code them with your desired subcode by dropping the selection in the "Code System" window.
> - If you are working with Overview of Coded Segments, you can drag and drop one (or more) row onto a target subcode to differentiate your coded segments. Alternatively, you can also select text parts in the preview window of the Overview of Coded Segments and drag them onto a code.
> - Steps 2 and 3 can then be repeated for each code.

Many MAXQDA users ask themselves whether the coded segment should remain in the parent code once it has been differentiated or not. A point in favor of this is that it will then always be possible to trace which and how many segments were first created within the broader code. However, since the presence of codes in the parent code often complicates further analytical tasks, for example, because the number of codes is taken into account for visualizations and you may have to laboriously recalculate them or somehow ignore them, it is usually recommended to delete the assignment of the coded segments to the parent code after completing the differentiation process. Neither should coded segments remain in the parent code because they could not be reasonably assigned to a subcode or the content of which only occurred very seldomly. Such segments are much better placed in a new subcategory named "Other." To ensure transparency and traceability of the analysis, a project copy with a descriptive file name can be saved just before you begin the differentiation process in order to document and view this version of your project at a later time. Alternatively, you could of course also transfer the coded segments of the parent code into another "Archive Code" and leave it in the project.

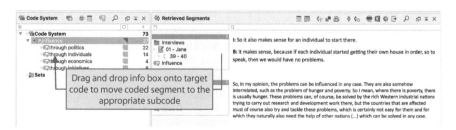

Fig. 9.8 Moving a coded segment from one code to another

Merging Codes: Combine Coded Segments from Different Codes into a Single Code

The opposite process of differentiating a code consists of merging codes, especially when two categories are similar in content or can be combined under a more abstract code name. In Chap. 8 we explained how to combine two codes on a surface similar to a pinboard using the *Codes > Creative Coding* function: drag one of the two code icons onto a second code icon with your mouse. All the subcodes of the code you moved will then be transferred to the target code, and the empty code will be deleted. This procedure can also be carried out—with a little more manual work—in the "Code System," as described in Box 9.2.

> **Box 9.2: Merging Two Codes in the "Code System"**
> - Right-click one of the two codes whose segments you want to merge.
> - In the context menu, choose *Move Coded Segments.* MAXQDA will remember that you want to move all the segments from this code, but nothing further will happen for now.
> - Right-click on the second code, i.e., the target code.
> - In the context menu, select the entry *Move Coded Segments from "Source Code,"* and click OK in the confirmation box that appears. At this point the segments will be reassigned to the target code.
> - Delete the source code that no longer contains any coded segments.
> - If necessary, edit the name of the remaining code.

▶ **Please Note** In MAXQDA, the same place in a document may only be coded once with the same code. Hence, if you transfer segments from one code to another, the resulting number of coded segments may be smaller than the sum of the segments of both codes separately. This happens when one or more locations in a document were already coded with the target code.

Smart Coding Tool: Working Effectively with Codes and Coded Segments

The Smart Coding Tool can be used to edit, adapt, and supplement existing coded segments. The tool is suitable for the creation of categories, in which codes are differentiated, existing codes are merged, and code comments are used for the development of new categories. Moreover, it might be helpful while writing reports, when it is important that you are able to grasp the contents and interdependencies of your categories quickly. The advantage of working with the Smart Coding Tool is that a lot of coding-specific information (coded segments, assigned codes, and

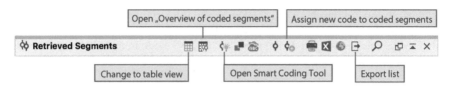

Fig. 9.9 The toolbar in the "Retrieved Segments" window

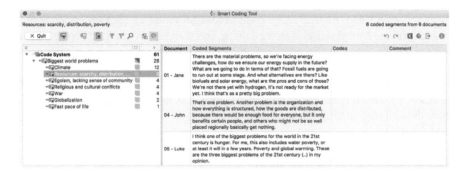

Fig. 9.10 Smart Coding Tool—working with coded segments

comments) can be displayed in a single overview, while the display of the code system is reduced to only currently relevant categories.

This tool can only be opened for compiled coded segments, i.e., in order to be able to use it, the coded segments you want to work with must first be compiled in the "Retrieved Segments" window or in the Overview of Coded Segments. Clicking on the *Smart Coding Tool* icon in the respective toolbar of either windows (Fig. 9.9) then opens a multicolumn view as shown in Fig. 9.10.

When you open the Smart Coding Tool, all codes displayed in the Overview of Coded Segments or "Retrieved Segments" window are automatically activated (if they haven't already been activated, yet). In the left window area, only these activated codes and, if applicable, their nonactivated parent codes are displayed so as to maintain the code system's hierarchical structure. On the right side, all the coded segments belonging to the currently selected code are displayed. In Fig. 9.9, you can see the segments of the code "Resources: scarcity, distribution, poverty." For each segment, you can see from which document it originates and which other codes have been assigned to it. To ensure that only the relevant codes are displayed in the "Codes" column, neither the currently selected code (which would always be the same) nor its parent code (which may also be coded) is displayed here.

To assign another code to a coded segment, for example, to dimensionalize a top-level code, simply drag a row with a segment from the right window pane onto a code in the code system on the left pane. MAXQDA immediately codes this segment, and the new assigned code is displayed in the "Codes" column. You can also code only a part of a segment with another (or new) code. To do this, double-click on the text in the column "Coded Segments," select the desired text, and drag it onto a code. Please note that you cannot code a segment by dragging a code onto the segment in this routine because as soon as you click on a code name, the display changes to show the segments assigned to that code. To remove an assigned code, hover your cursor over a code name in the "Codes" column, and click on the cross that appears. MAXQDA then deletes the assignment of this code to or within this segment.

In the "Comment" column, you can enter a comment to that segment or edit it at any time. For example, you can summarize the coded text as the first step in creating a category for the data. These comments can also be viewed in the "Document Browser" (see Chap. 6). The entire code list can be sorted by clicking on a column header, filtered by right-clicking on a column and searched by clicking on the search icon in the toolbar.

While working with the Smart Coding Tool, all other functions of MAXQDA are locked, but the tool is still connected to the project data. If you select a coded segment by clicking on a row, it will be displayed in the "Document Browser," including its surrounding context.

Exporting Retrieved Segments

To transfer individual coded segments as quotations into a research report, to be able to work through several segments on paper—on a train journey, for instance—or to discuss them together in a team, coded segments can be copied to the clipboard, exported, and printed. Both the coded segments compiled in the "Retrieved Segments" window and in the Overview of Coded Segments can be printed out and exported. Additional information can also be integrated, such as variable values of the source documents. You can access the export options via the toolbars of both windows, but the print option is only available in the "Retrieved Segments" window. There are several icons for exporting, and each has its own distinct use.

If you click on the Excel or the web page icon, the coded segments are opened directly in Excel or your default Internet browser—to save the generated file permanently, you must save these under a different file name from within either Excel or your browser. In table views, MAXQDA takes any existing selections into account: if you select one or more rows, only these are exported; if no row is selected, all coded segments currently displayed in the "Retrieved Segments" window are exported. If you want to have control over the additional information that is exported, it is best to choose the *Export* icon. In this case, a dialog box will open in which you can specify whether memos, code comments, time spans (for transcripts with timestamps), information about other codes assigned to the segment, and the values of selected variables in the source document should be exported with the segments. You can also export each segment's source information, including its code colors and weights, and specify a file name and location.

If you want to print out segments to work through on a train ride or discuss in a team, you can print them by clicking on the printer icon and then adjusting the contents of the header and footer in the print dialog box that appears. Since not all of the additional information that can be exported can be printed directly from MAXQDA, you may need to export these segments with the required additional information first, for example, into a text document for Word, and then print the text from there.

When writing a research report, there is often a need to integrate quotations from the analyzed material, as these have an illustrative effect—that is, as long as they are not overused (Kuckartz, Dresing, Rädiker, & Stefer, 2008, p. 45). For this purpose, you can copy individual segments from MAXQDA to the clipboard and paste them into the report. To do this, right-click on an info box in the "Retrieved Segments" window, a row in the Overview of Coded Segments, or a coding stripe in the "Document Browser" and select the entry *Copy Segment with Source Information to Clipboard* in the context menu. When you then paste the segment into a report, both the document name and the position in the document are automatically added too, since quotations from your data material should always include source references for the sake of transparency.

Smart Publisher: Presenting Coded Segments in a Report

A special form of exporting coded segments is the use of the Smart Publisher, which allows you to automatically generate a formatted report and is particularly well suited to presenting thematically coded segments. The structure of the report follows the arrangement of the codes in the "Code System":

- Each code at the top level has its own chapter.
- All subcodes of a code become subchapters.
- Each (sub)chapter contains the segments coded with this code. The coded segments are numbered consecutively per code (Fig. 9.11).

The Smart Publisher can be accessed via *Reports* > *Smart Publisher*. In the first dialog box, you can select the top-level codes in the "Code System" to be included in the report, and you can also limit the report to the codes of activated documents. In the second dialog box, you can assign headings and subheadings, select one or two image files to be placed on the title page, and define page headers and footers. In addition, the display and sequence of the codes can be set, and the report can be limited to codes of a certain weight. Instead of using regular code names, your report

Climate

1.

"And then, of course, there's climate change, although there's a lot of hysteria at play there too. It's not as if we need to turn the ship around and just reverse the last 60 years of emissions within a single year, so I don't think we need to take such a hectic, hasty approach."

[Interviews\01 - Jane; Position: 5 - 5; Author: Emily; 8/31/18 11:40; Weight score: 0]

Fig. 9.11 Extract from a "Smart Publisher" report: first segment in the "Climate" category

can be published with so-called code alias names, which is useful if you were working with very short code names but ideally want more detailed code names in the report. The *Codes > Code Alias Table* function lists all codes in a project in a table. Here you can enter an alias name up to four times as long (up to 255 characters) in the "Code Alias" column to stand in lieu of the code name, which is limited to 63 characters.

On Mac computers, MAXQDA saves the report in RTF format and opens it directly in Word (if installed) once the export is finished. In Windows, a DOCX document is created and opened with the corresponding program. On Windows computers, it is also possible to use document templates in DOTX format to determine the layout of the finished report, for example, to adapt the design of the report to the corporate design of your company, university, or research institute.

Keeping Track of Memos and Their Content

Memos can perform various tasks in the research process. In the "Document System" of MAXQDA, memos are ideal, for example, for recording a postscript with the notable details and general framework and conditions of an interview or for recording case summaries. Memos in the "Code System" usually contain category definitions, and memos within documents or videos can be used to record distinctive details, hypotheses, theories, and much more. Furthermore, there are the free memos that can be created via the *Analysis* ribbon tab. They are not assigned to a fixed location in MAXQDA and are often used for general, overarching information, ideas, observations, and interpretations.

Any memo can be opened by double-clicking on its yellow memo icon. But it is hardly feasible to keep track of the contents of all your memos and to know which memo contains what information. If you have written more than 20 longer memos, it can already be difficult to access them all via their icons alone, which may be distributed across several documents. For this reason, other ways to access memos are included in MAXQDA to help you manage them and work with their contents.

Via *Reports > Overview of Memos*, you can open a table list of all the memos in your project (Fig. 9.12). This overview is structured exactly like the Overview of Coded Segments. It contains one row for each memo and displays the contents of the currently selected memo in the upper window. A double-click on a memo opens it for editing.

Like all table overviews in MAXQDA, this overview can be sorted by left-clicking on the column headings and filtered by right-clicking on a heading. In addition to the freely definable filters available for each column, a drop-down menu with predefined filters is also available. For example, the view can be reduced to code memos or document memos, memos within documents (including audio and video files), and memos created by selected users. If individual memos have been linked to a code, the filter *Memos connected to an activated code* may be used. Just as the activation of codes ensures that only the coded segments of this code appear in the "Retrieved Segments" window, the use of this filter means that only memos to

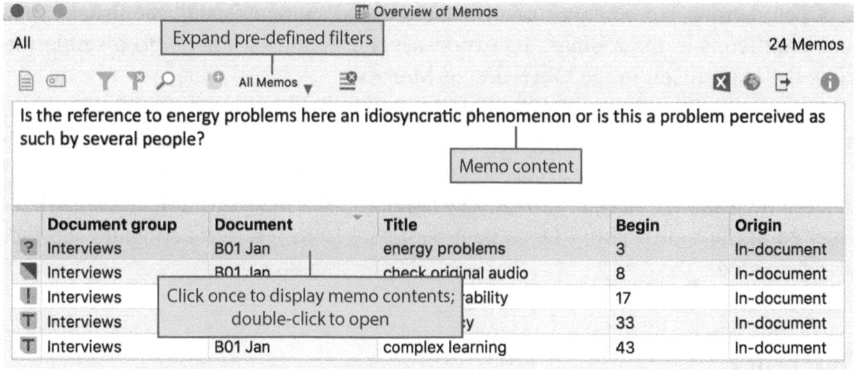

Fig. 9.12 The Overview of Memos includes a row per memo

which one of the activated codes has been assigned are displayed in the Overview of Memos. In addition to the predefined filters, the display of the memos in this overview can also be reduced by using the two icons *Only activated documents* and *Only activated codes* on the far left of the toolbar.

MAXQDA offers a total of 11 different memo icons for different types of memos. If you have assigned the label "unclear assignment" or "check again later" to the icon with the exclamation point and used it for corresponding text passages and codes, you can sort the overview by icon in the first column to find the corresponding memos quickly.

To explore your memos for a document, document group, or document set, the Overview of Memos can also be opened at all levels in the "Document System." If you open it from the context menu of a document, only the memos in this document will be displayed together with the memo on the document name to provide you with a case-specific overview.

You can search through your memos at any time, for example, to find important notes you wrote some time ago. To open the search function, choose *Analysis > Lexical Search* and select *In memos* as the search area in the upper field. As a result, all memos corresponding to your search criteria will be listed in an Overview of Memos. Double-clicking a memo opens it and jumps to the first location within the memo that corresponds to your search.

Working with and Printing Memos

Memos often contain important analytical considerations and ideas. It makes sense to export these contents, to print them out, or to transfer them directly into a research report. The latter can be done most easily via the clipboard: simply select the desired section in your memo, copy it to the clipboard, and paste it into the research report. The clipboard can also be used to integrate several memos into one.

Open memos can be saved or printed as text documents using the usual export and print icons in the toolbar. To export several memos at once into a single file, click the export icon in the Overview of Memos.

If you want to analyze the contents of a memo using the advanced techniques available for text documents, you can convert the memo into a document at any time (by right-clicking on a memo icon or a row in the Overview of Memos and selecting the option **Convert *Memo into a* Document**). The new text document will be inserted at the top of your "Document System," from where its contents can then also be coded.

Reference

Kuckartz, U., Dresing, T., Rädiker, S., & Stefer, C. (2008). *Qualitative Evaluation: Der Einstieg in die Praxis* (2nd ed.). Wiesbaden: VS Verlag für Sozialwissenschaften.

Adding Variables and Quantifying Codes

10

Even in strictly qualitative research, a set of standardized (quantitative) data will usually be collected, e.g., to record sociodemographic characteristics such as age, gender, education, number of children, religious affiliation, and much more. This data can be used very well to form groups and compare them with one another. What do women say about a certain topic, for example, and what do men say? Quantitative data, referred to as "variables" in MAXQDA, is of course also used in mixed methods projects, where qualitative and quantitative methods, data, and analyses are combined and interlinked. A third area that involves numbers also directly relates to qualitative analysis. Each time you assign a code to a segment of data, you are essentially classifying it, which in turn generates information about the frequency of code assignments per code and per case. You can then use this information in your analysis, for example, to find out who spoke about which topic and how often.

> **In This Chapter**
> - Understanding the meaning and purpose of quantitative data (variables)
> - Getting to know MAXQDA's variable functions: the "List of Variables" and "Data Editor"
> - Entering and editing variable values
> - Transforming code frequencies into variables
> - Statistically analyzing and visually presenting quantitative data

Benefits of Using Variables for Quantitative Data?

There are many examples of how standardized, quantitative information can be integrated into qualitative research, even beyond mixed methods strategies. Anyone who conducts an interview study will have information about the people they have

© Springer Nature Switzerland AG 2019
U. Kuckartz, S. Rädiker, *Analyzing Qualitative Data with MAXQDA*,
https://doi.org/10.1007/978-3-030-15671-8_10

interviewed, be it just the location the interview was conducted. Questionnaires are often used in parallel to interviews to alleviate the need to cover standardized information in the latter and to allow more time for interactive questions instead (Witzel & Reiter, 2012; Kuckartz, 2014). If you conducted a qualitative study in which you interviewed the educators, leaders, and financiers of a kindergarten in a socially deprived area, for example, you would automatically have access to information about grouping criteria, in this case the professional positions of those surveyed. As in this example, it is clear that qualitative studies often rely on standardized characteristics in their selection of qualitative samples, whether it is through a conscious selection process, quota system, or a strategy based on theoretical sampling (Corbin & Strauss, 2015). When carrying out a focus group study, sometimes homogeneous, other times heterogeneous compositions of groups are chosen. In other words, some additional information about the individual participants must also be available in these cases. When importing Twitter feeds into MAXQDA, standardized information about the authors of the tweets and the tweets themselves is automatically available in addition to their 280-character qualitative texts. This standardized data, such as the number of followers the author has, the language of the tweet, or whether it is a retweet, opens up extensive filtering and contrasting possibilities with respect to the qualitative data. The same applies to online surveys with closed and open questions: for each case, there is a set of standardized information available along with the answers to the open questions.

MAXQDA uses the term "variable" for standardized, quantitative data; you could also use the terms "attributes" or "characteristics," which are available as supplementary and descriptive information to the individual cases. This is because, in contrast to quantitative research, where the primary objective is the aggregation and consolidation of data using mean, standard deviation, and other statistics, qualitative data analysis focuses more on individual cases. In view of the examples mentioned above, quantitative data in the form of variables in MAXQDA can offer significant benefits for qualitative data analysis, including:

- They can be used for individual case analyses as supplementary information to help classify, explain, and interpret the available data and can also be integrated as descriptive features when creating case summaries.
- They can be used to form groups and allow you to contrast and compare cases.
- In addition to group formation, they can also be used for group descriptions, especially if the groups are derived from the qualitative data itself. This would be the case, for example, if respondents in an interview study are divided into three groups on the basis of their qualitatively analyzed responses to questions concerning their self-esteem—i.e., those with high, medium, or low self-esteem. Subsequently, these groups can be compared according to sociodemographic variables, such as the average age or the proportion of men.
- They can support the formulation of hypotheses about a given case that need to be tested.
- They can be used for sorting and filtering—especially when it comes to large volumes of data.

- They serve as a central link between qualitative and quantitative data in mixed methods analyses. When working with MAXQDA Stats, the add-on module for descriptive and inferential statistics, document variables provide this link between qualitative and quantitative data and enable further mixed methods analyses.
- They can be used to record quantitative information about a case, e.g., how often a topic has been coded for that case.

MAXQDA allows you to define variables not only for documents but also for codes in your code system. Code variables were originally introduced in MAXQDA 10 to store standardized information for the participants in group interviews. MAXQDA 12 introduced especially designed focus group variables for this purpose, which are described in detail in Chap. 15. Code variables have continued to be available in versions since MAXQDA 12 and can be used, for example, to trace the origins of codes (concept-driven vs. data-driven), or their creation date, and this information can in turn be useful for your analysis. The procedure for working with variables is the same for all variable types, so in this chapter we will limit ourselves to describing the most frequently used document variables.

Managing Variables in the "List of Variables"

By selecting *Variables* > *List of Document Variables* you can open a list of the available document variables in MAXQDA, as shown in Fig. 10.1. Here you can create new variables and edit or delete existing ones.

When you open the "List of Document Variables" for the first time, it will already contain six variables that MAXQDA automatically creates in each project and which cannot be deleted. You will recognize them by the red square in the first column. MAXQDA stores important information about your imported documents in these: the document group, document name, date of import, current number of coded segments and memos within the document, as well as the name of the "author,"

Variable	Variable type	To be displayed	Source	Missing value	Categorical	Display as tooltip
Document group	Text	✓	System		✓	
Document name	Text	✓	System		✓	
Creation date	Date/Time	✓	System			
Number of coded segments	Integer	✓	System			
Number of memos	Integer	✓	System			
Author	Text	✓	System			
Gender	Text	✓	User		✓	
Age	Integer	✓	User	999		✓
Age group	Text	✓	User		✓	
NGO member	Boolean (True/False)	✓	User		✓	✓
Scale environmental awareness	Floating point	✓	User	99.00		✓

Labels in figure: "Switch to Data Editor", "Add new variable", "List of Document Variables", Document Variables, "Red square" = MAXQDA standard variable, "Blue square" = project-specific variable, 14 Variables

Fig. 10.1 The "List of Document Variables"

i.e., the person who imported the respective document. In Fig. 10.1, five project-specific variables have already been defined in addition to the so-called "system variables." The values of the additional variables can be changed and are therefore marked with a blue square as "user variables" in the list.

A new variable is added to a project using the icon of the same name at the top of the window. A dialog box will then open in which you can enter a descriptive variable name of up to 63 characters and specify the variable type. While you can change the name later, the variable type can only be changed to a limited extent, which is why it is important to consider this choice of type carefully before adding a new variable. The following types are available:

- Text—This variable type allows you to enter any text of up to 63 characters as a value for each document. While in statistics programs standardized information is usually represented with numbers (e.g., 1, female; 2, male), this can prove very impractical in MAXQDA, because then you would always need a table of correspondence at hand to interpret the data. Instead, it is usually more helpful to work with plain text labels for the variable values in MAXQDA—which is why, in the example in Fig. 10.1, the gender has been defined as a text variable—so that you can enter "female" and "male" or "w" and "m" as immediately identifiable text.

- Integer—This variable type lets you specify (positive and negative) integer values. A classic example of this "integer" type is age. Negative values are less common than positive values but do occur, for example, when assessing the level of a student's seminar on a scale from "too low (-3)" to "too high $(+3)$," where negative values can be chosen.

- Floating point—Whenever you want to enter numbers with decimal places as additional information, you need this variable type. For example, this type can be used "for mean values of attitude scales or other test values." MAXQDA allows the input of two decimal places and always displays entered values with two decimal places.

- Date/time—This type is suitable for all situations in which you want to record the date and time for a case. For each case, you can enter both a date with a time and a date without a time. It is not possible to enter only a time. MAXQDA automatically recognizes most input formats and displays the values entered according to the current operating system settings. It makes no difference whether you enter the year as two or four digits; MAXQDA saves this date in a uniform, universal format and displays it as such.

- Boolean (true/false)—This variable type only has two values, namely, the logic values "true" and "false," which in a concrete case can also mean "yes" vs. "no" or "applies" vs. "does not apply." This variable type is not used as often, since it also comes with some restrictions, e.g., missing values cannot be defined using the Boolean variable type. Usually, the types "Integer" and "Text" offer more flexibility, as you can work with "0 vs. 1" or with "yes vs. no" and achieve the same results.

What Are "Missing Values"?

Once you have created a new variable, you can define further settings in the "List of Variables." In the "missing value" column, you can enter a variable value that will not be taken into account in subsequent case selections and other analyses based on variable values. Let us assume that in an interview study, there is no information on age for two cases. You can then assign the value "999" (or "−99") to these cases and enter this value in the column "missing value." If you then use MAXQDA to select people over 40 years of age, the cases with the values 999 will automatically be ignored. In addition to the values defined as missing, empty cells are also considered missing by MAXQDA. Empty cells can only occur for text and date variables. For Boolean variables, it makes no sense to define missing values, because here MAXQDA only lets you set a check mark denoting "yes" or "applies" or not; other values cannot be entered.

▶ **Please Note** For the variable types "integer" and "floating point," there can be no empty cells in MAXQDA. Hence, when a new variable is created, the value 0 is entered as the initial value in all cells. You should always take this into account if the value "0" may also occur as a real value and you do not know whether an existing 0 was deliberately entered for a case or whether it already existed as an initial value. For example, if you were to define the number of a person's children as a variable, you should define the missing value as "−99" to be able to distinguish people with no children from those for whom the number of children is unknown.

What Does the Variable Property "Categorical" Mean?

In general, different measurement levels are used for quantitative variables (Kuckartz, Rädiker, Ebert, & Schehl, 2013, pp. 16–20):

• With *nominal-scaled variables*, individual variable values cannot be sorted; each value is of equal importance, for example, "Gender: female, male."
• With *ordinal-scaled variables*, individual values can be ranked, for example, "Education levels: low, medium, high."
• With *interval-scaled variables*, individual values can be ranked and the intervals between values are always identical, for example, "Age: 10, 11, 12, 13 years." (In fact, ages in years are ratio-scaled, since they have an absolute zero point, but ratio-scaled variables in the social sciences are often only treated as interval-scaled.)

Nominally and ordinally scaled variables are also referred to as "categorical" variables; their categories, i.e., their individual variable values, are central to them, and you cannot calculate statistical measures, like mean values, for them as you could for interval-scaled variables. When you set the "categorical" property for a variable, you are instructing MAXQDA not to interpret its values as interval-scaled.

This would be necessary, for example, if you wanted to create the variable "education level" with the values 1, low; 2, medium; and 3, high. These values are ordinally scaled, and it does not make sense to calculate averages for them. By setting the property "categorical," certain functions in MAXQDA will calculate percentages for cases—for example, the percentage of people with a high level of education—instead of calculating their mean values.

Setting the "categorical" property is only useful in the case of "integer" or "floating point" variables, since MAXQDA sets the other variable types as categorical anyway. In other words, only in the case of numerical variables does the question arise as to whether they should be interpreted as categorical or interval-scaled.

What Is the Benefit of Setting the "Tooltip" Option for a Variable?

In computer programs, the "tooltip" is the information that appears when you place your cursor over an object. In MAXQDA, there are tooltips in several places: when you hover your cursor over a memo, a preview of the memo will appear; for a document link, a preview of the link target will appear; and for a document in the "Document System," information about who imported the data and how many memos are assigned to it is displayed. If you select the option "Display as tooltip" for a variable in the "List of Variables" (Fig. 10.1), the selected variable name and the variable value entered for the document will additionally appear in this document's tooltip (Fig. 10.2). This is particularly practical for quickly exploring cases, because instead of needing to read the variable information from a table when writing a case summary, for instance, you can simply hover your cursor over the document name to display the relevant context information about the case. The "Tooltip variable" setting also proves useful in other places in MAXQDA. Coded segments from the "Retrieved Segments" window or the Overview of Coded Segments can be exported together with their tooltip variables as additional information. For interviews, for example, you can include important case information on every retrieved or exported coded text passage, such as the age of the person interviewed.

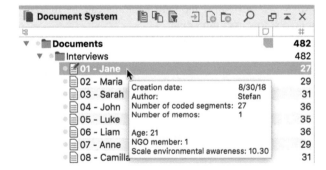

Fig. 10.2 Tooltip variable information in the "Document System"

Entering, Changing, and Viewing Variable Values Within the "Data Editor"

In MAXQDA's "List of Variables," you can organize your variables, while in the "Data Editor," you can edit and view the data for all or only selected cases. The "Data Editor" is opened either via the *Variables* ribbon tab or by clicking on the icon ⬚ with the same name at the top of the "List of Variables." The icon ⬚ switches back to the "List of Variables", so that you can switch between the variable and data views at any time. The structure of the "Data Editor" corresponds to a typical rectangular data matrix: cases (documents) form the rows, while variables form the columns (Fig. 10.3). As in all MAXQDA table overviews, columns whose values can be changed by the user have a blue header, while columns that cannot be changed and are set by MAXQDA have a black header.

If you only have a few variables and cases, you can usually enter the data quite quickly and conveniently by hand once you have created the relevant variables. To enter the data, click in a cell with the mouse, either a single or double-click will do, and enter a value. If you are entering this data column by column, it is best to confirm the entry with the *Enter* key (↵) as MAXQDA will then automatically select the next row. If you plan to enter the data on a case by case basis, you should press the *Tab* key (→) after the entry; then MAXQDA will jump to the next column in the "Data Editor."

By default, the "autocomplete" function is switched on for all variables, with the exception of the "Boolean" type. When you start to enter a value, the entered letters will be supplemented with suggested variable values that already exist in the column, just like in Excel. You can see this, for example, in the column "Gender" in Fig. 10.3. All you need to do is type an "m" and MAXQDA will automatically complete this value to "male," so that you only need to press the enter or tab key to accept the value.

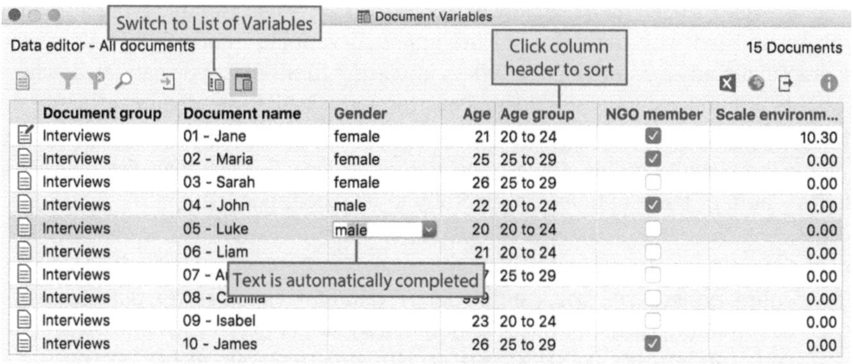

Fig. 10.3 The "Data Editor" for editing the variable values per individual case, here: documents

Explore Variables for Individual Documents, Document Groups, or Sets

You can easily set constraints over the rows shown in the "Data Editor." To explore only the variable values of documents in a document group, right-click on a document group in the "Document System," and select the *Overview of Variables*. The "Data Editor" which is displayed in this case will only contain the documents from the selected document group. You can also restrict the view to a single document or the documents in a set. Alternatively, you can restrict the displayed rows via activations in the "Document System" and the left-hand icon **Only activated documents** in the Data Editor toolbar.

It is also important to note that the "Data Editor" and "Document System" are interactively linked. If you select a document in the "Document System," the corresponding row is selected in the open "Data Editor" and vice versa. You can use this feature to explore documents if you prefer not to work with tooltip variables, which might be very useful when working with data from online surveys.

Import an Existing Data Matrix from Excel or SPSS

In studies, the standardized data are often already available in a data matrix of "cases x variables," and it is not necessary to reenter such data by hand. MAXQDA lets you import this data, as long as it is available in Excel or in the SPSS format, which is often used by statistical software. To make sure the data is assigned to the correct cases when importing it, MAXQDA requires the imported matrix to contain two columns for the assignment of cases, one for the document group and one for the document name. For imports from Excel, these columns should be titled as such; for SPSS imports, these columns can be selected as desired.

The import function is available via the *Import Document Variables* option in the *Variables* ribbon tab or via the corresponding icon in the "Data Editor" or "List of Variables." A file dialog box will then open in which you can select an Excel or SPSS file. MAXQDA will open the file, list all the variables contained in it, and allow you to specify for each new variable which variable type should be used.

If a given variable name already exists and has the same variable type, its values will be updated with the values of the imported variable—and empty values also overwrite already existing values! When importing SPSS files, you can select which variable column contains the document group and which the document name. In addition, you can specify that the variable labels should be imported, instead of the often-abbreviated variable names, and the value labels rather than the numerical codes—both of these options are generally to be recommended.

▶ **Please Note** Document variables are always defined globally for the entire project, i.e., you cannot define different variables for different document groups. But this is seldom necessary, because you can create any number of variables and only assign variable values to the documents for which they are relevant. For other documents, these cells will simply remain empty or the defined "missing value" will be displayed.

Transforming Code Frequencies into Document Variables

In the course of the coding process with MAXQDA, quantitative information about how often a code was assigned to a case is generated for each document. MAXQDA allows you to create document variables that reflect the frequency distribution of a code across individual documents. These variables are dynamic and are always automatically adapted to the current status of the project.

Let us assume that all text passages in which interviewees describe their environmentally conscious behavior were coded with the category of "personal behavior." By right-clicking on this code in the "Code System" and selecting the option *Transform into Document Variable*, you can create a new document variable whose values reflect how often that code has been assigned in individual documents (Fig. 10.4). The code name is used as the variable name, which can be changed at any time in the "List of Document Variables." While the name of this option in the context menu may suggest otherwise, the code is completely preserved by this action and will not be changed in any way.

▶ **Please Note** The values of a transformed code are updated automatically by MAXQDA whenever the code is assigned to a new segment or deleted from an existing one and so always reflect the current status of the project.

The variable can serve as an indicator of the extent to which people behave in an environmentally conscious manner, but it is immediately clear that these purely quantitative results should be interpreted with a degree of caution, since the frequency with which a topic is mentioned is not solely dependent on how important it is considered to be. The interview situation, the extroversion of an interviewee and, above all, the coding rules on how to deal with repeated occurrence of identical statements also have an effect on the number of times a code is assigned.

Document group	Document name	Age group	Personal behavior	
Interviews	01 - Jane	20 to 24	1	
Interviews	02 - Maria	25 to 29	1	
Interviews	03 - Sarah	25 to 29	1	
Interviews	04 - John	20 to 24	2	For Luke, the code
Interviews	05 - Luke	20 to 24	4	"Personal behavior"
Interviews	06 - Liam	20 to 24	0	was assigned 4 times;
Interviews	07 - Anne	25 to 29	1	for Liam not at all
Interviews	08 - Camilla		1	
Interviews	09 - Isabel	20 to 24	2	
Interviews	10 - James	25 to 29	2	

Fig. 10.4 Code transformed into a document variable in the "Data Editor"

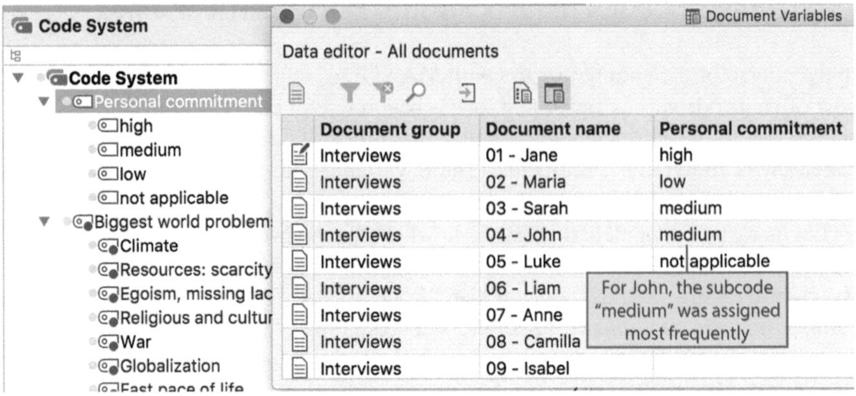

Fig. 10.5 Code converted to a categorical document variable (left) in the Data Editor (right)

The transformation of the frequencies of qualitative codes into variables with numerical values is also described in mixed methods literature as "quantitizing" (Kuckartz, 2017). Accordingly, the ***Mixed Methods*** ribbon tab also contains an icon bearing the same name, which can be used to transform several codes into document variables at once.

Transforming Codes into Categorical Document Variables

To continue our example, where the interviewees' personal engagement in environmental protection has been coded using scaled subcategories such as "low," "medium," "high," and "unknown," MAXQDA offers you the option of transforming the parent code "Personal engagement" into a document variable. The values of this variable will then be set to the subcategory which was assigned most frequently in each document (Fig. 10.5). To create such a variable, click on the parent code and choose ***Transform into Categorical Document Variable***. Transforming the parent code in this way provides an overview of the levels of personal engagement per document, which can be used for evaluative content analyses (Kuckartz, 2014; Mayring, 2014; Schreier, 2012) or to group documents together and contrast them, for example, the less committed vs. the highly committed.

Creating Frequency Tables and Charts for Document Variables

For the first analysis of the variables, you can use frequency tables and charts in which the individual variable values are listed and counted. They allow you to get an idea of the distribution of variable values and can be integrated into reports describing the sample and results. You can create tables and charts by going to

Document Variable Statistics			
Variable: ← ■ Age group ➡			
	Frequency▼	Percentage	Percentage (valid)
20 to 24	7	46.7	50.0
25 to 29	7	46.7	50.0
TOTAL (valid)	14	93.3	100.0
Missing	1	6.7	
TOTAL	15	100.0	

Fig. 10.6 Frequency table for a document variable

Variables > Document Variable Statistics. In the dialog box that opens, simply select several or all the available variables. The result is a window with a frequency table as shown in Fig. 10.6.

All variable values that occur are listed in the first column of the result table—in the example in Fig. 10.6, the two age groups "20–24 years" and "25–29 years." The second column indicates how many documents contain these variable values—in the example, there are seven interviewees (documents) per age group. The "Missing" row indicates how many documents contain either an empty value or a value defined as missing. In the example, this is the case for an interviewee for whom there is no age information available. The "Percentage" column contains the relative frequencies of the variable values with respect to all the values, including the missing ones. Usually, however, you will ignore the missing values in your analysis and therefore refer to the values in the "Percentage (valid)" column, which only takes into account the number of documents with valid values.

If the first column only contains numbers, which would be the case with a numeric variable, for example, the "number of children" variable, you can click the *Descriptive statistics* icon ⊘ to request the mean value, standard deviation, quartile values, and other statistical measures to describe the variable's distribution in addition to the frequency table.

The *Chart view* icon ıl switches the display of this data from a frequency table to a chart (Fig. 10.7). Once you have changed to this view, you can choose between a vertical or horizontal bar chart and a pie chart. The display can be adjusted using the icons at the top of the window; for example, you can toggle between displaying absolute values and relative frequencies as percentages, and you can also hide or display any missing values. The order of the columns, bars, and circle segments is always dependent on the order of the rows in the frequency table—there you can sort the variable values by frequency or by alphabetical order by clicking on the column headings. Both charts and frequency tables can be exported in numerous formats via the usual icon at the top right-hand corner of the window.

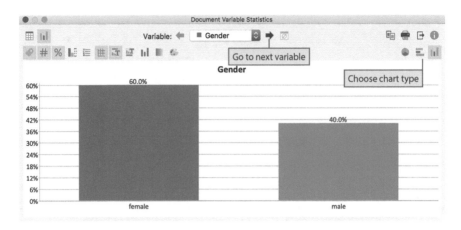

Fig. 10.7 Bar chart for the document variable "Gender"

▶   **Tip** You can also generate a frequency table or a chart directly from the
     "List of Variables" by clicking on the Statistics icon ılı after selecting one
     or more variables with your mouse (see Fig. 10.1).

References

Corbin, J. M., & Strauss, A. L. (2015). *Basics of qualitative research: Techniques and procedures for developing grounded theory* (4th ed.). Thousand Oaks, CA: SAGE.

Kuckartz, U. (2014). *Qualitative text analysis: A guide to methods, practice & using software.* Thousand Oaks, CA: SAGE.

Kuckartz, U. (2017). Datenanalyse in der Mixed-Methods-Forschung: Strategien der Integration von qualitativen und quantitativen Daten und Ergebnissen. *KZfSS Kölner Zeitschrift für Soziologie und Sozialpsychologie, 69*(S2), 157–183. https://doi.org/10.1007/S11577-017-0456-Z.

Kuckartz, U., Rädiker, S., Ebert, T., & Schehl, J. (2013). *Statistik: Eine verständliche Einführung* (2nd ed.). Wiesbaden: VS Verlag für Sozialwissenschaften.

Mayring, P. (2014). *Qualitative content analysis: Theoretical foundation, basic procedures and software solution.* Klagenfurt. Retrieved from http://nbn-resolving.de/urn:nbn:de:0168-ssoar-395173

Schreier, M. (2012). *Qualitative content analysis in practice.* Thousand Oaks, CA: SAGE.

Witzel, A., & Reiter, H. (2012). *The problem-centred interview: Principles and practice.* Thousand Oaks, CA: SAGE.

Working with Paraphrases and Summaries, Creating Case Overviews

11

One of the primary aims of the analysis process is to summarize and compress the data. This chapter will focus on two strategies for achieving this: firstly, paraphrasing sections of data and using the resulting paraphrases to develop categories and, secondly, the development of thematic summaries based on previous code assignments. The former is primarily used to form categories, the latter for descriptive analyses of previously categorized data. By coding and working on the category system, the empirical data is made accessible in a way that generates a conceptual classification system with a network of connections. Classification systems and taxonomies have a value in and of themselves. Think of the periodic table of elements in chemistry, for example, they contain highly concentrated information and allow you to classify elements and identify phenomena. Category systems in empirical social research do a similar job. If you imagine these systems as a grid with nodes that each contain a collection of all the information on a particular topic, then you may also face the problem that the volume of this information could be overwhelming. To bridge this vast gap between a category and the data coded with it, it often makes sense to work with summaries, i.e., to create a second grid that compresses and summarizes the information with the research question(s) in mind. This chapter focuses on the basic idea of a "summary grid" of this kind, as well as the presentation of summaries in "summary tables."

In This Chapter
- Compiling, editing, and categorizing paraphrases
- Writing thematic summaries
- Exploring the uses of the Summary Grid
- Creating case overviews using Summary Tables
- Create document variables from Summary Tables
- Preparing Summary Tables for publications and posters

© Springer Nature Switzerland AG 2019
U. Kuckartz, S. Rädiker, *Analyzing Qualitative Data with MAXQDA*,
https://doi.org/10.1007/978-3-030-15671-8_11

Writing and Categorizing Paraphrases

The two summarizing strategies discussed in this chapter—working with paraphrases and creating thematic summaries—have different prerequisites. The first strategy is relatively free of prerequisites and does not demand that the data has been coded in advance, while the thematic summary strategy that involves working with the Summary Grid is based on a prior coding of the material. When is either of these procedures more appropriate? It is difficult to provide a universal answer. If you are pressed for time and forming a category system and coding the data is out of the question, it is best to use paraphrases as a means of summarizing the data. On the other hand, it cannot be said for all cases in which categories have been formed and the data has been coded that the Summary Grid is always the best option. This is certainly often the case, but paraphrasing can also serve as a form of inductive category building. Detailed descriptions of how this is done in practice can be found in Mayring (2014), Kuckartz (2014), and Schreier (2012).

Paraphrasing texts is an effective way of summarizing their content, especially when there is no time to code this material or you need to produce a condensed version of the text at short notice, as is often the case in journalism, for example. We have described how texts can be paraphrased in MAXQDA in Chap. 5, "Exploring Data," which also covers further options for working with paraphrases.

Compiling All the Paraphrases Assigned to a Document

Assuming that everything considered important from a certain perspective has been paraphrased, these paraphrases should, in sum, contain the "substance" of a text. There are several ways in which you can review this substance, that is, compile all the paraphrases and read them at once. First, you can use the Overview of Coded Segments. To access this, right-click on the relevant text in the "Document System," and select *Coded Segments* in the *Overviews* section. If text passages have already been coded in this text, you must additionally activate the code "Paraphrases," and click on the *Only activated codes* icon in the overview window. Of the large amount of information that can be displayed in the columns of the Overview of Coded Segments, only three columns are required: first, the column "Begin," and if necessary also the column "End," to sort the order of the paraphrases according to their order in the text itself; second, the column "Comment," since the paraphrases are stored in this column in MAXQDA; and, third, the "Preview" column, in which the text that has been paraphrased is listed. You can right-click on the header row, i.e., the row in which the column names are located, to hide the columns that are not required. Figure 11.1 shows the corresponding result for a newspaper article. The paraphrases are listed in the "Comments" column in the lower window, while the original text that has been paraphrased is displayed in the upper window. From here, all the options provided for MAXQDA's overview tables are available to you. For example, you can search for certain words within the paraphrases and filter them thematically. The word "migration" was searched for in Fig. 11.1 and found in two paraphrases.

Comment	Document name	Begin	End
confidence in a coalition's success is on the decline	Newspaper Article 03	3	3
chances are 50/50	Newspaper Article 03	5	5
fear of losing face should be disregarded	Newspaper Article 03	6	6
migration issue is still controversial	Newspaper Article 03	13	13
everyone is gambling on fresh elections being called, that can cause chaos	Newspaper Article 03	8	8
limit of	Newspaper Article 03	14	14
no agre	Newspaper Article 03	17	17
special asylum recognition procedures for specific groups	Newspaper Article 03	20	20
highly qualified people are to be recruited	Newspaper Article 03	11	11
agreement on migration must be reached by Friday	Newspaper Article 03	21	21

Fig. 11.1 Compiling paraphrases in the Overview of Coded Segments

Analyzing and Summarizing Paraphrases

Having compiled this set of paraphrases, you can then go through them a second time. Redundant or even contradictory paraphrases can be found via the versatile options for filtering overview tables. To filter paraphrases thematically, right-click on the column heading "Comment," and define the appropriate filter, for example, all paraphrases containing the word "migration." Only these paraphrases will then remain visible, and you can edit them as required. Following the technique of summarizing as described by Mayring (2014), this second phase (S2)—once you have finished paraphrasing the material—is about generalizing paraphrases to the required level of abstraction for which Mayring sets out the following rules (Mayring, 2014, p. 68):

S2.1 Generalize the referents of the paraphrases to the defined level of abstraction, so that the old referents are implied in the newly formulated ones.
S2.2 Generalize the sentence kernels (predicates) in the same way.
S2.3 Leave those paraphrases standing which are above the intended level of abstraction.
S2.4 In cases of doubt make use of theoretical preconceptions.

You can follow this procedure in the Overview of Coded Segments as shown in Fig. 11.1: once you have double-clicked on a paraphrase, you can edit it and—if necessary—generalize it. Alternatively, this generalization step can also be carried out with the *Categorize Paraphrases* function, as described below.

In the third phase of Mayring's technique of summarizing ("S3: First reduction"), the paraphrases are condensed according to the following rules (Mayring, 2014, p. 68):

S3.1 Cut semantically identical paraphrases within units of evaluation.
S3.2 Cut paraphrases which are not felt to add substantially to the content on the new level of abstraction.

S3.3 Adopt the paraphrases which continue to be thought of as vitally content-bearing (selection).
S3.4 Resolve cases of doubt with the aid of theoretical preconceptions.

This procedure can also be carried out using both the Overview of Coded Segments and the *Categorize Paraphrases* function. If this technique of summarizing is used to form categories inductively, it is not necessary to delete any paraphrases, because the aim here is a consistent category system, not the coding of the data. Aside from this, one should also be aware that deleting paraphrases deletes the link to the original material, i.e., it will no longer necessarily be apparent that the content captured in a generalized paraphrase occurs several times throughout the material.

The fourth phase of Mayring's technique of summarizing, the so-called second reduction, can be implemented in the same way. In this phase, the aim is to bundle and integrate paraphrases not only on a case-by-case basis but across several cases and to delete redundant paraphrases if necessary. For this step, you must first activate all documents in MAXQDA the paraphrases of which you want to process in this way. Then double-click on the "Paraphrases" code, and filter the display by clicking on the *Only activated documents* icon. From here, the procedure mirrors that of the "first reduction," i.e., you can use either the Overview of Coded Segments or the "Categorize paraphrases" function. Again, the step of deleting paraphrases needs to be thought through carefully in advance; especially when it comes to summarizing the contents of your data, the deletion of paraphrases should be treated with caution.

In order to keep track of and comment on your summarized paraphrases as well as your categories, it is best to create a new free (unassigned) memo in which their contents—in the above example on the subject of "migration"—can be summarized. All edited paraphrases are accessible in the Overview of Coded Segments such that particularly significant paraphrases can be transferred to the free memo as quotations via the clipboard.

From Paraphrases to Categories
The systematization and grouping of paraphrases is a proven method for arriving at categories. This inductive, data-based category formation through paraphrasing can admittedly be quite time-consuming. However, especially for newcomers to the field of qualitative content analysis, this is a path that can be taken without major difficulties, because here you are always working very closely with the original text. The MAXQDA function "Categorize Paraphrases" not only supports the creation of categories but can also be used in general to categorize paraphrases in the context of qualitative content analyses. You can find this function in the *Analysis* ribbon tab via *Paraphrases* > *Categorize Paraphrases*. If you only want to work with one or a certain number of selected documents, you must activate them beforehand. Figure 11.2 illustrates what the window for categorizing paraphrases looks like.

The "Categorize Paraphrases" window is divided into two areas. In the left area, you will see the category system; at the beginning of the category formation process,

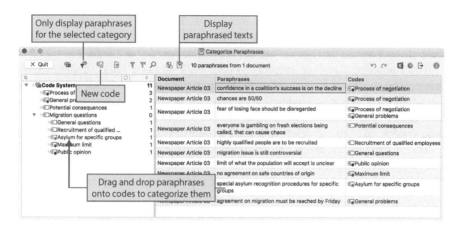

Fig. 11.2 Creating categories from paraphrases in the "Categorize Paraphrases" window

it will still be empty, of course, provided that the activated documents have not yet been assigned any codes. New categories can now be inserted and assigned to individual paraphrases. The number at the end of each line of code indicates how often the category has been so far assigned in the selected documents. Unlike the code frequency in the "Code System," this number does not indicate the total number of assignments of this code throughout all your documents but only the number of codes in the documents you have activated for the paraphrase categorization process. In the right window area, the paraphrases contained in all or only the activated documents are listed—each in a separate row. By default, three columns are displayed in the right window: the first column contains the document name, the second the paraphrases, and the third the assigned codes. A fourth column "Paraphrased text" can be added via a corresponding icon in the toolbar, which in turn contains the original text that has been paraphrased.

Like all MAXQDA tables, the table can be adapted: you can change the width and position of the columns with the mouse and hide them by right-clicking on them. Clicking on the header sorts the column in ascending order, another click in descending order.

▶ **Please Note** While the window for categorizing paraphrases is open, the other functions of MAXQDA are locked. When this window is closed, all changes made to the code system, including the addition of new codes, are adopted directly in MAXQDA's "Code System."

Assigning Categories

To assign a new category to a paraphrase, right-click on it and select the option *Create and Assign New Code* in the context menu. To assign an existing code to a paraphrase, simply drag the row containing the paraphrase onto this code in the code system. This new categorization is indicated immediately, as the code will then appear in the "Codes" column. To remove a category from a paraphrase, hover your cursor over the code in the "Codes" column and click on the "x" that appears. To create a new code for categorization, click on the ***New code*** icon in the toolbar and enter your desired code name in the usual dialog box. You can also assign a color to the code and enter a description for it in the "Code Memo" text field.

You can reorganize your category system while working with paraphrases: the order of the codes can be changed with the mouse and parent/subcode relationships can be adjusted. When you right-click on a code, many of the familiar functions from MAXQDA's main "Code System" window are also available here for adapting the code system, i.e., you can delete codes and change their color or create a code memo.

The current display, that is, all the paraphrases in the right area of the window, can also be opened or exported as an Excel or HTML table. An overview of this kind can be useful for documenting the content behind a particular category or subcategory.

Summary Grid: Writing Thematic Summaries Based on Coded Segments

Anyone who analyses texts will often decide to distinguish important from unimportant information and summarize what is important from the perspective of the research question at hand. These summaries therefore capture something that is considered significant from a specific point of view. On the other hand, this also means that there is no universal way of composing summaries; what a summary looks like will depend on the situation and its purpose within the analysis process. Hence, summaries can vary greatly in terms of their length. The keywords that help you to find relevant texts while conducting literature research are very succinct. These keywords compress the information contained in a text into a few terms. Abstracts, on the other hand, are more detailed in this respect and can summarize the key content and arguments of an article in a scientific journal, for example, in a few sentences. Both keywords and abstracts refer to the entire text or, to use social research terminology, to the entire unit of analysis. In MAXQDA, keywords can be assigned to a unit of analysis (= document) in the form of codes. Abstracts that summarize an entire text are best assigned to the respective document in the form of a document memo in the "Document System." A very detailed and concise technique of summarizing is the technique of paraphrasing we have already described, which serves to render individual statements or sections of a text in the researcher's own words. This can result in a large number of paraphrases—depending on the research question—which can then be ordered and further summarized at a higher level of abstraction.

Paraphrasing is a technique that has no prerequisites, that is, a prior thematic coding of the material is not necessary. Instead, uncoded text sections are reproduced in the analyst's words in a condensed form. Another summarizing method in the context of content analyses works with already coded text passages. MAXQDA offers a special function for this purpose, namely, the Summary Grid. The basic idea of the Summary Grid is that it allows you to write thematic summaries, building on an already existing thematic coding of the data. The principle of thematic summaries is illustrated in Fig. 11.3. For each case, a specific topic, i.e., the segments coded with a specific category, is brought into focus. For example, what did the person

	Case 1	Case 2	...
Topic A	*All coded text segments* from Case 1 on Topic A	*All coded text segments* from Case 2 on Topic A	
Topic B	*All coded text segments* from Case 1 on Topic B	*All coded text segments* from Case 2 on Topic B	
...	...	...	...

⇓   ⇓

	Case 1	Case 2	...
Topic A	*Summary* of text segments from Case 1 on Topic A	*Summary* of text segments from Case 2 on Topic A	
Topic B	*Summary* of text segments from Case 1 on Topic B	*Summary* of text segments from Case 2 on Topic B	
...	...	...	...

Fig. 11.3 The principle of the Summary Grid (summaries for cases x topics) as an additional level of analysis

"Peter Berkemper" say about the topic, "Confronting Global Challenges," during the course of an interview? It may be that he mentioned this topic at ten different points throughout the interview. With the help of MAXQDA's Summary Grid function, you can compile all these places in the interview and then write a thematic summary for all of them combined.

These thematic summaries can in turn be used for further analyses, in particular for systematic case comparisons, case contrasts, and case overviews. Case-oriented approaches of this nature are typical techniques in qualitative social research. You can perform analyses like this using MAXQDA's Summary Tables; these are based on the coded segments and corresponding summaries as they have been formulated by the respective researchers.

Writing summaries can take a long time. You should therefore think carefully about which topics (codes) are actually worth summarizing. There is certainly no imperative to create summaries for every topic.

To create and edit summaries, go to *Analysis* > ***Summary Grid***. The Summary Grid window (Fig. 11.4) has three areas:

- In the left column, the thematic grid is displayed in a format similar to the "Code Matrix Browser," a visual tool of MAXQDA. A blue square indicates the presence of some coded segments in that document for that code. A green shading around it indicates that a summary of those segments has been created already. A red rectangle indicates for which document and which code in the thematic grid the coded segments are currently being displayed.
- The middle column displays the full content of these coded segments.
- The right column, which is initially empty, is where you can write your summary.

The columns and rows of the thematic grid shown in the left column can be reduced using two icons. The ***Only activated documents*** icon 📄 ensures that only

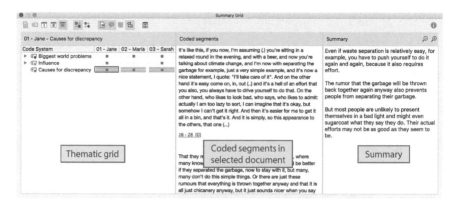

Fig. 11.4 The three columns of the Summary Grid window

those documents you have activated in the "Document System" are displayed as grid columns. The **Only activated codes** icon ▬ has a similar effect—only codes activated in the "Code System" are displayed as grid rows. Furthermore, the **Summary Tables** icon ▤ opens the Summary Tables window described below.

So how do you write a summary or edit an already existing summary? If you hover your cursor over the nodes of the Summary Grid in the left window, a tooltip will appear with information about the document and the number of segments in the document that have been assigned this code. Clicking on a cell in the matrix selects it for editing. In fact, this is almost like opening a drawer and revealing its contents; in this case you will now see the corresponding coded segments in the middle window. At the end of each segment, there is a reference to the source (the paragraph number of the segment highlighted in blue). Clicking on this source reference will display the corresponding section within the document in the "Document Browser," so that you can see the segment in its original context—which can be of help when interpreting the segment.

You can now enter a summary in the right window. Summaries are automatically saved when another node is clicked in the left window or when you close the Summary Grid window.

▶   **Tip** Selected text passages can be dragged and dropped from the middle window into the summary window by holding down the left mouse button. This makes it easy to insert original quotes into a summary.

Summary Tables: Creating Case Overviews

The Summary Tables function is used to contrast cases and create case overviews. It can be accessed either via **Analysis > Summary Tables** or by clicking on the icon of the same name ▤ in the Summary Grid window. In a Summary Table, the associated

Fig. 11.5 Options for creating a new Summary Table

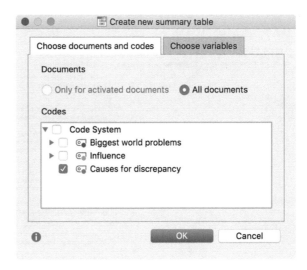

summaries for selected documents and codes are displayed together with document variables. Summary Tables are ideal for presentations and publications.

In Fig. 11.6 you can see the Summary Tables window: on the left side, there is a list of all Summary Tables created so far, and on the right side, there is a table window in which the Summary Table is displayed according to your chosen settings. Of course, this list will be empty if no Summary Table has been created yet. Click on the icon of the same name ⊞ to create a new table; next, you need to choose from various options (Fig. 11.5):

- Select whether all or only activated documents are to be included. This defines the rows of the Summary Table.
- Select which codes to include. This defines the columns of the Summary Table.
- Select which document variables are to be included as additional information. The variables selected for the "Variable for first column" window area will be displayed in the first column together with the document name. All variables selected in the "Variables in own column" window area will be added as separate columns behind the codes.

Once you have configured these settings, the finished table will appear, listing the summaries for the selected codes (Fig. 11.6). The first column will contain the document group and the document name as well as the values of the selected variables. This way, additional information about the case in question can be displayed in the Summary Table. The table is created in a uniform, plain text format with the same font throughout.

▶   **Please Note** The individual cells in MAXQDA's Summary Table can be edited. The displayed summaries can be changed, and all changes made

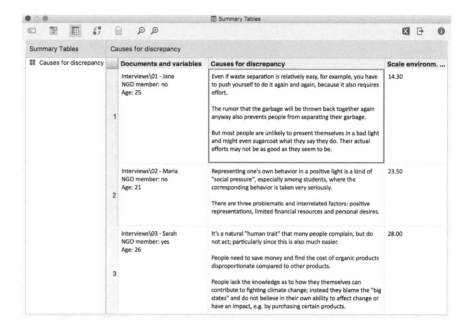

Fig. 11.6 MAXQDA's Summary Table window

to their contents are, in turn, applied to the summaries in the Summary Grid, i.e., the contents of the corresponding cells here are also changed. The values of the variables, which are displayed in their own columns, can also be changed, but this has no effect on the document variables themselves.

The cells displayed in the Summary Table are linked to their corresponding coded segments. Clicking on a cell displays the coded segments associated with that cell in the Summary Grid window. If you right-click within a cell, a context menu will appear, which includes the option ***Display associated coded segments***; these are then displayed in the "Retrieved Segments" window.

As with all tables in MAXQDA, you can adjust the display of your Summary Tables. For example, you can change the order of the columns by dragging and dropping the column to the desired position. You can also hide columns and sort the entire table in ascending or descending order according to the values in a column.

Creating Document Variables From a Summary Table

From these already highly condensed summaries, you can automatically generate document variables. Take the following example: in preparation for a workshop, the participants were asked in an online survey whether they had any previous

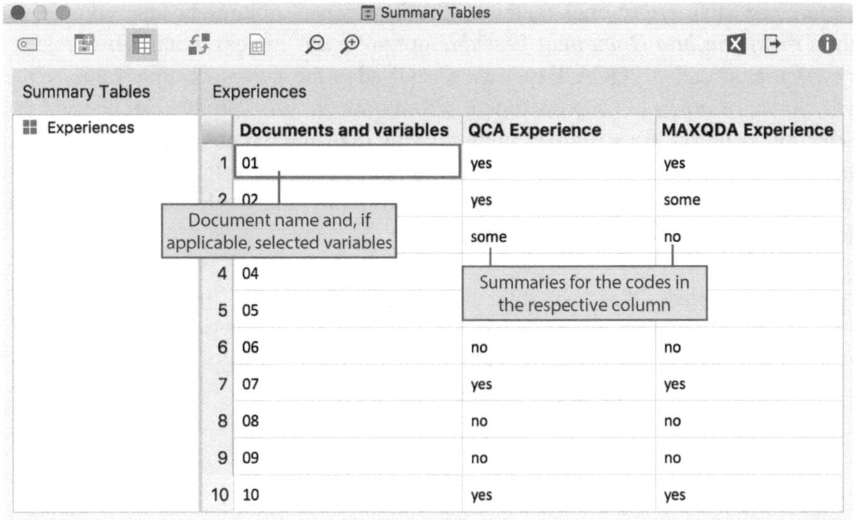

Fig. 11.7 A Summary Table with assessments for the codes "QCA Experience" and "MAXQDA Experience"

experience with the "qualitative content analysis" method. One of the responses states, "I analyzed guided interviews with the method of qualitative content analysis as part of my bachelor's and master's theses." This person seems to have had quite a lot of experience working with this method. Now you want to evaluate the answers on the scale "QCA Experience" with the possible results of "yes," "some," and "none." In this case, the experience gained during the participant's BA and MA studies results in the assessment "yes," which is entered as a summary for the person. The survey asks a similar question about previous experience with MAXQDA. Rather conveniently, the same options can also be chosen here, namely, "yes," "some," and "none."

All the documents are processed in this way and the appropriate value is entered in the respective summary column. The resulting Summary Table can be seen in Fig. 11.7. The first column of the table contains the names of the documents—variables were not selected here. The second column contains the assigned values for the question about each participant's previous experience with qualitative content analysis, and the third column contains the assigned values for the question about their previous experience with MAXQDA.

At first glance, you might already be able to detect some interrelationships: barring one exception, all those who have experience with qualitative content analysis also have experience in working with MAXQDA. Very often there is a coincidence of two "none" answers, i.e., the participant has no experience in either area. Clicking on the header line of a column causes the table to be sorted according to this column. This makes it easy to find out that five people have experience with qualitative content analysis, five have no experience, and two people have some experience. If you right-click on the "QCA Experience" column header, you will see the *Transform into Document Variable* option in the context menu. This creates a new variable called "QCA Experience" and adds the corresponding value (either yes, some, or none) to each document. From now on, this variable can be used as a selection criterion, for example, to answer the question "What do participants who have no experience with qualitative content analysis want to learn?" Of course, the variables formed in this way can also be statistically analyzed, for example, in the form of a frequency table or bar chart.

▶   **Please Note** The variable values displayed in the Summary Table window are static, i.e., changes made here will not be permanently stored in the database. To change these values permanently, use the Data Editor for Document Variables (see Chap. 10).

Alternative Display of Case Overviews

For some questions and comparisons, especially when contrasting selected cases, it makes sense to swap the arrangement of rows and columns so that the cases (documents) appear in the columns and the topics (codes) appear in the rows. You can do this by clicking on the icon of the same name in the toolbar at the top of the window. The best way to select cases to compare is to use the "Select columns" option, which you can access by right-clicking any column header. In Fig. 11.8 four cases are being compared, two with "QCA experience" and two with none; the participants "01" and "04" have experience with the qualitative content analysis method, and "08" and "09" have no experience. In addition to the codes that cover the level of experience, the summaries on the topic, "What do you want to learn in the workshop?", are also listed in the table. The two people with no experience are particularly interested in the topic of "category formation," while the two experienced participants have more specific learning goals and even want to work with their own data.

		01	04	08	09
1	Documents and variables	01	04	08	09
2	QCA Experience	yes	yes	no	no
3	MAXQDA Experience	yes	no	no	no
4	What do you want to learn?	How exactly can I create and edit excerpts in MAXQDA?	I would like to deepen my understanding of qualitative content analysis. It would be nice if we could practice this using our own data.	How do I create categories?	I'm particularly interested in how to form categories (category types, the category system) and structural content analysis (the procedure to begin with).

Fig. 11.8 Summary Table for four selected people in the columns

Creating Integrative Summaries

It is often the case that summaries relate several topics that need to be integrated, that is, combined to form an overall assessment. This is the case, for example, if you want to develop classification types (a typology) based on several codes or their summaries. As a simple example, take the summaries above for "QCA Experience" and "MAXQDA Experience." The aim is to integrate these two topics (= columns in Fig. 11.9) into a "Type of previous experience." How do you do this? It would actually be helpful to be able to add another column to the Summary Table and write this integrative summary there, for example, the combination "yes" + "yes" would be assigned to the type "Experienced" and the combination "none" + "none" to the type "Beginners." However, no further columns can be inserted into a MAXQDA Summary Table. Even if this were possible, you would face the question of where these newly generated values would be stored. If they were only added to this Summary Table, they would be lost for all subsequent analyses. So, you need to use the tools MAXQDA provides for such analyses—and these tools are the codes and variables. Since the changes made to variable values in Summary Tables are not permanently stored in the corresponding document variables, the only available option is to use codes. This means that you need to define a new code "Type of previous experience," recreate the Summary Table to include this code, and then—in the table's "Type of Previous Experience" column—enter the type which should be assigned to each respective person. Figure 11.9 illustrates the result: three groups were formed, namely, "Experienced," "Beginners," and a mixed group of people who already have some previous experience; for these participants, the type "Some Experience" was entered. In this way, the "Type of previous experience" remains permanently stored, is available for further analyses, and can be statistically analyzed—and, last but not least, it is also available in the summary overviews.

	Documents and variables	QCA Experience	MAXQDA Experience	Type of previous experience
1	01	yes	yes	Experienced
2	02	some	yes	some experience
3	03	no	some	some experience
4	04	yes	no	some experience
5	05	no	no	Beginner
6	06	no	no	Beginner
7	07	yes	yes	Experienced
8	08	no	no	Beginner
9	09	no	no	Beginner
10	10	yes	yes	Experienced

Fig. 11.9 Creating an integrative summary in an additional column

The Overview of Summaries

In the "Document System," you can access a *case-related* overview of the summaries you have written by opening the Overview of Summaries. In this context, case-related means that you can see the summaries of selected documents, document groups, or document sets. This overview is available at all levels of your "Document System" via the context menu. In this menu, you will find the entry *Summaries* in the bottom row of the *Overviews* section. You can also access this overview via the *Overview of Summaries* option in the *Reports* ribbon tab.

In this overview you will see a table list, similar to many in MAXQDA, that contains all existing summaries of the respective document in the lower window area and displays any summary you select in full in the upper window area.

The columns "Document" and "Code" indicate the source of these summaries, the "Preview" contains the first 63 characters of the summary, and the column "Locations" lists all locations in the document from which the underlying coded segments originate. Selected in Fig. 11.10 is the first summary from the document "B01 Jane"; here, all text passages assigned with the code "Causes for the discrepancy" were summarized. Two text passages in the document were assigned with this code, namely, paragraphs 28 and 30.

At the end of this chapter on summaries, it is worth turning to the question of standards and quality criteria. Are there rules for writing a summary, for example? And can you assume that several people will agree on how a given summary should be formulated?

First, as regards the question of rules, it is difficult to define universal guidelines for writing summaries. However, a research team may decide together how best to write summaries for the purposes of their project, what information their summaries should contain, and how comprehensive they should be. Measured against these criteria, which should be set down in writing, you can then judge the quality of a summary.

As far as the agreement of two summaries written by different researchers is concerned, the first question to be asked is what exactly is meant by "agreement." A literal match is impossible. However, you should be able to expect a summary to

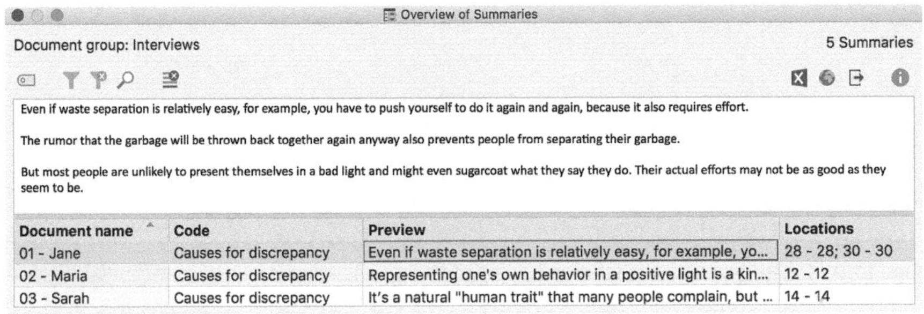

Fig. 11.10 The Overview of Summaries

contain important, valuable information from the perspective of the research question(s) at hand. This should be practiced by the research group until—true to the principle of intersubjectivity—sufficient agreement in view of this goal has been reached.

References

Kuckartz, U. (2014). *Qualitative text analysis: A guide to methods, practice & using software.* Thousand Oaks, CA: SAGE.

Mayring, P. (2014). *Qualitative content analysis: Theoretical foundation, basic procedures and software solution.* Klagenfurt. Retrieved from http://nbn-resolving.de/urn:nbn:de:0168-ssoar-395173

Schreier, M. (2012). *Qualitative content analysis in practice.* Thousand Oaks, CA: SAGE.

Comparing Cases and Groups, Discovering Interrelations, and Using Visualizations

12

Creating categories, coding data, defining variables, and determining code frequencies are key steps in the analysis process. It would be far from accurate to view these steps merely as "preliminary work" for the actual analysis process. This is especially clear if you consider how the category system is constructed, because it usually takes a lot of work and careful reflection to arrive at a sound and effective category system that suits the research question. The category system itself and the assumptions and hypotheses about the relationships between codes both represent independent results of the analysis process and are vital to answering the questions at the heart of a project. Nevertheless, the question "What comes next?" will inevitably arise, or more specifically "What comes after coding the data?" This chapter will address the latter question, while paying special attention to case-oriented and cross-case visualizations, which each play particularly significant roles.

In This Chapter
- Comparing cases and groups
- Using sets to form groups for analysis
- Using quantitative data for qualitative and quantitative group comparisons
- Visually displaying the relationships between cases (documents) and codes
- Comparing the frequency of specific content or statements between groups
- Examining overlaps and interrelationships between codes
- Asking complex questions about the data
- Discovering more types of visualizations

© Springer Nature Switzerland AG 2019
U. Kuckartz, S. Rädiker, *Analyzing Qualitative Data with MAXQDA*,
https://doi.org/10.1007/978-3-030-15671-8_12

About Case and Group Comparisons

Consistently comparing cases and groups is one of the core techniques of qualitative data analysis and plays an important role in many analytical methods—especially in grounded theory, in the form of the "constant comparison method" (Glaser & Strauss, 2009, pp. 102–113). These comparisons can be conducted in MAXQDA both as qualitative and quantitative comparisons.

For *qualitative comparisons*, the coded segments of one or more selected categories in cases or groups are compared with each other. For example, "What do Maria, Isabel and Anna say about environmentally conscious nutrition?" or "What do students say about this topic?" Qualitative comparisons work with the coded original texts or with the summaries provided in the Summary Grid and do not require any numeric data.

Quantitative comparisons focus on the number (or the extent) of coded segments. The questions are "How often do Maria, Isabel and Anna talk about the topic of environmentally conscious nutrition?" or "To what extent is the topic covered in the relevant interviews?"

In the simplest case, the groups you want to compare will correspond to your document groups, i.e., the groups that are displayed in the "Document System." For example, if a study was conducted in two cities and the interviews were assigned to two different document groups, let us say "Tokyo" and "New York," then you would be able to compare the coded segments between these two groups.

Another way to form groups is to use *document sets*. In MAXQDA, these are groups that are put together especially for analysis. You can do this by creating a new set (right-click on the word "Sets" in the "Document System" and select the *New Set* option) and simply dragging and dropping documents into that set. In most situations, sets are created on the basis of certain characteristics. Sometimes you may want to create sets of documents that contain a particular code or a combination of codes. More often, however, you will probably use certain standardized data stored as document variables in your MAXQDA project to form a document set. For example, you could form the sets "Women in the 30–40 age group," "People with a test result outside the simple standard deviation," or "High-school students who received a mathematics grade of A– or above in their final exams."

Forming Groups Based on Variable Values

As described above, document sets can be put together manually or according to document variable values. Even for purely qualitative studies, it makes sense to store the sociodemographic characteristics of your research participants, as well as other standardized information, in the form of document variables. Indeed, mixed methods studies usually have their own data set containing the quantitative data collected. We will now look at how these document variables can be used to form groups to conduct comparisons.

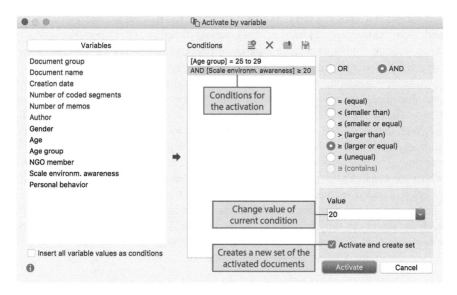

Fig. 12.1 Formulating conditions for the automatic activation of documents

In MAXQDA, you can group documents in this way by selecting **Activate by Document Variables** in the context menu that appears when you right-click the top row in the "Document System" or via the corresponding icon in the toolbar of the same window or the first option in the "Mixed Methods" menu ribbon. Once you select this option, the dialog box shown in Fig. 12.1 will appear, where you can configure logical conditions for the activation process.

These conditions have to be defined according to the following rule:

$$\text{"Variable Name Operator Value"}$$

If you recorded your participants' ages, for instance, by creating age groups like "25–29 years," and then named the corresponding variable "Age group," the formula for selecting people in this age range would need to be configured as follows:

$$\text{"Age group} = 25 \text{ to } 29 \text{ years"}$$

Multiple selection conditions can also be linked according to the AND combination. This way individuals in the age group 25–29 can be selected who, for example, have also been attributed a certain minimum value on the "Environmental awareness" variable scale. In Fig. 12.1 a value of 20 has been set as a minimum selection value.

Selecting the **Activate and create set** option not only activates the relevant documents but also creates a new set in the "Document System," which contains all documents that meet the applied variable conditions—a set which is then available for further analysis. The selection formula is automatically added as the new set's name, but this name can of course also be replaced by a name of your choice.

Compared to creating sets manually, this automatic method is clearly much faster and more convenient. Moreover, this analysis function is invaluable, especially when you are analyzing a large number of documents, as may be the case if you have conducted a mixed methods online survey, for example.

A further interesting analysis option can be to transform the frequencies of codes into document variables; you can do this via the context menu for codes (see Chap. 10). After completing the transformation, you can form groups of documents to which certain codes have been assigned or where the frequency of an assigned code exceeds a given threshold value. Please note that the document sets are not dynamically connected to the document variables, unlike the variables themselves which are dynamically linked to the codes and which are updated each time you add or delete a coded segment of a code that has been transformed into a variable.

Document sets differ considerably from document groups in one respect: while each document can only belong to a single document group and is deleted when the group is deleted, a document can belong to any number of document sets. Sets can be removed without deleting the associated documents.

Qualitative Contrasting: Comparing Statements of Cases and Groups

The function *Analysis* > *Compare Groups* > *Qualitative* is used to compare the contents of statements made by individuals or groups. The dialog box that appears (Fig. 12.2) consists of three areas.

Drag and drop at least two document groups, document sets, or individual documents from the "Document System" into the "Groups" area (at the top). Then drag and drop one or more codes from the "Code System" into the middle section "Codes." In the "Compare" section below these, you can select which data you want to compare: the coded segments of the selected codes or the coded segments combined with the comments that have been written for each code. MAXQDA will then generate and display an Interactive Quote Matrix.

If two groups have been formed as document sets as described above, e.g., "Environmental NGO membership = yes" and "Environmental NGO membership = no," the Quote Matrix presents the statements of these two groups side by side in a table format. In Fig. 12.3 this has been done for the code "(Influence) through individuals." In the second column, the corresponding statements made by individuals who are not NGO members are listed, while the third column lists those of NGO members. The previously selected codes are listed in the leftmost column, and from here you can switch between them. You can also choose whether you want the source information and memos to be displayed as well as the code comments displayed below the coded segments.

The Interactive Quote Matrix is connected to the original data: clicking on the source information below a segment displays it in its original context in the "Document Browser." If you want to use this comparison for a presentation or publication, or to integrate it into a poster, you can save it as a text file for Word (RTF format) or as an Excel table.

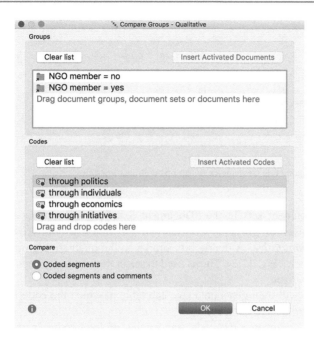

Fig. 12.2 The dialog box for comparing cases and groups

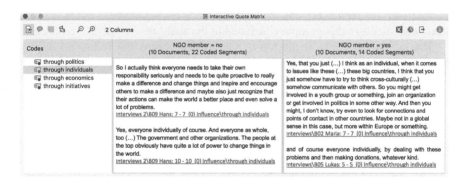

Fig. 12.3 Compare statements made by groups with the Interactive Quote Matrix

Quantitative Contrasting: Comparing Frequency of Statements of Cases and Groups

The Interactive Quote Matrix depicted in Fig. 12.3 allows you to make purely qualitative comparisons of cases and groups. However, you may also be interested in comparing the frequencies of codes for both cases and groups. As with the qualitative comparison, the groups you want to compare must first exist as document

	NGO member = no	NGO member = yes	Total
through politics	29	25	54
through individuals	22	14	36
through economics	10		10
through initiatives	5	10	15
Σ SUM	66	49	115
# N = Documents	16 (61.5%)	10 (38.5%)	26 (100.0%)

Fig. 12.4 Compare code frequencies for groups with the crosstab

groups or document sets in the "Document System." To conduct a quantitative contrast of cases or groups, you can use the function *Analysis > Compare Groups > Quantitative*. A dialog box similar to the qualitative group comparison dialog will appear (Fig. 12.2). This is used to select the cases or groups and the codes for your comparison.

MAXQDA will then generate a crosstab table in which the code frequencies of cases and/or groups are compared.

Figure 12.4 compares the code frequencies of four codes, namely, "through politics," "through individuals," "through economics," and "through initiatives", for members and nonmembers of environmental organizations. The "Σ SUM" row contains the number of coded segments for the respective groups (i.e., 49 coded segments for the members), and the bottom line "# N (Documents)" indicates how many documents in this group are included in the analysis.

The toolbar available at the top of the window opens the following display options, which allow a variety of further analyses:

- *Display codes with hierarchy*—If you select this option, MAXQDA automatically adds the parent codes of the selected codes to preserve the hierarchical structure of the code system. This has the advantage that the code groups can be aggregated by collapsing them. If this option is switched off, all the codes selected for the analysis are displayed without their hierarchy. This gives you the option of removing unwanted, nonactivated parent codes from the display.
- *Number of segments*—Shows absolute frequencies, i.e., the number of segments of the respective code for the respective group.
- *Row percentage*—This is the percentage share of the cell calculated in comparison to the whole row (i.e., the figure in column "Total"). The row shows how the number of coded segments is distributed as a percentage across the selected groups.
- *Column percentages based on the sum of coded segments (row "SUM")*—This is the percentage of the cell calculated in comparison to the whole column (i.e., the figure in row "SUM"). The column shows how the number of coded segments in the individual groups is distributed as a percentage across the selected codes.

🖼 *Column percentages based on the number of documents (row "N = Documents")*—Indicates the percentage of documents within the respective group in which each code occurs (the option *Count hits only once per document* is selected automatically in this case).

Count hits only once per document—The documents are used as the unit of analysis. For each document, the system only registers whether the corresponding code has been assigned or not; it does not matter how often a code occurs within a document.

Using Visualizations for Analyses and Presentations

Bar charts and pie charts are ubiquitous as a means of presenting results in both scientific and nonscientific publications. For Eurobarometer surveys, for example, the data of thousands of respondents are summarized in a chart, allowing the data of 27 EU countries to be presented and compared at a glance. It is hard to believe that it has been more than 200 years since William Playfair, a Scottish engineer, invented these forms of representation (Tufte, 2001, p. 3). Bar and pie charts are still used today in quantitatively oriented research—though with far more beautiful designs and more complex structure than originally conceived. These charts also play a role in the analysis of qualitative and mixed methods data, but only for qualitative data if it has been transformed into quantitative data, for example, as frequencies of the occurrence of a particular category. While visualizations for the analysis of qualitative data are still discussed relatively rarely (Kuckartz, 2014; Miles, Huberman, & Saldana, 2013), MAXQDA contains some very useful tools in this respect, which are described below. You can find a detailed discussion on visualizations and how to use the visual tool MAXMaps in Chap. 17.

Code Matrix Browser: Visualizing the Distribution of Codes Per Case or Group

The following question often comes up during analyses: which codes have been assigned to which documents and how often? What you need here is a presentation of these results in a "documents x codes" format, preferably as a table or matrix. In MAXQDA, you can do this with the Code Matrix Browser, a visualization tool you can access via *Visual Tools > Code Matrix Browser*. Figure 12.5 illustrates an example that includes seven documents and the category "Biggest world problems" along with its subcodes. The documents are arranged in the columns of the matrix and the code "Biggest world problems" and its subcodes in the rows. The top row contains the names of the seven documents displayed in the columns (here I01 to I07). The individual nodes indicate how many times the relevant code has been assigned in the respective document. The larger the node, the more often the code has been assigned. In Fig. 12.5 a binarized view has been selected, i.e., the Code

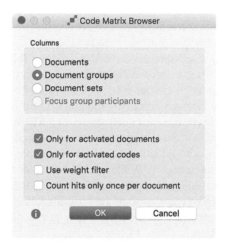

Code System	I01	I02	I03	I04	I05	I06	I07	SUM
▼ Biggest world problems								0
Climate	■	■	■	■	■	■	■	7
Resources: scarcity, distributic	■		■	■	■	■	·	5
Egoism, lacking sense of comr	■			■				2
Religious and cultural conflicts	■		■					2
War	■	■				■	■	4
Globalization		■					■	2
Fast pace of life	■					■		2
Σ SUM	6	3	3	3	2	4	3	24

Fig. 12.5 The binarized view in the Code Matrix Browser

Columns

○ Documents
◉ Document groups
○ Document sets
○ Focus group participants

☑ Only for activated documents
☑ Only for activated codes
☐ Use weight filter
☐ Count hits only once per document

OK   Cancel

Fig. 12.6 Code Matrix Browser options

Matrix Browser displays whether the relevant code is present in the document or not but not how often it is present in each case. Hence, the nodes displayed are all the same size. Interview B05 only mentions two global problems: "Climate" and "Scarcity of resources." The bottom row is a summary row; it indicates how many of the displayed codes are present in each document. Here you can see that interviewees one and six mention a lot of the problems: six and four, respectively.

Before opening the Code Matrix Browser, you have to decide what you want to display in the columns and rows (Fig. 12.5). To select these documents and codes, simply activate them, as usual, in the "Document System."

The Code Matrix Browser can be used not only to generate "documents x codes" matrices for individual documents, but you can also compare groups of documents. In the dialog box that appears when you open the Code Matrix Browser, select either the "Document groups" or "Document sets" option (Fig. 12.6). It is best to reset all activations in the "Document System" window (using the icon at the top left of the

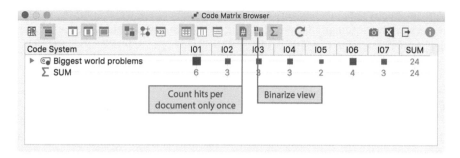

Fig. 12.7 The Code Matrix Browser once the subcodes have been aggregated

window) and then activate the document groups or document sets you want to compare. The weight filter can be used to analyze only the codes that lie within a certain weight range.

Further display options are also available in the Code Matrix Browser:

- You can determine the column width and design of the nodes (as squares or circles).
- You can choose whether the hits per document are counted only once, i.e., where there is no difference whether someone has named environmental issues as the world's biggest problem in three different text segments or only one.

The subordinate levels of the code system can be collapsed in the same way as they can in the "Code System." When you do this, the code frequencies will be aggregated at the upper level. Figure 12.7 illustrates what occurs when the subcodes are collapsed: now the nodes appear in different sizes. The greater the number of codes that have been assigned to a given document, the larger the node. To get this result, the option *Count hits only once per document* must be selected, and the option *Binarize view* must be deselected. In Fig. 12.7 you can see then that interviewee one mentions the most problems, while interview six also mentions quite a few; the SUM row demonstrates that six and four problems are mentioned in each respective case.

This display of the codes assigned per document in the Code Matrix Browser should demonstrate that visualizations are far more than just eye-catching gimmicks. The visual representation shown in Fig. 12.5 makes it easier for researchers to identify patterns and exceptional or extreme cases. In this example, for instance, it is easier to identify people who only cite "climate" and "scarcity of resources" as the biggest global problems. The display of the nodes in Code Matrix Browser can also be switched from symbols to their numerical values. If you switch back and forth between these two forms of representation, the major advantage of such graphics should become clear: it is much easier to recognize contexts, patterns, and special cases in a visual representation than it is in a large, unmanageable sea of numbers.

The Code Matrix Browser can not only be used for analyses but also for "quality control" purposes. If, for example, you want to differentiate a main category in one step of inductive coding, it is very easy first to visually check whether the documents in question have actually been coded with at least one of the subcodes or if some documents have been forgotten.

Code Relations Browser: Visualizing Co-occurrences of Codes

Searching for connections and interrelationships between the categories, and not just describing the categories and their subcategories, is certainly one of the most interesting aspects of any research project. Such interrelationships can be examined in MAXQDA in various ways. One option is to investigate the co-occurrence of codes. Now, "co-occurrence" can mean very different things, for example (Fig. 12.8):

- Two codes were *both assigned to a specific document*, for example, someone talks about environmental problems as being the most serious problems facing the world, and the same interview also includes a section on the need for education concerning sustainable development.
- Two codes were assigned to the same text segment, image segment, or video clip, i.e., the code assignments *intersect*.
- Two codes have been assigned *in close proximity to each other*: first someone talks about environmental problems as the biggest global problem and in the next section about education.

Of course, further variations of co-occurrences are also conceivable. You can search for these using the function *Analysis > Complex Coding Query*, and they are discussed in detail in the following section "Discovering complex interrelationships of codes."

Various options exist for analyzing the co-occurrence of codes in text, image, or video segments, i.e., intersections or overlaps. Code intersections involving a

Fig. 12.8 Co-occurrence of codes

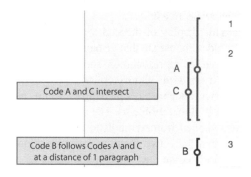

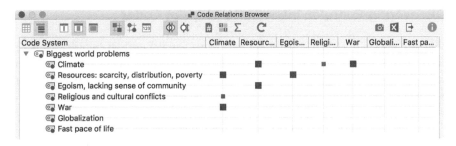

Fig. 12.9 The Code Relations Browser

specific code can be quickly and easily identified by right-clicking on the code in question in the "Code System" and selecting ***Intersections*** in the context menu. The result is a list of intersecting codes sorted by frequency. If you select a code from that list, the relevant intersecting segments are displayed in the "Retrieved Segments" window.

The most important tool for displaying code intersections is the Code Relations Browser, which generates matrices, code by code (Fig. 12.9). You can open this tool via ***Visual Tools > Code Relations Browser*** and then determine the codes to display in your matrix's rows and columns (all or only activated codes). You can also determine the documents to be used in the analysis via activations; the default is all documents. For the columns, there is the additional option ***Choose top-level code***. If you choose this option, MAXQDA will subsequently open a dialog box in which you can select any number of code groups on the top level of your code system. As with the Code Matrix Browser, you can determine how the column headers and the nodes of the matrix (squares or circles) are to be displayed. The size and color of these individual nodes symbolize how many intersections occur for each respective pair of codes. The larger the node in the corresponding cell, the more intersections occur for those codes across all documents or only the activated documents. Double-clicking on a node displays the relevant segments in the "Retrieved Segments" window. Further options for adjusting the display of these matrices are available in the Code Relations Browser toolbar:

- ⬡ ***Near (codes)***—searches for codes in close proximity to each other, rather than intersecting codes.
- ⊞ ***Count hits only once per document***—in this case, the display is not based on the respective number of coded segments, but on the number of documents in which at least one intersection occurs.
- ⬛ ***Binarize view***—only indicates whether there is any intersection between these codes or not. No matter what the number of intersections, the node will have a uniform size.

Discovering Complex Interrelationships of Codes

Whereas the Code Relations Browser examines the relationships between pairs of codes, the ***Complex Coding Query*** (available in the ***Analysis*** ribbon tab) allows you to examine relationships between several codes. Additionally, beyond searching for intersections and the proximity of codes, you can also ask more complex questions about your data.

In Fig. 12.10 you can see the dialog box that appears when you access the Complex Coding Query function; the first analysis setting, *Intersection*, is selected by default. Functionally, this does the same as the Code Relations Browser, however, not just for two but for any number of codes. MAXQDA then finds the places in all your documents (or only in the activated documents) where all of these codes intersect. If you select four codes and *Intersection*, then only segments where all four codes are present together will be reported. The image to the right of the dialog box outlines how each setting works: only the simultaneous occurrence of the two selected codes results in a hit, and only the inner, intersecting area of these two codes is displayed in the "Retrieved Segments" window.

Various settings can be configured for your analysis: the subcodes of the selected codes can be included, and the search can also be limited to activated documents or code assignments made by specific users.

The analysis settings *Intersection (Set)* and *Overlapping* are used to investigate further forms of the co-occurrence of codes. If there is an *Intersection (Set)*, the system checks whether at least a predefined number of selected codes have been

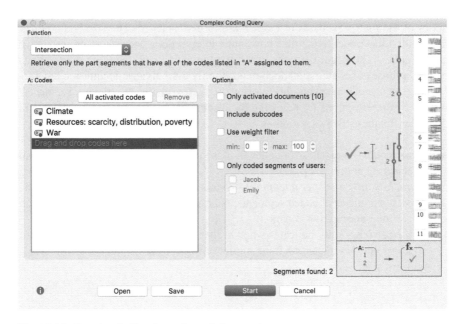

Fig. 12.10 Complex Coding Query for code intersections

Table 12.1 Additional settings for the Complex Coding Query

Analysis setting	Description
Only one code	Search for segments that have been assigned one—and only one—code from a predefined list of codes
Only this code	Search for segments to which only one specific certain code has been assigned and no other
If inside	Search for segments that have been assigned a certain code, but only those segments that are completely within the coded segments of a different, specified code
If outside	The counterpart to "If inside": search for segments that have been assigned a certain code, but only those that are completely outside coded segments of a different, specified code
Followed by (ignores code assignments in PDFs and images)	Search for segments of a certain code that are followed, at a specified maximum distance, by text passages assigned with a different, specified code
Near (ignores code assignments in PDFs and images)	Very similar to "Followed by," but this analysis function does not depend on the sequence (B follows A), but only on the proximity of the assignments of two different codes

coded simultaneously. The *Overlapping* setting works in a similar way to the *Intersection* setting: not only the inner, intersecting area of the segments is displayed in the "Retrieved Segments" window, but instead the larger section between the outer segment boundaries is displayed.

The functionality of the other six analysis settings is explained in Table 12.1. By careful selection of documents, codes, settings, and parameters, an enormous range of detailed questions about your coded data can be answered. Note that while you are specifying the parameters, the dialog displays the number of segments found to match the current settings ("2" in Fig. 12.10), so you need not run a query which you can see has no hits.

Code Configurations: Identifying Multidimensional Patterns

The *Analysis > Code Configurations* function can be used to determine how often selected codes were assigned simultaneously to a segment or within the same document. Code Configurations are a powerful tool for analyzing the interrelationships of several aspects or dimensions. These different dimensions are to be found in almost every research project. In classroom research, for example, the dimensions "teaching phase," "teacher action," and "student reactions" may all be the focus of a study. And in a research paper on the effects of the increasing digitization of vocational trades, the following question might be asked: "Which 'new technologies' are used in which 'work processes' and which 'skills' are required for this?"

	Anna	Harry	Josh	Segments	Percent	Number of codes	Day 1	Day 2
◆			■	9	45.00	1	50.00	40.00
◆	■	■		5	25.00	2	30.00	20.00
◆		■		2	10.00	1	10.00	10.00
◆	■			2	10.00	1	10.00	10.00
◆		■	■	1	5.00	2	0.00	10.00
◆	■		■	1	5.00	2	0.00	10.00
Σ				20	100.00	9	100.00	100.00

Fig. 12.11 Simple Code Configurations results table for the unit "Segments"

In order to use the Code Configurations function, you need to have defined these dimensions as codes and their partial aspects as subcodes in the "Code System," and you need to have coded the data with these categories. Let us take a look at a simple example to illustrate this: during a video analysis conducted at a day care center, three top-level categories were used to code which teachers (1) played which game (2) with which child (3). The function *Analysis > Code Configurations > Simple Code Configurations* will then show how often these individual codes co-occur. Figure 12.11 illustrates the result of one such analysis, in which you can easily see how often the individual children played together or by themselves. Each row contains one of the configurations of codes found in the data; for example, you can see from the second row that Anna and Harry played in pairs during five observations. Throughout the observation period as a whole, the children never played together as a group of three—no row contains a square in all three code columns. The number of code configurations that occurred from all the theoretically possible configurations is shown at the top right of the results window.

In the options dialog box that appears when you open this function, you can restrict the analysis to currently activated documents, and you can opt to have the table differentiated by document, by document group, or by document set. A differentiation of this kind was also chosen for this example, so that the two observation sessions could be displayed in two additional columns and analyzed separately. The icons in the example allow you to toggle the display of the values in the columns for documents, document groups, and document sets between absolute values and row and column percentages, making systematic comparisons easier. As always, the results table is interactively linked to the original data: double-clicking on the second row will list all five segments in which Anna and Harry played together in the "Retrieved Segments" window.

When you open the function *Analysis > Code Configurations > Complex Code Configurations*, an options dialog box will appear into which you can drag and drop several parent codes for your analysis. MAXQDA will then generate a table, which displays how often combinations of the respective subcodes of these codes were assigned to the same segment in your data. Figure 12.12 illustrates the result of such an analysis. Each row represents one combination of the subcodes that occur in the data material. In the first row, you can see that in seven observations (coded

● ○ ●   xox Complex Code Configurations

10 (of 27 theoretically possible) combinations

Ỵ Ỵᵖ ⅠⅠ [#] [→] [↓] Cᐢ   ⌧ ◔ [→]   ⓘ

	Which teacher	plays what	with whom?	Segments ▾	Percent	Day 1	Day 2
◆	Ms. Whitford	Hide and seek	Josh	7	25,00	3	4
◆	Mr. Thompson	Board game	Harry	5	17,86	2	3
◆	Ms. Jones	Hide and seek	Anna	4	14,29	2	2
◆	Mr. Thompson	Board game	Josh	3	10,71	2	1
◆	Mr. Thompson	Board game	Anna	2	7,14	1	1
◆	Ms. Jones	Hide and seek	Harry	2	7,14	1	1
◆	Ms. Jones	Ball game	Anna	2	7,14	1	1
◆	Ms. Whitford	Ball game	Josh	1	3,57	1	0
◆	Ms. Jones	Ball game	Josh	1	3,57	0	1
◆	Ms. Jones	Ball game	Harry	1	3,57	1	0
Σ				28	100,00	14	14

Fig. 12.12 Complex Code Configurations results table for the unit "segments"

segments), Ms. Whitford played hide and seek with Josh. This corresponds to 25% of the total of 28 observations that were analyzed.

The Simple and Complex Code Configurations tables can be set to display their results using either coded segments or documents as a unit. To do this, choose the appropriate setting in dialog box once you have opened either function. If you choose documents as the unit, the co-occurrence of codes in a document as a whole is analyzed. It does not matter whether the code was assigned more than once or where in the document. If two codes occur at least once in the document, this is treated as a co-occurrence.

The benefit of all four variants of MAXQDA's Code Configurations (simple/complex, segments/documents) is clear: they effectively support the discovery of patterns in the data and provide a good foundation for developing types and typologies.

Document Portrait: Visualizing the Encodings of a Case

If you have assigned colors to the codes following a logical scheme of some kind, it can be very interesting from an analytical perspective to display the coded segments within a document visually as an image. The Document Portrait (opened via *Visual Tools > Document Portrait*, or a document's context menu) is an innovative visualization tool in MAXQDA with which you can generate a case-oriented visualization of selected documents. The Document Portrait is based on the idea that codes can be assigned a color or, if you use the emoticode function, a symbol in the style of an emoji. This means that a connection has already been established between a category and a visual element, that is, either a color or an emoji symbol.

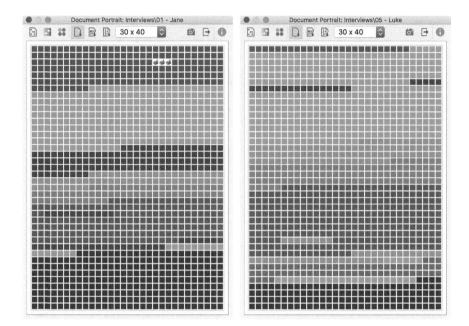

Fig. 12.13 Document Portraits for two guided interviews

The document portrait thereby displays a document as an image of its coded segments in sequential order; in other words, the image starts at the top left with the color (or symbol) of the first code assigned to a text or video (Fig. 12.13).

How the Document Portrait Works

A document portrait always consists of a certain number of tiles (30 × 30, 30 × 40, 40 × 30, 40 × 40, or 40 × 60), which can be displayed as squares or circles of a certain color or as emojis. The Document Portrait visually represents the coded segments of the selected document, i.e., the same segments that would be listed in the Overview of Coded Segments for that document. The first column of the latter overview table contains small colored circles, namely, the color of the corresponding code. The sequence of colors in this overview table is the starting point for the Document Portrait; however, the length of a segment is used as a weighting factor for this visual representation, while in the Overview of Coded Segments, each segment always corresponds to exactly one row of the table, regardless of the length of the coded segment. Moreover, in the Document Portrait, the code colors are not displayed one below the other, but next to each other. The picture, consisting of 900, 1200, 1600, or 2400 tiles, depending on the setting you choose, is similar to a classic TV screen, structured line by line and starting at the top left. In a television screen, the electron beam scans the screen line by line from left to right. In the same way, the Document Portrait starts in the upper left corner and builds up a portrait line by line, i.e., at the end of a line, the system jumps back to the start of the next line.

And, since it does make a difference here whether a coded segment is 3 or 30 lines long, the length (or size) of a segment is taken into account when calculating the number of tiles allocated to that segment.

Figure 12.13 shows example Document Portraits for two guided interviews. The presentations allow you to make a direct comparison of the progression of the key topics covered in each interview. In both portraits you can also see how individual topics come up again and again in the course of the interview. Extensive use of the Document Portrait was made by d'Andrea, Hodgen, and Heaton (2016) in a study on the communication of consultants, in which their use of skills and the timing of their application were brought into focus.

As shown in Fig. 12.13, all of the existing coded segments of a document are visualized immediately one after the other—without any space between the individual segments. Using the *Visualize entire document or coded text* option (at the far left of the toolbar), parts of the document that have not been coded can also be included in the display. With this option, the entire document is projected onto the tiles of the portrait, and sections of the document that have not been assigned a code appear as white tiles in proportion to their length.

The appearance of the Document Portrait can be adjusted via the following settings:

- Mixed colors for overlapping codes yes-no: this determines how the tiles are displayed if several codes are assigned to a segment instead of just one. If this setting is switched off, the coded segments (i.e., the colors) are displayed sequentially one after the other. If this setting is switched on, however, the colors of the codes involved are mixed to form a new color, reflected in the corresponding tiles.
- You can choose circles instead of squares as tiles.
- Ordered by document: the order of the coded segments in the Document Portrait is determined by the order of the coded segments in the document (default setting and the one used in Fig. 12.13).
- Ordered by color: the order of the coded segments in the Document Portrait is sorted by color, i.e., the same colors are grouped together. In this display it is not apparent if any topic has arisen several times.
- Sorting by color frequency: in this display setting (Fig. 12.14), the document portrait is "tidied up." First, the tiles of the same color are stacked as individual columns. The column with the most tiles, i.e., with the largest coded portion of the document, is placed on the far left, the column with the least coded portion on the far right. Only the most common 20 colors are displayed.

The Document Portrait is also interactively linked to your project data: clicking on one of the tiles with the left mouse button displays the corresponding coded segment in its original context in the "Document Browser." By right-clicking and selecting the option *Retrieve Coded Segments with this Color*, MAXQDA compiles all the coded segments of this color within the displayed document in the "Retrieved Segments" window.

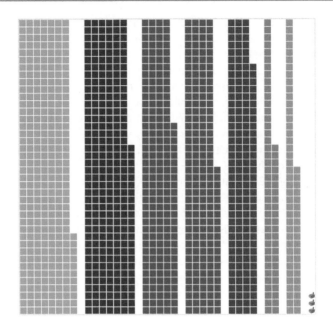

Fig. 12.14 Document Portrait ordered by color frequency

On the right side of the Document Portrait toolbar, you will find two additional icons for exporting and saving the displayed image. By clicking on the "Camera" icon, you can copy the current display to the clipboard and paste it into a PowerPoint presentation, for example. By clicking on the "Export" icon, you can export the current display as a PNG or SVG file, among other formats.

Codeline: Representing Timelines and Sequences of Codes

While the Document Portrait converts an entire document, such as an interview, into an image, the Codeline visualization tool (opened via *Visual Tools > Codeline*, or via the document's context menu) focuses on displaying the progression of interviews or focus group discussions. The resulting visualization is structured like a musical score in which the individual instrumental parts are arranged one below the other, so you have an overview of each musical moment. In the columns texts are divided into sections (paragraphs) for the Codeline, tables into their rows, and videos into minutes or seconds.

In Fig. 12.15 you can see a Codeline from a research project by Hatani (2015) that analyses the first 14 sections of a panel discussion on global health. Six speakers are arranged in the top rows, namely, the moderator and the five participants of the focus group. Below, the coded topics of the panel discussion have been visualized. As with the Document Portrait, the code colors here have both an aesthetic and analytical function. You can use two icons in the Codeline toolbar and the slider to customize

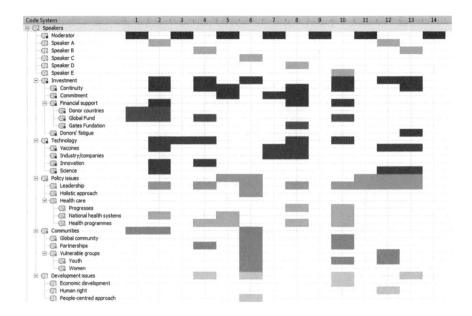

Fig. 12.15 The sequence of contributions to a group discussion (source: Hatani, 2015, http://www.qualitative-research.net/index.php/fqs/article/view/2208, Creative Commons Attribution 4.0 License)

the display on the x-axis. For example, you can adjust the width of the Codeline to suit the size of your window; it will then be "compressed" horizontally so that it perfectly fits your screen.

What can you tell from the Codeline above? The first thing you might notice is that the moderator—at least at the beginning of the focus group—tries to let all participants speak one after the other, because the moderator and speakers alternate up to and including paragraph 10. Then, once they have completed a full round, the moderator addresses "Speaker A" again, and in paragraph 13, there is direct interaction between two speakers: "Speaker B" reacts to "Speaker A" without being addressed by the moderator. Let us now look at the topics of discussion: the topics "Financial Support" and "Communities" are talked about by the moderator at the outset. Speaker A expands on the topics and—like the speakers that follow—immediately addresses the topic of "Leadership." This presentation allows a very detailed analysis of the sequence of speakers and the progression of the topics covered in the discussion. So, what can the Codeline be used for?

- First, the Codeline can display the sequence of speakers very clearly for analyses of focus group discussions and can also make the connection between speakers and certain topics apparent.

- Second, this visual tool can be used analytically to track certain codes throughout the course of a text. If you display activated codes only, you can make targeted comparisons between different codes.
- Third, using the Codeline during the exploration stage of a project can help you detect the simultaneous appearance of certain codes.
- Fourth, the tool provides a general overview of your code assignments, which makes it universally applicable. It is particularly useful for systematic comparisons of the temporal progression across multiple cases.

If you hover your cursor over one of the blocks of a particular color, a tooltip will appear; double-click on it to jump to the corresponding text position in the "Document Browser." Like all MAXQDA visual tools, the current Codeline display can be exported or copied to the clipboard by clicking on the camera icon and then pasting it into Word, PowerPoint, or other programs.

References

D'Andrea, L. M., Hodgen, C. M., & Heaton, M. (2016). Visualizing communication patterns among expert and novice counselors. *Journal of Professional Communication, 4*(2), 37–56. https://doi.org/10.15173/JPC.V4I2.2345.

Glaser, B. G., & Strauss, A. L. (2009). *The discovery of grounded theory: Strategies for qualitative research* (4th ed.). New Brunswick: Aldine.

Hatani, F. (2015). Analyzing high-profile panel discussion on global health: An exploration with MAXQDA. *Forum Qualitative Sozialforschung/Forum: Qualitative Social Research, 16*(1). https://doi.org/10.17169/fqs-16.1.2208.

Kuckartz, U. (2014). *Qualitative text analysis: A guide to methods, practice & using software.* Thousand Oaks, CA: SAGE.

Miles, M. B., Huberman, A. M., & Saldana, J. (2013). *Qualitative data analysis: A methods sourcebook* (3rd ed.). Thousand Oaks, CA: SAGE.

Tufte, E. R. (2001). *The visual display of quantitative information.* Cheshire, CT: Bertrams.

Analyzing Mixed Methods Data

13

Mixed methods approaches are becoming increasingly popular in practical empirical research. At the beginning of the 2000s, a global and interdisciplinary mixed methods community was formed, presenting mixed methods approaches and research projects at many international conferences. A large number of publications and textbooks were written, and a special journal, the *Journal of Mixed Methods Research* (JMMR), was founded in 2007. How can mixed methods data analysis be implemented within MAXQDA? Since the first program versions, MAXQDA has always paid great attention to the combination and integration of methods. Thus, from the very beginning of the program, it was possible to manage an associated data set of quantitative data parallel to the qualitative data and to link qualitative and quantitative data during the analysis. Special functions for mixed methods research are summarized in a separate ribbon tab "Mixed Methods"; these functions are the subject of this chapter.

In This Chapter
- Integration during analysis as a challenge for mixed methods approaches
- Combination of qualitative and quantitative data in MAXQDA
- Strategies for integrating both data strands
- Joint displays in mixed methods data analysis
- Results-based integration strategies
- Data-based integration strategies
- Further options for integration

© Springer Nature Switzerland AG 2019
U. Kuckartz, S. Rädiker, *Analyzing Qualitative Data with MAXQDA*,
https://doi.org/10.1007/978-3-030-15671-8_13

Integration as a Challenge of Mixed Methods Research

For a long time, literature on mixed methods has focused on questions of research design and the development of design typologies (Creswell & Plano Clark, 2011; Morgan, 2014; Teddlie & Tashakkori, 2009). The question of the fundamental compatibility of qualitative and quantitative paradigms has also been discussed repeatedly as has been, in this context, the question of what is to be understood by a paradigm at all (Creswell, 2016; Morgan, 2007). In comparison, relatively little attention has been paid to the analysis of mixed methods data. However, a number of scholars have been dealing with questions of data analysis in mixed methods research for some time. These include Pat Bazeley (2009, 2013, 2017) and Tony Onwuegbuzie (Onwuegbuzie & Dickinson, 2008; Onwuegbuzie, Slate, Leech, & Collins, 2009; Onwuegbuzie & Teddlie, 2003). Kuckartz (2017) also deals extensively with the topic of data analysis in mixed methods research and gives numerous examples. At this point we will restrict ourselves to references to these methodological texts, especially to the special issue "Mixed Methods" of the Cologne Journal for Sociology and Social Psychology (Baur, Kelle, & Kuckartz, 2017), because a detailed treatment of this topic would go beyond the scope of this book.

The fact that the mixed methods literature now increasingly focuses on the phase of data analysis can certainly be interpreted as a sign of the growing maturity of this approach. The crucial point in the analysis phase is the integration of the two research lines; Creswell (2015, p. 75) formulated the following definition:

> Integration refers to how one brings together the qualitative and quantitative results in a mixed methods study. The way the researcher combines the data needs to relate to the type of mixed methods design used.

Tashakkori and Teddlie (2003) formed the term "meta inferences" in this context, with the help of which the conclusions of both studies—or "strands," as it is often called in the literature—are to be integrated into a coherent whole. Some authors have already described integration as a key aspect of mixed methods research at an early stage, for example, Bryman (2006) and Collins et al., who spoke of the "integration challenge," a formulation that was also taken up again by Fetters and Freshwater (2015) in the JMMR editorial in 2014. There they explicitly demanded that all future contributions submitted to the JMMR must meet this challenge of integration and clearly formulate what analytical benefits will be achieved compared to "monostrand research."

In the following, the relevant "points of integration" for the mixing in the data analysis phase are considered; possible integration strategies are shown, and their implementation with MAXQDA is discussed. Special forms of integrative display, the "joint displays" (Creswell & Plano Clark, 2018, pp. 227–232; Guetterman, Creswell, & Kuckartz, 2015), perform a special role here. These support the presentation, integration, and analysis of qualitative and quantitative data and results. In a review article by Guetterman et al. (2015), 11 different joint displays and their application in different mixed methods designs are presented; most of these joint displays are now implemented in MAXQDA.

Combining Qualitative and Quantitative Data in MAXQDA

Before we specifically discuss the combination of qualitative and quantitative data in MAXQDA, it makes sense to consider the different motivations for the choice of a mixed methods approach. Greene, Caracelli, and Graham (2008, p. 127) identified five different tasks of mixed methods purposes in an often quoted paper:

- *Triangulation* aims at convergence, the agreement of the results of both research strands; this is the classical perspective of validating research results by including a second perspective.
- *Complementarity* aims to complement, illustrate, and better understand the results of one method through the results of a second study using different methodology. This is therefore about a more complete picture, a better understanding, and thus a more comprehensive answer to the research question. Other authors also speak here of the motif of *additional coverage*.
- *Development* means that the results of a method are used to develop or improve a subsequent study. The goal of the development can refer both to the sampling strategy and directly to the development of instruments (e.g., a questionnaire).
- *Initiation* aims at the discovery of contradictions and paradoxical results. The research results are reconsidered and "reread" from the perspective of another method, which may lead to new conclusions.
- *Expansion* aims to broaden the breadth and scope of research by using the most appropriate methods for the components of research.

The combination of methods is associated with the claim (or hope) that more than the sum of the individual parts, "QUAL" + "QUAN", can be achieved (Bazeley, 2010, p. 432; Bryman, 2007; Woolley, 2009). To identify the points of integration between QUAL and QUAN, we first take a look at a classic parallel design, often also referred to as "convergent design" (Fig. 13.1). This is typically chosen for the first of the above motivations (triangulation). With such a design, integration can be based on the data or on the results; the former assumes that both data types are available to the research participants: for example, people took part in narrative interviews and also completed a standardized questionnaire.

So how do we link the two types of data for each person? In MAXQDA the identification is done by means of the variables "document name" and "document group." Whenever a new document with qualitative data (such as a narrative interview) is imported into MAXQDA, so-called system variables are defined at the same time: for the imported document, the name of the document group into which it was imported, and the document name are saved. When adding a corresponding data set with quantitative data (e.g., sociodemographic variables) from an Excel or SPSS file using the routine *Variables* > *Import Document Variables* (see Chap. 10), this must contain two variables called "document name" and "document group." If the names of the document and document group are identical in both data sources, MAXQDA links the qualitative data with the quantitative data.

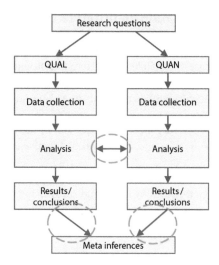

Fig. 13.1 Points of integration in parallel design (highlighted with circles)

Possibilities and Strategies for Integration in MAXQDA

MAXQDA's special analysis functions for mixed methods approaches are summarized in the ribbon tab *Mixed Methods* (Fig. 13.2).

A simple way of integrating quantitative and qualitative data is already created by the option *Activate via document variables*. In this way, the variables of the quantitative data set are used for targeted access to the qualitative data. This is done by formulating one or more logical conditions according to the "Variable Operator Value" pattern. How this has to be done is described in Chap. 12. The logical conditions can be simple, for example, if only a certain characteristic of a variable serves as a selection criterion ("membership in the liberal party = yes"), but they can also combine two or more variables ("gender = female" and "membership in the liberal party = yes") or be the result of a preceding statistical calculation ("value on the factor conservatism > 1.96"). For integrative data analysis, it is particularly interesting that the selection of documents created by activating them via document variables can be saved in MAXQDA as "document sets" and are thus available for later analyses without the groups having to be formed again by formulating the selection conditions for each analysis.

Home	Import	Codes	Variables	Analysis	**Mixed Methods**	Visual Tools	Reports	Stats	MAXDictio

Activate by Document Variables · Quote Matrix · Interactive Quote Matrix · Crosstab · Quantitizing · Typology Table · Similarity Analysis for Documents · Side-by-side Display · QUAL Themes for QUAN Groups (Coded Segments) · QUAL Themes for QUAN Groups (Summaries) · Statistics for QUAL Groups

Fig. 13.2 The various functions of the "Mixed Methods" tab

In addition to this simple way of combining quantitative and qualitative data, a large number of integration strategies exist. With each new version of the program, MAXQDA has extended the set of tools with which these strategies can be realized.

Numerous authors have dealt with theoretical questions of integration and practical integration strategies (Bazeley, 2012; Creswell, 2015; Creswell & Plano Clark, 2011; Erzberger & Kelle, 2003; Guetterman et al., 2015; Kelle, 2007; Onwuegbuzie & Teddlie, 2003; Plano Clark & Ivankova, 2016). Three types of integration strategies are distinguished below: results-based, data-based, and sequence-oriented strategies (Kuckartz, 2017). The first two types are described in more detail in the following.

Results-Based Integration Strategies

One way of integrating qualitative and quantitative studies is to link the results of the two studies. This is the adequate variant of integration when data from studies with two independent samples are analyzed in the context of a triangulation design. In this case, the comparison of the findings can achieve the objective of increased validity because it only takes place after those findings have been made. Two integration strategies can be used, and corresponding joint displays can be created: firstly, the results of both sub-studies can be connected with the help of hyperlinks and, secondly, results can be compared in a table.

Linking of Results via Hyperlinks

The integration strategy of connecting text passages of both research strands via hyperlinks is the first choice when little time is available for the analysis phase. For both parts of the study, written reports, or at least analytical outputs such as frequency counts or statistical tables, must be available.

The task now is to link the respective results of both studies with respect to the topics most interesting for comparison. In MAXQDA this is done as follows:

1. The report with the results of the qualitative study is opened in the "Document Browser."
2. The report with the results of the quantitative study is opened in a second "Document Browser" (by right-clicking on the document name and selecting the function of the same name from the context menu).
3. Both "Document Browsers" are arranged next to each other.
4. The local search function of the first "Document Browser" is used to find topics of interest (e.g., "personal contribution to climate protection") within that document using suitable search terms.
5. The local search function in the second "Document Browser" is used to find corresponding content.
6. The relevant text passages of the qualitative and quantitative results report are linked using "document links"; to do this, the text passages are marked, and from the context menu, ***Insert Document Link*** is selected.

The links in MAXQDA have the same function as hyperlinks in an Internet browser. When a link is clicked later, MAXQDA jumps to the corresponding target position, in this case to the corresponding statements of the study of the other method branch. The inserted links provide a net-like structure over the two research reports, which is very useful for the drafting of the final integrative report. Significant text passages can be copied for the joint presentation of both results and contrasted in the results report.

Side-by-Side Display of Results for Coded Segments
While the technique of linking the results is immediately available, the technique of contrasting the results of both studies in tabular form requires some preparatory work; both research reports or result materials must first be thematically coded (Creswell & Plano Clark, 2018, pp. 228–232; Kuckartz, 2014b, pp. 69–88), whereby the research questions determine the thematic codes. This means that not only the results report of the qualitative study but also the results report of the quantitative study is reviewed with regard to the occurrence of the topics of interest; the relevant text passages are marked and coded with the corresponding thematic code. The search functions of MAXQDA can also be used in this procedure to search for specific terms. It is also possible to automatically code the text passages found. If no written reports on the results of the two sub-studies are yet available, the existing preparatory work can be used instead. For example, the statistical tables can be coded for the quantitative results.

In the start dialog, which appears after calling the function *Mixed Methods > Side-by-side Display > ... of Results (Coded Segments)*, the two reports are dragged from the "Document System" window into the corresponding fields of the dialog by clicking and dragging with the mouse. The same happens with the codes of interest: these are dragged from the "Code System" window into the left field "Themes" (Fig. 13.3).

Side-by-Side Display of Results for Summaries
If the reports contain many pages, as is the case with larger studies such as the Eurobarometer studies, the tabular comparison of the coded segments with the topics

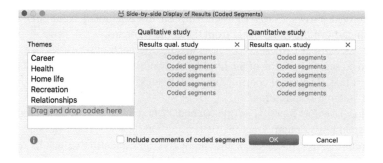

Fig. 13.3 The dialog to create a side-by-side display of the results

of interest may become very extensive. In the case of very important topics, it can also happen that many passages of text are coded throughout the report, but some of these may be quite redundant. In this case it can be very useful to first write thematic summaries with the function *Analysis > Summary Grid* (see Chap. 11) and then use these thematic summaries in place of the original text passages in the side-by-side displays. Another advantage of this method is that the tables created in this way already have a very high degree of compression, so that they can be easily transferred to the final integrative report without major changes.

After selecting the option *Mixed Methods > Side-by-side Display of Results (Summaries)*, the same dialog appears as for the side-by-side display of the coded segments of the original text: the two reports and the codes of interest are dragged with the mouse into the corresponding dialog boxes.

Data-Based Integration Strategies

Transformation of Qualitative Data into Quantitative Data: Quantitizing

The conversion of qualitative, i.e., linguistic, information into a number is also called "quantitizing." This is a process that respondents already practice (unconsciously) when they convert their answer to a certain statement into a numerical value in a standardized survey and, for example, tick the value "7" on a scale from "(0) total rejection" to "(10) total approval."

A good example of the strategy of quantitizing is the mixed methods study by Fölling-Albers and Meidenbauer (see Kuckartz, 2014a, pp. 89–90), which examines which aspects of teaching students still remember in the evening. The study by Mayring, König, Birk, and Hurst (2000, pp. 28–30) on teacher unemployment in the new states of the unified Germany also transforms qualitative information into numbers. How is the quantification done in practice with MAXQDA? Whenever you code a segment, MAXQDA increases the count of how often the code is assigned to the document. The total number of all assignments of a code is visible beside each code in the "Code System" and beside each document in the "Document System." This creates a matrix of "documents by codes" in the background without the user noticing. This matrix or parts of it can be displayed with the "Code Matrix Browser" (called in the ribbon tab *Visual Tools*). If a code is now to be transformed into a quantitative variable, simply click on it and select the *Transform into Document Variable* option in the context menu (see Chap. 10). A new variable is created, and the code name is selected as the name for the new variable. The frequencies of coding with this code are stored as values of the variables for each document and can then be statistically analyzed. The MAXQDA module "Stats," which is not described in this book, can be particularly useful for analyses using mixed methods. "Stats" is only included in the "MAXQDA Analytics Pro" version and can be used directly with the code frequencies, i.e., without converting code frequencies into variable values. Stats allows the combination of quantitative data with the quantified qualitative data and offers a variety of descriptive and inferential statistical methods.[1]

Quantifying qualitative data is a common integration strategy. Kuckartz (2014a), Sandelowski, Voils, and Knafl (2009), and Vogl (2017) deal in great detail with the different possibilities of quantification.

Qualitative Exploration of Extreme Cases of the Quantitative Study

This integration strategy of QUAL and QUAN identifies extreme cases, mostly on the basis of quantitative data. Then the qualitative data, focused on certain important topics, are analyzed in detail for these extreme cases (Creswell & Plano Clark, 2018, p. 235; Bazeley, 2012, p. 821). MAXQDA makes it easy to find extreme cases even with large samples: click on the column heading of the desired variable (e.g., the factor value for "Neuroticism") in the "Data Editor," and all rows (i.e., documents) are then sorted in ascending or descending order. In the first and last rows, after sorting, you will find the persons with particularly high and particularly low values on the factor "neuroticism." If you click on the rows, the documents are also highlighted in the "Document System" (with a blue bar); they can now be compared with each other and you can compare their statements on specific topics using the *Compare Groups* function on the *Analysis* ribbon tab.

The possibility described above of transforming codes into document variables opens up the possibility of also using the code frequencies to identify extreme cases. After the transformation and sorting of the table, it is easy to identify the people who have talked about a specific topic extremely frequently during the interview.

Compare Statements on Qualitative Topics According to Quantitative Groups

This integration strategy requires qualitative and quantitative data to be collected for the same research units. In many cases, sociodemographic variables are included in the analysis as categorical variables, but they can also be scale or index values for which a categorization is previously carried out; corresponding examples can be found in Guetterman et al. (2015) and Creswell and Plano Clark (2018). In this strategy and the corresponding joint displays, the quantitative data serve to group the qualitative data, e.g., thematic statements from qualitative interviews are broken down separately according to an educational level recorded by a questionnaire used at the same time (university degree, high school diploma, intermediate school leaving certificate, lower secondary school leaving certificate). In principle, all variables of the quantitative study can be used as grouping variables; for metric variables, a meaningful reduction to a manageable number of categories must first be made. This type of joint display can be generated using *Mixed Methods > Quote Matrix > Quote Matrix with Coded Segments* or *Mixed Methods > QUAL Themes for QUAN Groups*; a schematic representation of the result is shown in Fig. 13.4.

---

[1]Further information on the functionality and mode of operation of the "Stats" module can be found, for example, in the online manual: www.maxqda.com/products/maxqda-analytics-pro.

Code	Variable: Awareness of climate change		
	High (N=5)	Moderate (N=12)	Low (N=4)
Personal behavior	Segments of this group coded with the code "Personal behavior"	Segments of this group coded with the code "Personal behavior"	Segments of this group coded with the code "Personal behavior"
Personal acceptance of responsibility	Segments of this group coded with the code "Personal acceptance of responsibility"	Segments of this group coded with the code "Personal acceptance of responsibility"	Segments of this group coded with the code "Personal acceptance of responsibility"

Fig. 13.4 Schematic structure of the display "qualitative themes for quantitative groups"

Quantitative Analysis of Code Frequencies Broken Down by Groups: Crosstabulations

This integration strategy or the joint display implementing this strategy has the same formal structure as the display described above, but now the cells of the matrix do not contain the text passages themselves, but only the information about the respective number of encodings. How many people with a certain variable value (such as university degree) talk about a certain topic (qualitative data), and how many text passages are coded? Do more people with a university degree talk about the influence of global problems than people with low education, and do they do this more often in the course of the interview? This aggregated numerical presentation corresponds to the logic of a statistical crosstabulation. With the help of row and column percentages, the respective comparative figures can be determined, and with the help of a chi-square test, it can be checked against the probability that this distribution across the different categories could also occur randomly. An example from social science environmental research can be found in Kuckartz (2014a, pp. 140–142). To create such a crosstabulation, choose *Mixed Methods > Crosstab*. The codes that you want to include in the group comparison must be activated before the call. After the start of the crosstab function, the groups that are to form the columns in the table are defined on the basis of variable values, e.g., awareness of climate change, high; awareness of climate change, moderate; and awareness of climate change, low (Fig. 13.5).

Code	Variable: Awareness of climate change		
	High (N=5)	Moderate (N=12)	Low (N=4)
Personal behavior	Number of segments in this group coded with the code "Personal behavior"	Number of segments in this group coded with the code "Personal behavior"	Number of segments in this group coded with the code "Personal behavior"
Personal acceptance of responsibility	Number of segments in this group coded with the code "Personal acceptance of responsibility"	Number of segments in this group coded with the code "Personal acceptance of responsibility"	Number of segments in this group coded with the code "Personal acceptance of responsibility"
Documents	N (%)	N (%)	N (%)

Fig. 13.5 Schematic structure of the display "number of coded segments for quantitative groups"

The cells of this display show the code frequencies per group. You can choose whether the absolute or the percentage frequencies (related to columns or rows) are listed. To prevent people for whom a code has been coded very often from distorting the result, it can be determined that coded segments are counted only once per document; now the frequency of a code in a particular group cannot be greater than its group size. The option of coloring the cells of the table depending on the code frequencies is particularly useful for large tables. In this way, the group-related differences can be identified at first glance.

Statistical Analysis of Quantitative Data Differentiated by Typology: The Typology Table

This data-based integration strategy is particularly suitable if a typology was first formed from the qualitative data or if codes were transformed into document variables. A well-known historical example of such an approach can be found in the study "The Unemployed of Marienthal" (Jahoda, Lazarsfeld, & Zeisel, 2002). In this study, attitude types were formed on the basis of various qualitative data on the experience of unemployment. A current example of such an analysis can be found in Creswell and Plano Clark (2011, p. 292).

In a typology table, a connection is established between quantitative data in the sense of dependent variables (these form the rows of the table) and transformed codes or categorical variables. This function was given the name "Typology table" because of its ability to display several variables and their percentages or characteristic values (mean value and standard deviation) broken down for certain types (which are stored as the values of a categorical variable). Figure 13.6 shows the structure of the table with independent variables in the columns and the dependent variables in the rows.

In Fig. 13.6, three groups with different time use behavior ("time use types") are compared in the columns, namely, "optimizers" (12 persons), "postponers," and "hedonists" (16 persons each). The first line calculates the average age for the groups (44, 33, and 27 years), followed by the standard deviation in brackets. The following line "Siblings" contains the average number of siblings per type; the fourth line contains the percentage of employed persons in the respective group, all optimizers are employed, for example. The highest value of the line is highlighted in green for easier interpretation.

The rows consist of variables, either metric variables or selected values of categorical variables. The columns follow the pattern of the crosstabs; here you

	Time use type = Optimizer (N=12)	Time use type = Postponer (N=16)	Time use type = Hedonist (N=16)
Age, Mean (SD)	44.4 (8.4)	32.5 (6.2)	27.2 (3.7)
Siblings, Mean (SD)	1.3 (0.5)	0.8 (0.8)	2.3 (0.4)
Education level: University degree	8 (66.7)	5 (31.3)	8 (50.0)
employed?: yes, Number (%)	12 (100.0)	11 (68.8)	9 (56.3)
N (Documents)	12 (27.3%)	16 (36.4%)	16 (36.4%)

Fig. 13.6 Comparison of different types with regard to statistical values in the typology table

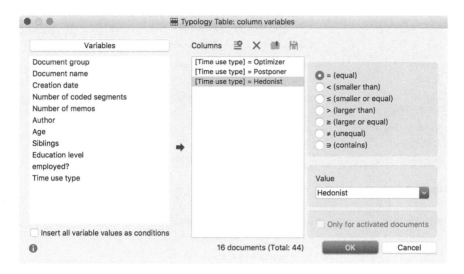

Fig. 13.7 Dialog for determining the columns of a typology table

can select not only type affiliations but the values of any categorical variables. The function is started from the ribbon tab *Mixed Methods* > *Typology Table*; two dialogs appear in succession, in which the selection of the rows and columns is controlled. Figure 13.7 shows the selection process for the three columns of the table shown in Fig. 13.6.

The typology table is interactively linked to the data of MAXQDA: double-clicking *on a result cell* activates the documents with this categorical variable value, e.g., in Fig. 13.6 with a corresponding click on the nine professionals of the "hedonist" type. Double-clicking *in the first column* activates all documents with the selected variable value for a categorical variable.

Statistics for Qualitative Groups

This joint display integrates qualitative groups (subcodes) with quantitative data: similar to the typology table, the groups are compared with regard to statistical characteristics such as mean value, standard deviation, or their relative proportions. Figure 13.8 shows the schematic structure of this joint display. For a metric variable, the cells will show the mean and the standard deviation, and for categorical variables, the cells will show its absolute and relative frequencies.

The documents for which the selected grouping code was assigned are evaluated in each column. It is therefore important to ensure that only a single subcode from this group of codes is assigned to each document to ensure that the documents belong uniquely to the groups. Assuming that an evaluative, scaling content analysis was carried out, a code "personal acceptance of responsibility" with the characteristics "low," "medium," and "high" as subcodes was formed, and corresponding segments were coded in each document. Then this coding can be used as a basis for forming the groups.

	Coded with …		
	Subcode A	**Subcode B**	**Subcode C**
Variable 1 (metric)	Mean (Standard Dev.)	Mean (Standard Dev.)	Mean (Standard Dev.)
Variable 2 (categorical)	Number (%)	Number (%)	Number (%)
Variable 3 (categorical or metric)	..	..	..
Documents	N (%)	N (%)	N (%)

Fig. 13.8 Schematic structure of the display "statistics for qualitative groups"

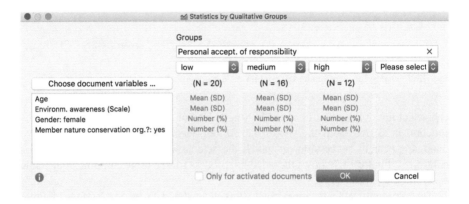

Fig. 13.9 Selection dialog for "Statistics for qualitative groups"

After starting ***Statistics for QUAL groups*** (in the ***Mixed Methods*** ribbon tab), the variables for the rows of the table are selected and then the grouping code and the desired subcodes for the columns of the table (Fig. 13.9).

The joint display "statistics for qualitative groups" can be used for parallel, explanative, and explorative mixed methods designs. In principle, the result of this display corresponds to the result of the typology table, but here the columns are formed by the presence of the subcodes instead of the values of a variable.

Overview of Integration Strategies and Joint Displays

Table 13.1 gives an overview of the integration strategies described above. However, the spectrum of possible integration strategies is by no means exhausted with the joint displays shown, as there are many other possibilities for integration; for example, the article of Guetterman et al. (2015) contains further proposals, such as joint displays that make it possible to construct the questionnaire of a quantitative study from the results of a qualitative study. Many suggestions for mixed methods data analysis can also be found in the old and new editions of the extensive book by Miles, Huberman, and Saldaña (2013).

Table 13.1 Integration strategies in MAXQDA

	Integration strategy	Description	Based on
1	Activation via document variables	Selection of qualitative data by using variable values	Data
2	Linking the results of QUAL and QUAN	The results of the qualitative and quantitative studies are linked using "hyperlinks" ("document links")	Results
3	Side-by-side Display (Coded segments)	Comparison of the results of the qualitative and quantitative study (based on coded segments in a table)	Results
4	Side-by-side Display (Summaries)	Comparison of the results of the qualitative and quantitative studies (based on thematic summaries) in a table	Results
5	Quantitizing: data transformation QUAL→QUAN	Qualitative data is transformed into quantitative data, e.g., presence of a code or frequency of a code per case	Data
6	Qualitative exploration of extreme cases of the quantitative study	Based on the statistical analysis of quantitative data, extreme cases are identified, and their qualitative data is analyzed in detail	Data
7	Grouped thematic display	Statements on qualitative topics are presented in matrix form, broken down by variables from the quantitative study (e.g., sociodemographic characteristics)	Data
8	Statistics on qualitative topics broken down by quantitative groups: Crosstabulation	The frequencies of qualitative topics are compared, broken down by variables from the quantitative study (e.g., sociodemographic characteristics)	Data
9	Qualitative typology as grouping variable for quantitative data: Typology Table	Descriptive statistical analysis of quantitative data, broken down by the types formed in the qualitative study	Data
10	Statistics for qualitative groups	Descriptive statistical analysis of quantitative data, broken down for the subcodes of a code	Data

MAXQDA provides a set of tools that can also be used to design new forms of these strategies of integration, as is the case with strategy "qualitative exploration of extreme cases of quantitative study" described above. The basic functionality of MAXQDA is used here—in this case sorting the table of quantitative data while retaining direct access to the associated qualitative data. The ***Mixed Methods*** ribbon tab contains some frequently used joint displays with the necessary setting options. Table 13.2 gives an overview of these functions, explaining how qualitative and quantitative data are linked using these functions and what the results look like. This should help to make an informed choice when designing joint displays among the options MAXQDA offers.

Table 13.2 Overview of joint displays in the ribbon tab "Mixed Methods"

	Columns	Rows	Results in the cells of the table	Maximum number of groups to be compared
Crosstab	Groups formed by variable values	Codes	Code frequencies per group, different calculation, and percentage variants	No limit
Typology table	Groups formed by variable values. Often, a typology was previously formed on the basis of the qualitative data, whereby the assignment to a type was saved as a variable value	Metric and categorical variables	For metric variables, mean values and standard deviations; for categorical variables, percentages of the selected variable value (type affiliation)	No limit
Statistics for QUAL Groups	Groups formed by the subcodes of a selected code	Metric and categorical variables	For metric variables, mean values and standard deviations; for categorical variables, frequencies and percentages of the selected variable value	4
Qualitative themes for quantitative groups (Coded segments)	Groups formed by variable values	Codes	List of coded segments of the selected codes for the documents of the respective group	4
Qualitative themes for quantitative groups (Summaries)	Groups formed by variable values	Codes	Thematic summaries of the selected codes for the documents of the respective group	4

References

Baur, N., Kelle, U., & Kuckartz, U. (Eds.). (2017). *Mixed methods*. Wiesbaden: Springer VS.

Bazeley, P. (2009). Editorial: Integrating data analyses in mixed methods research. *Journal of Mixed Methods Research, 3*(3), 203–207. https://doi.org/10.1177/1558689809334443.

Bazeley, P. (2010). Computer assisted integration of mixed methods data sources and analysis. In A. Tashakkori & C. Teddlie (Eds.), *SAGE Handbook of mixed methods in social and behavioral research* (2nd ed., pp. 431–467). Thousand Oaks, CA: SAGE.

Bazeley, P. (2012). Integrative analysis strategies for mixed data sources. *American Behavioral Scientist, 56*(6), 814–828. https://doi.org/10.1177/0002764211426330.

Bazeley, P. (2013). *Qualitative data analysis: Practical strategies*. Thousand Oaks, CA: SAGE.

Bazeley, P. (2017). *Integrating analyses for mixed methods research*. Thousand Oaks, CA: SAGE.

Bryman, A. (2006). Integrating quantitative and qualitative research: How is it done? *Qualitative Inquiry, 6*, 97–113. https://doi.org/10.1177/1468794106058877.

Bryman, A. (2007). Barriers to integrating quantitative and qualitative research. *Journal of Mixed Methods Research, 1*(1), 8–22. https://doi.org/10.1177/2345678906290531.

Creswell, J. W. (2015). *A concise introduction to mixed methods research*. Thousand Oaks, CA: SAGE.

Creswell, J. W. (2016). Reflections on the MMIRA: The future of mixed methods: Task force report. *Journal of Mixed Methods Research, 10*(3), 215–219. https://doi.org/10.1177/1558689816650298.

Creswell, J. W., & Plano Clark, V. L. (2011). *Designing and conducting mixed methods research* (2nd ed.). Thousand Oaks, CA: SAGE.

Creswell, J. W., & Plano Clark, V. L. (2018). *Designing and conducting mixed methods research* (3rd ed.). Thousand Oaks, CA: SAGE.

Erzberger, C., & Kelle, U. (2003). Making inferences in mixed methods: The rules of integration. In A. Tashakkori & C. Teddlie (Eds.), *Handbook of mixed methods in social and behavioral research* (pp. 457–488). Thousand Oaks, CA: SAGE.

Fetters, M. D., & Freshwater, D. (2015). Publishing a methodological mixed methods research article. *Journal of Mixed Methods Research, 9*(3), 203–213. https://doi.org/10.1177/1558689815594687.

Greene, J. C., Caracelli, V., & Graham, W. F. (2008). Identifying the purposes for mixed methods designs. In V. L. P. Clark & J. Creswell (Eds.), *The mixed methods reader* (pp. 121–148). Thousand Oaks, CA: SAGE.

Guetterman, T., Creswell, J. W., & Kuckartz, U. (2015). Using joint displays and MAXQDA software to represent the results of mixed methods research. In M. T. McCrudden, G. J. Schraw, & C. W. Buckendahl (Eds.), *Use of visual displays in research and testing: Coding, interpreting, and reporting data*. Charlotte, NC: Information Age Publishing.

Jahoda, M., Lazarsfeld, P. F., & Zeisel, H. (2002). *Marienthal: The sociography of an unemployed community*. New Brunswick, NJ: Transaction Publishers.

Kelle, U. (2007). *Die Integration qualitativer und quantitativer Methoden in der empirischen Sozialforschung: Theoretische Grundlagen und methodologische Konzepte*. Wiesbaden: VS Verlag für Sozialwissenschaften.

Kuckartz, U. (2014a). *Mixed methods: Methodologie, Forschungsdesigns und Analyseverfahren*. Wiesbaden: Springer VS.

Kuckartz, U. (2014b). *Qualitative text analysis: A guide to methods, practice & using software*. Thousand Oaks, CA: SAGE.

Kuckartz, U. (2017). Datenanalyse in der Mixed-Methods-Forschung: Strategien der Integration von qualitativen und quantitativen Daten und Ergebnissen. *KZfSS Kölner Zeitschrift für Soziologie und Sozialpsychologie, 69*(S2), 157–183. https://doi.org/10.1007/S11577-017-0456-Z.

Mayring, P., König, J., Birk, N., & Hurst, A. (2000). *Opfer der Einheit: eine Studie zur Lehrerarbeitslosigkeit in den neuen Bundesländern*. Opladen: Leske + Budrich.

Miles, M. B., Huberman, A. M., & Saldaña, J. (2013). *Qualitative data analysis: A methods sourcebook* (3rd ed.). Thousand Oaks, CA: SAGE.

Morgan, D. L. (2007). Paradigms lost and pragmatism regained: Methodological implications of combining qualitative and quantitative methods. *Journal of Mixed Methods Research, 1*(1), 48–76. https://doi.org/10.1177/2345678906292462.

Morgan, D. L. (2014). *Integrating qualitative and quantitative methods: A pragmatic approach*. Thousand Oaks, CA: SAGE.

Onwuegbuzie, A. J., & Dickinson, W. (2008). Mixed methods analysis and information visualization: Graphical display for effective communication of research results. *The Qualitative Report, 13*(2), 204–225.

Onwuegbuzie, A. J., Slate, J. R., Leech, N. L., & Collins, K. M. (2009). Mixed data analysis: Advanced integration techniques. *International Journal of Multiple Research Approaches, 3*(1), 13–33. https://doi.org/10.5172/MRA.455.3.1.13.

Onwuegbuzie, A. J., & Teddlie, C. (2003). A framework for analyzing data in mixed methods research. In A. Tashakkori & C. Teddlie (Eds.), *Handbook of mixed methods in social and behavioral research* (pp. 351–383). Thousand Oaks, CA: SAGE.

Plano Clark, V. L., & Ivankova, N. V. (2016). *Mixed methods research: A guide to the field.* Thousand Oaks, CA: SAGE.

Sandelowski, M., Voils, C., & Knafl, G. (2009). On quantitizing. *Journal of Mixed Methods Research, 3*(3), 208–222. https://doi.org/10.1177/1558689809334210.

Tashakkori, A., & Teddlie, C. (2003). The past and future of mixed methods research: From data triangulation to mixed model designs. In A. Tashakkori & C. Teddlie (Eds.), *Handbook of mixed methods in social and behavioral research* (pp. 671–701). Thousand Oaks, CA: SAGE.

Teddlie, C., & Tashakkori, A. (2009). *Foundations of mixed methods research: Integrating quantitative and qualitative approaches in the social and behavioral sciences.* Thousand Oaks, CA: SAGE.

Vogl, S. (2017). Quantifizierung: Datentransformation von qualitativen Daten in quantitative Daten in Mixed-Methods-Studien. *KZfSS Kölner Zeitschrift für Soziologie und Sozialpsychologie, 69* (S2), 287–312. https://doi.org/10.1007/S11577-017-0461-2.

Woolley, C. M. (2009). Meeting the mixed methods challenge of integration in a sociological study of structure and agency. *Journal of Mixed Methods Research, 3*(1), 7–25. https://doi.org/10.1177/1558689808325774.

Working with Bibliographic Information and Creating Literature Reviews

14

Working with specialized literature is a core element of many scientific disciplines. It is difficult to imagine a report for a project, master's thesis, or dissertation in which previous research has not been systematically analyzed and presented (Creswell, 2016, pp. 58–66). As more and more publishers make their journals and publications accessible online, the creation of literature reviews has become easier and more efficient. MAXQDA is suitable for day-to-day work with literature as well as the creation of literature reviews (e.g., the preparation of theory chapters and research reports) as well as for systematic reviews for the preparation of research results for meta-analysis. In particular, MAXQDA can be used to manage notes and create summaries to support the writing process. When working with literature, bibliographic information (author, year of publication, etc.) must be distinguished from the content of the literature. MAXQDA focuses primarily on the content and is not a specialized reference management software; however, data from such programs can be imported into MAXQDA for further processing.

> **In This Chapter**
> - Working with bibliographic data
> - Importing data from reference management programs and (online) databases
> - Everyday tasks with literature and summaries
> - Conducting literature reviews
> - Possibilities for the creation of systematic reviews

© Springer Nature Switzerland AG 2019
U. Kuckartz, S. Rädiker, *Analyzing Qualitative Data with MAXQDA*,
https://doi.org/10.1007/978-3-030-15671-8_14

Working with Bibliographic Data from Reference Managers

MAXQDA offers the possibility to import bibliographic data from reference management software such as Mendeley, Endnote, Citavi, and Zotero. Like MAXQDA, these reference managers use project files, meaning databases, containing all collected bibliographic information. The smallest unit of such a project is a bibliographic reference (author, title, etc.) which may also contain links to websites, keywords, abstracts, full texts, and other information.

MAXQDA can work with all reference management programs that are able to export their databases in RIS format, a standard format for bibliographic data. For Citavi, this can be done via the "File" menu with "Export > Export" and for the free Zotero program via "File > Export Library." A detailed description of the RIS format can be found on Wikipedia under https://en.wikipedia.org/wiki/RIS_(file_format). RIS data contains tags, each consisting of two letters, to which the corresponding information is attached.

Some important tags include:

- TY—Type of reference, always introduces a new entry
- ID—Unique identification number for the entry
- AU—Author
- TI—Title
- PY—Publication date
- ER—Must appear at the end of an entry for closure of said entry

Source specification in RIS format appears as follows:

```
TY - BOOK
AU - McLuhan, Marshall
AU - Fiore, Quentin
TI - The medium is the message
PY - 1967
CY - New York
PB - Bantam Books
ER -
```

A detailed description of all RIS tags can also be found on Wikipedia.

Import and Automatic Pre-coding in MAXQDA

RIS data can be imported via the option *Bibliographic Data* in the *Import* ribbon tab of the main menu. First, a dialog window with import information will appear, followed by a dialog window, in which the file with the extension RIS or TXT can be selected. During the import process, the following occurs (Fig. 14.1):

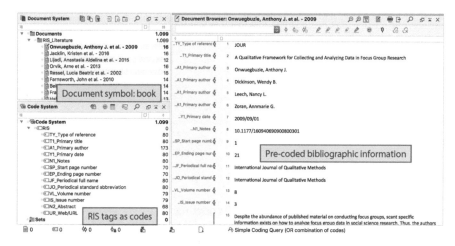

Fig. 14.1 Imported RIS data in MAXQDA

- A new document group is created in MAXQDA, whose name begins with "RIS" and is supplemented with the name of the import file.
- Each reference from the RIS file is added to the newly created document group as a separate document. The entries remain in their original order. The imported documents are identified with a book symbol in the "Document System."
- The document names are structured as follows: <Author>—<Year>—<ID>. Empty fields may be indicated with the "?" symbol. In the case of multiple authors, only the first author's (last and first) name will appear, followed by the abbreviation "et al."
- The newly created documents contain the information to the right of the tags. The tags themselves will not be imported.
- A new top-level code, "RIS," will appear in the "Code System," which contains all the RIS tags used in the import file as subcodes, for example, "TY—Type of reference."
- Upon import, all documents will be automatically pre-coded, meaning each text element will be coded with the corresponding tag code.

Five pieces of information which may also be important for future selections are also stored as document variables:

- RIS_Type (Type of reference)—Text
- RIS_Author (First author)—Text
- RIS_Title (Title)—Text
- RIS_Reference-ID (Identification number)—Integer
- RIS_Year (Year of publication)—Integer

These variables are created as system variables and cannot be changed by the user (Fig. 14.2).

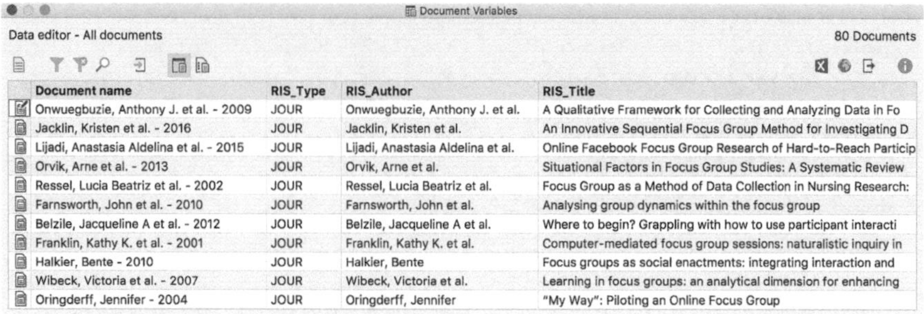

Document name	RIS_Type	RIS_Author	RIS_Title
Onwuegbuzie, Anthony J. et al. - 2009	JOUR	Onwuegbuzie, Anthony J. et al.	A Qualitative Framework for Collecting and Analyzing Data in Fo
Jacklin, Kristen et al. - 2016	JOUR	Jacklin, Kristen et al.	An Innovative Sequential Focus Group Method for Investigating D
Lijadi, Anastasia Aldelina et al. - 2015	JOUR	Lijadi, Anastasia Aldelina et al.	Online Facebook Focus Group Research of Hard-to-Reach Particip
Orvik, Arne et al. - 2013	JOUR	Orvik, Arne et al.	Situational Factors in Focus Group Studies: A Systematic Review
Ressel, Lucia Beatriz et al. - 2002	JOUR	Ressel, Lucia Beatriz et al.	Focus Group as a Method of Data Collection in Nursing Research:
Farnsworth, John et al. - 2010	JOUR	Farnsworth, John et al.	Analysing group dynamics within the focus group
Belzile, Jacqueline A et al. - 2012	JOUR	Belzile, Jacqueline A et al.	Where to begin? Grappling with how to use participant interacti
Franklin, Kathy K. et al. - 2001	JOUR	Franklin, Kathy K. et al.	Computer-mediated focus group sessions: naturalistic inquiry in
Halkier, Bente - 2010	JOUR	Halkier, Bente	Focus groups as social enactments: integrating interaction and
Wibeck, Victoria et al. - 2007	JOUR	Wibeck, Victoria et al.	Learning in focus groups: an analytical dimension for enhancing
Oringderff, Jennifer - 2004	JOUR	Oringderff, Jennifer	"My Way": Piloting an Online Focus Group

Fig. 14.2 Variable values for each document

Working with Bibliographic Data and Exporting

Following import and automatic pre-coding, the bibliographic data is made available in MAXQDA as normal text. This means the data can be searched, coded, linked, and edited and have memos added for further qualitative and quantitative content analysis. Now one can answer questions such as:

- How often are specific authors named?
- Which topics are represented?
- How has the focus on specific topics shifted?
- Are there more journal articles or monographs on a specific topic?
- To what extent have journal article titles changed over time?

Naturally, ***Visual Tools*** and all of the other MAXQDA functions, such as graphics and statistics functions, can be applied to this data. On the basis of the automatic pre-coding, documents of a specific type can be selected, for example, only journal contributions or only articles in compilations.

Bibliographic data can be exported from MAXQDA in RIS format, for example, to a reference management program. The export function can be accessed via ***Reports*** > ***Export*** > ***Bibliographic Data as RIS File***. All documents of a project containing bibliographic data and therefore identified with a book symbol will be exported in a RIS file (encoding: UTF-8).

Organizing and Analyzing Literature and Summaries with MAXQDA

Working with literature—both online and offline—is one of the most important activities not only in research and teaching but also in NGOs and institutions and for the purpose of market research. Characteristics of working with literature are finding and reading relevant works, identifying and marking important points, understanding arguments, and extracting, compiling, and comparing texts. MAXQDA is an excellent tool for these daily tasks. Elgen Sauerborn (2014) and Uta-Kristina Meyer

(2014) reported in their blog posts how they created summaries and notes while reading relevant literature for their research and managed them with MAXQDA. Based on their work and our own experiences, we suggest the following procedure:

- As far as possible, all available literature sources for the research are imported into a MAXQDA project.
- Summaries are created as individual documents in MAXQDA, whereby the reference information (author, year, title) is used as the document name, ideally in the exact citation style which will be used in the later bibliography. Consequently, authors can be easily searched for in the "Document System" by means of the document name.
- In-document memos, further information about the sources, can be managed, such as questions arising from particular arguments, criticism of particular works, or whether the source is important for one's own work.
- The "Code System" is created following the chapters of the report, with codes following the same order as in the later work. Summaries or parts of the original documents suitable for citation will be coded with these codes.
- As the report is written, the corresponding codes are activated so all of the important coded segments are compiled in the "Retrieved Segments" window.
- This basis makes writing easy, eliminating the risk of overlooking an important point or reference and helping the user to "write up" the work.
- After completing the work, the sources, summaries, notes, and coded segments remain available. When one is working on a similar topic at a later date, this work can be accessed, creating a foundation on which to add further references and summaries.

Creating Literature Reviews with MAXQDA

What is meant by the term "literature review"? Arlene Fink provides the following definition: "A research literature review is a systematic, explicit, and reproducible method for identifying, evaluating, and synthesizing the existing body of completed and recorded work produced by researchers, scholars, and practitioners." (Fink, 2010, p. 3)

A literature review as explained in this way is conducted on a specific topic or research question. The objective is to determine the current state of research and/or the scientific discussion with regard to a particular field of knowledge. The focus may be on different predetermined aspects, for example, theoretical or methodological aspects. A literature review represents a specific form of secondary analysis, as it is not a matter of new, independent research but rather a review of research that has already been conducted. A literature review, like an essay, is frequently written by an individual researcher. It systematically presents substantial research results, identifies controversies, and summarizes the state of scientific discourse in a specific field. A literature review is always an explanatory text, not simply a list of sources.

Literature reviews can be created as embedded reviews (e.g., embedded within a dissertation or research report) or as stand-alone reviews. The latter are frequently referred to as "systematic reviews." As a rule, systematic reviews are concerned with the research results in relation to a specific question and with identifying any gaps in the research. This is not usually the case with general embedded reviews, which is not to say that these are unsystematic or eclectic. Traditionally, however, stand-alone reviews focus more heavily on quantitative aspects.

Work Phases for the Creation of a Literature Review
Based on the work of Fink (2010, pp. 4–7); Hart (2017); Gough, Oliver, and Thomas (2017); and Heyvaert, Hannes, and Onghena (2016, pp. 6–8), six phases for the creation of a literature review can be identified:

1. Formulation of research questions and objectives of the review. The research question should be precisely formulated in order to lead the review.
2. Selection of bibliographic databases, which today are normally online databases.
3. Determination of search terms within these databases.
4. Application of practical and methodological criteria for the selection of high-quality scientific literature.
5. Conducting the review. This includes, among other aspects, import of bibliographic data and eventually full texts; definition of variables such as author, year of publication, etc.; thematic coding of significant text segments; and writing of notes and summaries.
6. Synthesis of results and writing of the review, either in the form of a qualitative description of results or in case of a quantitative meta-analysis as a calculation of statistical characteristic values and measures.

MAXQDA can provide valuable support in all phases, particularly in the thematic and content development of primary sources in phases 5 and 6. Before describing the possibilities offered by MAXQDA for this type of work, the differences between MAXQDA and reference management programs such as Endnote, Citavi, Mendeley, Zotero, etc. should be considered. Endnote and the like allow the collection, management, and citation of primary online and offline sources. The focus of these programs is the management of bibliographic input and the creation of bibliographies corresponding to the different regulations of a large number of scientific journals and publishers. For example, the widely used Zotero program (www.zotero.org) searches for bibliographic information in online catalogs and booksellers such as Amazon and allows this information to be stored in a local database and to be provided with keywords and metadata. Reference lists can later be exported in various citation styles (e.g., in the widely used APA style). While reference management programs focus on the *bibliographic data*, MAXQDA focuses on the *content* and allows for the thematic coding and systematic, qualitative, and quantitative analysis of this content. MAXQDA is therefore not primarily used for the collection of bibliographic data (although this is possible) nor for the creation of reference lists for publications. However, as described above, MAXQDA allows the user to import bibliographic data from reference management programs.

But now, we return to a description of the phases of creating a literature review with MAXQDA. The literature review is valuable not only as it provides an overview of current knowledge in the field, but it also situates the research within a wider context and discussion within the scientific community. The six phases of the creation of a literature review are described in greater detail below.

Phase 1: Formulation of Research Questions and Objectives of the Review

Similar to a research project, a literature review begins with the formulation of the research field and question(s) as well as the objectives. However, the question is formulated somewhat more broadly than would normally be the case for a research project. If the focus is overly narrow, sources that are relevant but do not initially appear to be central to the research could be overlooked. In MAXQDA, the research question and objectives are best presented in the form of a free memo (via **Analysis > Free Memo**) as in the following example:

Memo

Literature Search on Data Analysis and Integration in Mixed Methods Research

The goal of the literature search is to evaluate the current state of the discussion on the topic of data analysis/integration in mixed methods research. Well-known authors in the mixed methods research community see the integration of qualitative and quantitative as the primary challenge of mixed methods research. The review aims to compile the most important positions. Since mixed methods discourse is conducted in English, only English-language literature should be taken into account. The review will cover the years 2014–2016 and will be limited to the leading journal on this topic, the *Journal of Mixed Methods Research*.

Phase 2: Selection of Bibliographic Databases

The next step is a targeted search for sources that could present information about the topic in question. In a traditional library, literature is identified by means of keywords and keyword catalogs, retrieved from the shelves, then taken to the workspace, and placed on the desk. When working with computers and searching in appropriate databases, the principle is similar. The researcher explores databases and scientific journals, saves search hits, and selects sources that are presumed to contribute to the review.

Next, it is important to decide exactly where to search and what to look for, in other words, to select the *bibliographic databases* and define the *search terms*. Normally the databases are online, and hundreds of public and private databases exist. The most popular international databases are PubMed (medicine), MEDLINE (medicine), ERIC (education science), JSTOR (various), LexisNexis (economics and law), PsycINFO (psychology), and Social Science Citation Index and Sociological Abstracts (social sciences) (Fink, 2010, pp. 17–21). Also to be noted are private databases such as SpringerLink, the portal for the Springer International Publishing AG, and the databases of journals and periodicals such as that from SAGE Publications, which is indispensable for research in the fields of methods and methodology.

A further consideration is whether to include only English-language sources in the search.

Phase 3: Determination of Search Terms

After these specifications, the next step is to determine *search terms*. These could be single words or combinations of multiple words. Nearly all databases offer the possibility for advanced searches, in which one can formulate more complex conditions, for example, linking search terms with the logical operators AND and OR.

> **Example**
>
> In the *Journal of Mixed Methods Research* (JMMR), a search is conducted for all entries concerning the theme "data analysis." The search is restricted to the years 2014–2016. Other possible search terms would be "triangulation" and "integration," but in the following example, the search is restricted to "data analysis." The search on the JMMR website (http://mmr.sagepub.com/search) results in 57 hits.
>
> In the next step, the compilation of results on the website can be checked for relevance on the website, or the full list of results can be imported into MAXQDA and checked there. In this example, it is more efficient to import the results into MAXQDA. When exporting from the SAGE Publications website, it is important to ensure that both the citation and the abstract are exported. The RIS format should be selected from the list of available formats. The file can be imported into MAXQDA via the menu function *Import > bibliographic data*.

Phase 4: Application of Practical and Methodological Criteria for the Selection of High-Quality Scientific Literature

This phase concerns the selection of relevant literature, that is to say the literature that was found in the database search is now examined in order to determine if it falls within the narrower area of the research question and whether it fulfills the objectives of the review.

Practical as well as methodological criteria of this selection process should be documented. Practical criteria are those which relate to the practical accessibility, language, and type of publication. For example, for a study on environmental awareness in Europe, only results in the most common languages, possibly only in English, would be considered. In addition, the search would be restricted to only the

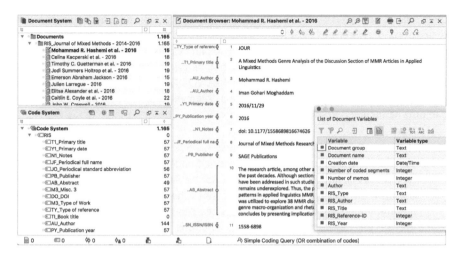

Fig. 14.3 Imported RIS file with search results in "*Journal of Mixed Methods Research*"

most important social science journals. Methodological criteria for this review could be, for example, the quality and manner of sampling or the "seriousness" of the institution carrying out the study. It is possible that for methodological reasons, sources based on online surveys would be excluded because they used a convenience sample.

For the earlier example of the literature review of data analysis in mixed methods research, all of the bibliographic search hits were imported into MAXQDA. The sources now appear in the "Document System." Figure 14.3 shows how MAXQDA appears after this information is imported.

The RIS format tags are found in the "Code System." Here it can be seen that an abstract is available for only 49 of the 57 sources. The list of document variables displayed on the right shows that five tags are also available as variables for later selections, namely, type of publication, author, title, ID, and year of publication.

The next step is to systematically read each abstract in order to decide if the source is relevant or not. It is advisable to set up two (or more) new document groups in the "Document System" to which the results can be moved according to their relevance. The names of the document groups should indicate their functions, for example, "Relevant sources" and "Less relevant sources." Sources that do not contribute to the review can be deleted immediately. If there is any doubt concerning where to assign a source when reading the abstract, the full text can be obtained by clicking the link coded with the tag "UR_Web/URL." This will open the information page in the SAGE Publications database, which contains a link leading to the full text (assuming you have access to the sources via your library). Reading the full text provides a solid basis on which to classify the text as relevant or less relevant.

Other variables which allow the user to make selections or comparisons and recognize trends can be defined in this phase of the literature review. For example, the variable "RIS_Year" allows for the creation of a table or chart showing the distribution of sources by year.

There may be other primary sources outside the results of the database search that should be included in the review. In principle, all types of sources, including audio and video sources, can be imported into MAXQDA. Sources such as books that cannot be borrowed may only be available as scanned copies. Such scanned sources can also be included in the literature review.

▶   **Hints for Scanned Sources** If no digitized version of a relevant source is available, the only option is to use scanned pages. This results in a photo or PDF file. Using software such as Adobe Acrobat, it is possible to perform an OCR text recognition (see Chap. 3). This is strongly recommended, as subsequently searches can be performed on words in the text and all word-related functions in MAXQDA including MAXDictio can be used.

If the sources have been classified according to their relevance, particularly relevant works can be imported as full texts. It is best to create a new document group (e.g., "Primary literature") and to download and import full texts into this folder. Ideally, the full text and bibliographic reference should be linked, as described in Box 14.1.

Box 14.1: Linking Full Text and Bibliographic Reference
- Open the full text.
- Open the bibliographic reference in the "Second Document Browser."
- Highlight the first word (or first paragraph) in the full text and select *Insert Document Link* from the context menu.
- Highlight the first word (or first paragraph) in the bibliographic reference, and select *Insert Document Link* from the context menu.

For many databases, particularly private databases, you may only download full texts if you have authorization to do so. This is the case at most universities, and all members of the university may have access. It may be necessary to log into the university network via VPN.

Phase 5: Conducting the Review

The process of conducting a literature review varies depending on the nature of the research questions and the objectives of the review as well as the range of the sources. In addition, the process depends on the time available for the preparation of the review. If little time is available, it is necessary to restrict the material and tighten the formulation of practical and methodological criteria (see Phase 4). In this case, the review will be based mainly on the abstracts and not on the more extensive full texts. The following are some of the possibilities MAXQDA offers for conducting a literature review:

Working with Word Clouds
What are the central themes of a text and the key terms that are used? These can be easily explored by right-clicking on the full text and selecting the option **Word Cloud**. Alternatively, one can create a word cloud for parts of the bibliographic data (titles or abstracts) by retrieving the relevant segments and starting the word cloud function in the "Retrieved Segments" window. Nonsensical words or words that are not relevant in the context of the review can be transferred to the stop list.

Exploring Full Texts and Working with Memos
In view of the abundance of publications available on almost every topic, one is often not able to read an entire book or journal article. Using the context search in the "Document Browser," one can search specifically for the presence of key terms, which greatly reduces the extent of text passages that need to be read intensively. Questions which arise, alongside ideas and core statements, can then be stored as memos attached to the corresponding text passages. The overall assessment, evaluation, and criticism of a text can be stored as a document memo in the "Document System."

Emphasizing Important Text Passages
Reading a text and underlining important points is a common practice. One can work in the same way when creating literature reviews in MAXQDA: five distinct colors are available for color coding text passages. The marked passages can be easily located at a later time. In some cases, it may be useful to mark the text passages with a thematic code rather than color coding.

Exploring the Frequency of Words and Terms Used in the Sources
Using the word frequency function (part of the MAXDictio module), one can analyze the frequency of words in one or more documents. In addition, a differentiated word frequency analysis can be performed on documents, document groups, and document sets. As with word clouds, nonsensical words can be transferred to the stop list and therefore excluded from the analysis.

Writing Summaries
Summarizing text and extracting interesting passages is one of the classic techniques of literature work. In MAXQDA, a document group "Summaries" should first be defined, in which all summaries and excerpts are stored. Next, select the option **New Text Document** from the context menu of this new document group. A new document will appear in the "Document Browser" in Edit Mode, where one can start to write a summary. If the full text has been imported, it can be opened in the "Second Document Browser," allowing the user to read the source text and write the summary concurrently. The text segment and the corresponding summary can be linked using document links.

The name of the summary should also contain the author and year; furthermore, the summary should be linked to the bibliographic reference using the procedure described above.

Automatic Coding of Text Segments
The text can be searched for interesting keywords and the results coded automatically using the function *Analysis > Lexical search*. The range of text passages to be coded can be freely selected by the user (search hit, sentence, several sentences, paragraph). Following automatic coding, the coded segments can be retrieved and explored further.

Manual Thematic Coding of Significant Text Passages
It is possible to code the relevant text passages when the primary text is available, which is normally the case with journal articles. In this case, working with thematic codes which are as close as possible to the research questions in the scope of the review is recommended. By means of specific labeling, it is possible to indicate the passages that are suitable for later quotation. For this purpose, a specific code, for example, "Suitable for quotation," can be defined. Alternatively, the comment function or a weight score can be used. For each coded segment, a short comment can be added, in this case, for example, "Quotation." Later, in the Overview of Coded Segments, you can sort by the comment column so that all potential quotes are listed together. It is also possible to assign a weight score to any coded segment. Later, one can retrieve just the text passages which have been coded to a selected theme and allocated a specific weight score.

Distinguishing, Coding, and Statistically Analyzing Different Dimensions
For a specific content area in the literature, for example, the research design, specific dimensions can be identified and defined as subcodes, for example, "Explanatory sequential design," "Exploratory sequential design," or "Convergent design." Using the option *Subcode Statistics* in the context menu of the "Code System," the frequency of the different design types can be determined and displayed as a table or graph.

Visual Representation of Themes and Sources
MAXQDA's visual tools can be used very effectively for literature reviews. We assume here that thematic coding of relevant texts has already taken place, either manually or using automatic coding of search items.

- The *Code Matrix Browser* displays the themes covered and their respective frequency per text in a comparative table.
- The *Code Relations Browser* displays the simultaneous occurrence of pairs of themes in a comparative table.
- The *Single-Case Model* (available in *Visual Tools > MAXMaps*) represents the coded themes and their respective frequencies for a selected source in a schematic diagram.

- The *One-Code Model* (also available in **MAXMaps**) displays a selected theme and its coded segments, the code memo, and the memos linked to the code in a schematic diagram.

Writing Thematic Summaries and Creating Summary Tables
This technique uses MAXQDA's function **Analysis** > **Summary Grid** (see Chap. 11). This makes it possible to write thematic compilations and present them in comparative tables ("Summary Tables"). In order to use this technique, it is a prerequisite that relevant text passages have been thematically coded beforehand.

Quantitative Evaluation of Themes
Quantitative aspects can also be relevant in a literature review. For example, it is possible to sort and count sources according to variables (e.g., year of publication) and answer questions such as "How are the sources distributed over time?" or "Has the investigation of the topic 'Data analysis/integration' increased or decreased during the period under study?" Statistical tables with absolute and relative frequencies as well as bar and pie charts can be created for thematic codes and subcodes in MAXQDA. More complex analyses including correlation analyses can also be carried out with the STATS module in MAXQDA.

Phase 6: Synthesis of Results and Writing of the Review
After most of the work has been completed in the first five phases, it is time to summarize the findings. When the review is written, the preparatory work of the first five phases comes into effect, that is to say, the results of the previous work prepare the researcher to write a well-structured text. Effectively, one can build on the memos prepared in phases 5 and 6, as well as the displays such as summary tables, and visual representations, in the review.

There are two types of reviews:

1. A review in the form of a qualitative description of *results (descriptive literature review)*; occasionally, quantitative results can also be included, such as the number of sources, their distribution over time, apparent trends, frequency of sub-topics, etc. The focus, however, remains a qualitative one.
2. A review in the form of a quantitative *meta-analysis* with calculations of statistical parameters and measures. Here, the results of statistical procedures are central, as in the case of a meta-analysis of attitude-behavior research, where average correlations in various spheres of activity are calculated and communicated.

Both types of literature reviews should always contain the following four parts (Fink, 2010, pp. 206–207):

- Purpose and objectives of the review
- Methods and sampling
- Results
- Conclusions

In the case of a quantitative meta-analysis, the methods section should be expanded with particular attention to the description and substantiation of the statistical methods used.

When writing the review, the following MAXQDA tools can provide valuable assistance:

- The Coding Query, with which previously classified text segments can be located.
- Memos, particularly the free memos written in phase 5 of the work on the review, from which passages can be copied and inserted into the final text.
- Summary tables, with which compressed summaries of sources can be effectively compared and represented. Summary tables can also be integrated into the review.
- The word frequency functions of MAXDictio, with which the usage of specific search items and semantic contexts can be represented.
- The graphical display options of MAXMaps, which in particular allow the creation of concept maps.

References

Creswell, J. W. (2016). *30 essential skills for the qualitative researcher*. Thousand Oaks, CA: SAGE.

Fink, A. (2010). *Conducting research literature reviews: From the internet to paper* (3rd ed.). Thousand Oaks, CA: SAGE.

Gough, D., Oliver, S., & Thomas, J. (2017). *An introduction to systematic reviews* (2nd ed.). Thousand Oaks, CA: SAGE.

Hart, C. (2017). *Doing a literature review: Releasing the research imagination* (2nd ed.). Thousand Oaks, CA: SAGE.

Heyvaert, M., Hannes, K., & Onghena, P. (2016). *Using mixed methods research synthesis for literature reviews*. Thousand Oaks, CA: SAGE.

Meyer, U.-K. (2014, May 28). *MAXQDA11 Tip of the month: How I manage my excerpts with MAXQDA [blog post]*. Retrieved November 5, 2018, from https://www.maxqda.com/tip-month-manage-excerpts-with-maxqda

Sauerborn, E. (2014, August 18). *MAXQDA11 Tip of the month: How I manage my literature with MAXQDA [blog post]*. Retrieved November 5, 2018, from https://www.maxqda.com/managing-literature-maxqda

Analyzing Focus Group Data

15

Focus groups have become increasingly popular in recent years, as they can provide you with a variety of voices and opinions on a subject within a relatively short period of time and also offer the advantage of encouraging participants to communicate and discuss their views with each other. Both the group and the individual levels are of interest when analyzing focus group data. In fact, such analyses often require you to alternate between these two levels and to keep an eye on one while focusing on the other. Accordingly, MAXQDA provides functions especially adapted for the analysis of focus group data, which provide easy access to the focus group transcript as a whole and to the statements and contributions made by individual participants. Progress analyses of the overall discussion are also available, and you can just as easily trace the development of the stated opinions of individuals. Moreover, since these functions can equally be used for other types of text involving two or more speakers—such as forum discussions—this chapter is worth reading even if you are not specifically analyzing transcripts of focus groups.

In This Chapter
- Getting to know the features and characteristics of focus group interviews and how to analyze them
- Preparing and importing focus group transcripts
- Exploring and coding focus group transcripts
- Comparing individuals and groups of participants
- Notes on how to approach the process of answering typical questions

© Springer Nature Switzerland AG 2019
U. Kuckartz, S. Rädiker, *Analyzing Qualitative Data with MAXQDA*,
https://doi.org/10.1007/978-3-030-15671-8_15

About Focus Groups and Group Discussions

Focus groups have a long history as modes of collecting data, going back to studies on the impact of mass communication in the 1940s and before (Morgan, 1997, pp. 4–5; Stewart & Shamdasani, 2015, p. 3). Since then, focus groups have been widely used in market research and more recently in many of the social sciences. With the increasing spread and development of the Internet, procedures for online data collection of group interviews have also been developed in which several people can express and exchange opinions on a given topic simultaneously, both verbally and in writing (Krueger & Casey, 2015, pp. 211–213; Liamputtong, 2011, pp. 149–155).

The terms used for focus groups in methods literature are just as diverse as the fields in which they can be applied. Sometimes they are referred to as "focused interviews," other times as "group discussions" or "group interviews." In some cases, there are different methods and methodologies based on distinct research traditions behind the term in question, some of which may influence how they are applied and how the data is collected and analyzed. In this chapter, we will concentrate on describing the functions for computer-assisted analysis of focus group interviews offered in MAXQDA and, for the sake of clarity, use primarily the terms that are used throughout the program, i.e., "focus group" and "participants."

Focus groups are usually conducted with about five to eight people and are led by one or sometimes two moderators who initially focus on a specific topic, often using a stimulus in the form of a film, an image, or a product presentation. The moderators ask questions based on structured, thematic guidelines and create a constructive atmosphere for discussion and interviews. The result of a focus group is at least one audio recording and, on some rare occasions, also a video recording, which may be partially or completely transcribed to varying degrees of accuracy, depending on the area of interest.

The complete spectrum of analysis methods for qualitative data can be used to analyze focus group data. The contents of the transcripts can be analyzed using techniques based on grounded theory method, thematic analysis, qualitative content analysis, or other analysis approaches. The more that attention is paid, not only to the topics and points of view mentioned during the focus group discussion, but also to the interactions of individual participants or overall group dynamics, the more important those analysis methods become that take into account the special characteristics of focus groups. Accordingly, textbooks that cover how to conduct focus groups, as well as journal articles and chapters in anthologies, will contain special advice for analyzing focus group data. Morgan and Hoffman (2018), for example, set out a coding scheme to code participants' interactions, and Onwuegbuzie, Dickinson, Leech, and Zoran (2009) have developed a "Qualitative Framework for Collecting and Analyzing Data in Focus Group Research," which contains proposals for tables depicting areas of consensus among participants as well as visual representations of response behavior.

MAXQDA supports both the analysis of focus group transcripts using standard analysis methods for qualitative interviews and special techniques developed for focus group analyses. The following is an introduction to the broad set of options for analyzing focus group data in MAXQDA, with a focus on the functions developed specifically for this form of data. At the end of this chapter, we will then address analysis questions that are independent of specific analysis techniques and describe how these questions can be answered effectively using MAXQDA.

Preparing and Importing Focus Group Transcripts

In MAXQDA, you have the option of importing a finished focus group transcript or creating one inside the project. As explained regarding texts generally in Chap. 3, focus group transcripts should be checked for spelling mistakes before you import them, anonymized if necessary, and prepared so that they are legible on screen, since this can save you a lot of work later on.

In order that MAXQDA can automatically code the contributions made to the discussion by each participant when you import the focus group transcript, these contributions must be prepared and identified according to two rules:

1. Each contribution begins with a new paragraph.
2. The name of the participant is written at the beginning of each contribution, followed by a colon. The names may not exceed 63 characters in length, but may contain spaces, so names such as "Mr. Anders" or "Ms. Berkempers" are possible. To make them easier to read, we recommend putting the names of the participants in bold type or emphasizing them in other ways. You need to be careful with colons in the transcript; if these are used within the first 63 characters of the beginning of a paragraph, MAXQDA interprets the preceding text as a name.

While it is helpful for most analyses in MAXQDA when contributions contain only one paragraph, it may be better for very long speech contributions to subdivide them into several paragraphs; the automated coding process will still easily recognize these as being part of the same contribution. If you want to import several focus group transcripts into MAXQDA, you should also assign identical names for the same participants across these transcripts so that you can later perform analyses for individual participants.

You can import prepared transcripts saved as Word, OpenOffice, or Rich Text files, just like other text documents. To start the import, go to **Import > Focus Group Transcripts** in the main ribbon menu. If transcripts contain timestamps, these are identified and removed once the corresponding audio or video file has been successfully assigned to it.

Figure 15.1 illustrates the view in MAXQDA once you have imported a focus group transcript. A new document has been created in the "Document System," and the file name "Democratic Candidates" has been adopted as its name. The

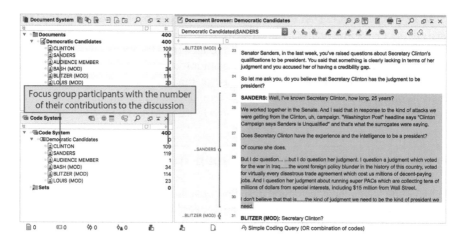

Fig. 15.1 Automatically coded contributions after importing a focus group transcript

document has its own icon, which indicates that this is a "focus group" document type. Below the document, the participants of the group discussion are listed individually, and these are permanently linked to the document. Like other documents in the "Document System," focus group documents can be moved and assigned to document groups and document sets. The participants are always moved with the document and can only be changed in order by clicking and dragging them with the mouse.

In the "Code System," a focus group code with the same name as the document is inserted at the top level, and the participants are defined as subcodes. The participants listed in the "Code System" and the "Document System" are permanently linked; if you change the order or names of the participants in one, the order and names in the other will change simultaneously. Focus group codes cannot be deleted; they are automatically removed when the associated document is deleted. If several focus group transcripts are imported, a document is inserted for each in the "Document System," and another top-level code is created in the "Code System."

As the coding stripes in the "Document Browser" in Fig. 15.1 illustrate, the contributions of participants are automatically assigned with the corresponding participant's code when the transcript is imported. The names of the speakers are not coded themselves to avoid artificially increasing the length of their contributions. The number behind a participant in the "Document System" and "Code System" indicates the number of contributions that participant made in the respective focus group discussion. This number will remain constant during the analysis, unless you delete the assignment of a participant's code after the import or add another—both are generally to be avoided.

▶ **Tip** After the import you should check the names of the participants in the "Document System" or "Code System" for typing errors. It would be annoying later if the same person appeared twice with different names, just because they were written differently. Please note that MAXQDA is case-sensitive. Since the participant codes cannot be deleted, if you detect any errors, you must delete the transcript, and then import it again, which is easily done as long as you have not assigned any further codes to the transcript in the meantime.

Immediately after the import, it is a good idea to write down information about the respective focus group in a document memo, for example, the basic conditions of the data collection procedure and any distinctive features of the process. Document memos are therefore an ideal place to store the moderators' minutes and a postscript, unless they have already been imported into the project file as separate documents. Memos can also be written for individual participants, but standardized information such as their age and occupation are better recorded as variable values in the Overview of Focus Group Participants (see below).

Transcribe Focus Group Discussion in MAXQDA
If you would like to transcribe an audio or video recording of a focus group in MAXQDA, first import the recording as a new document, and then proceed as described in Chap. 4 "Transcribing Audio and Video Recordings." The rules we mention above regarding the preparation of focus group transcripts for automatic coding should also be observed for these. When the transcription is complete, keep the transcript open, and go to *Import > Convert Text > Insert Displayed Text as a Focus Group Transcript*. MAXQDA then creates a copy of this text, processes it in the same way as when importing a ready-made focus group transcript, and automatically codes the discussion contributions with the names of each participant. Existing code assignments, memos, and timestamps are retained during this process. You can then delete the original document with the transcription.

Exploring Focus Group Transcripts

Once you have imported all the focus group data you want to analyze, you may want to conduct an explorative analysis of the focus group texts, for which the procedures and functions described in Chap. 5 are available. You can record all your findings and any hypotheses that arise during this exploration and subsequent analysis in memos (even for individual participants) or in the logbook, so that you can retrieve these at a later point in time. You can color-code interesting text passages with the available highlighters during your first reading; you can search for interesting words or use a word cloud to gain an interactive overview of frequently used terms. MAXDictio can also be used for keyword-in-context (KWIC) analyses.

In addition to these familiar explorative tools, the visual tools described in Chap. 12 can also be used to examine focus group transcripts, and MAXQDA provides several analysis tools specifically tailored to focus groups. The basis of these tools is that while focus group transcripts in the "Document System" can be selected for analysis just like normal text documents, MAXQDA also gives you access to the contributions of individual, several, or all participants within these transcripts and thus allows for a simple differentiation at the participant level.

Gain an Overview of the Participants in a Focus Group

The first exploration tool presented here is the Overview of Focus Group Participants, which provides important information about individual participants, such as the number and extent of their contributions to the discussion, and enables the storage of standardized data in the form of variables. You can open this overview from all levels in the "Document System" (with the exception of the Sets level), including for individual participants, for all the participants within a focus group, and for all the focus group documents in your project. To open this overview, right-click on the relevant level in the "Document System," and select *Focus Group Participants* in the *Overviews* section of the context menu.

The number of contributions corresponds to the number of code assignments per participant in the "Code System," and the displayed percentage allows you to easily compare these. When interpreting these results, you should consider whether many very short contributions were coded for a person—for example, if they interjected frequently—and a lot of very short paragraphs were coded as a result. Information about the comparative extent of participants' contributions, in the number of characters, as can be seen in the last two columns, can help you to accurately evaluate participants' contributions. For example, Fig. 15.2 shows that Clinton spoke 45% of everything that was said during the discussion, while she only made 27% of all the contributions, counted individually. Special consideration must also be given to comments and notes included in a transcript that are not actually part of the participant's contributions, such as "[applause]" or "(unintelligible)," but were automatically coded as if they were speech when importing the transcript. These are counted in the analysis of the characters but should have no major influence on the percentages if they have been used sparingly. If you want to display the distribution of the number and extent of speech contributions in a graphic, you can click on the

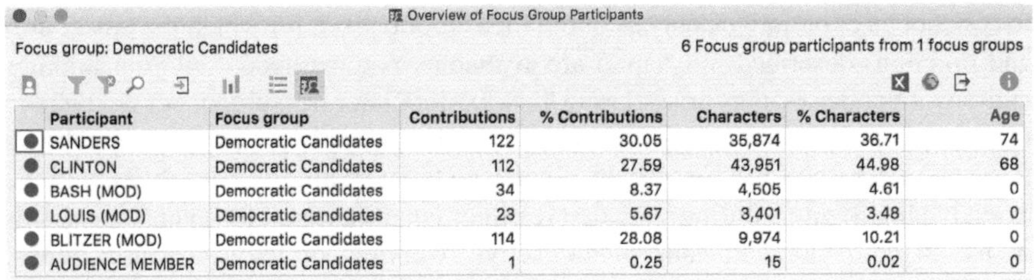

Participant	Focus group	Contributions	% Contributions	Characters	% Characters	Age
SANDERS	Democratic Candidates	122	30.05	35,874	36.71	74
CLINTON	Democratic Candidates	112	27.59	43,951	44.98	68
BASH (MOD)	Democratic Candidates	34	8.37	4,505	4.61	0
LOUIS (MOD)	Democratic Candidates	23	5.67	3,401	3.48	0
BLITZER (MOD)	Democratic Candidates	114	28.08	9,974	10.21	0
AUDIENCE MEMBER	Democratic Candidates	1	0.25	15	0.02	0

Focus group: Democratic Candidates — 6 Focus group participants from 1 focus groups — Overview of Focus Group Participants

Fig. 15.2 Overview of Focus Group Participants for a focus group

Statistics icon in the Overview of Focus Group Participants toolbar to open MAXQDA's statistics and chart functions, with which you can create and export horizontal and vertical bar charts and pie charts.

By default, all the participants at the selected level are listed in this overview. To restrict the display to selected participants or to exclude the moderators from the table, activate the participants in the "Document System" that you want displayed, and then click on the *Only activated focus group participants* icon at the far left in the overview toolbar. The percentages are then automatically recalculated. If you use the filter functions available in the context menu for each column header, rows are only hidden, that is, the percentages are not recalculated.

This overview operates in the same way as all overviews in MAXQDA, allowing you to search through, sort, and export it. It also lets you define variables in which standardized information can be stored for each participant. To do this, switch to the variables view (by clicking on the *List of variables* icon within the overview window), create your new variables, and enter the corresponding values for the participants. Alternatively, you can import this data from an Excel table in the same way as with document variables. In Fig. 15.2, an integer-type "Age" variable has been created to record the age of the individual focus group participants, which can then be used to select and compare the participants in a later analysis. The moderators were assigned the age "0," which was defined as a missing value, so that they could easily be disregarded.

Document Portrait: Graphical Representations of Focus Group Contributions
A tool for visually exploring focus group data is the Document Portrait, which can be used to visualize participants' contributions and, in the case of short focus group discussions, their progression. In order to achieve a meaningful visual representation, however, it is necessary to first assign different colors to the individual participants. You can do this by right-clicking on a participant (in either the "Document System" or the "Code System") and selecting a color from the context menu. The Document Portrait can be via the context menu when you right-click on the focus group document. If necessary, you can activate only those participants in the "Code System" that you want to include in the visualization.

To compare the spoken contributions of individual participants, you need to select *Ordered by color frequency* in the toolbar. In this display mode, the image is similar to a bar chart (Fig. 15.3).

Codeline: Visualizing the Progression of a Focus Group Discussion
The Codeline is ideal for visualizing the flow of a focus group discussion. When exploring these discussions, the first step is to examine only the progression and patterns of the spoken contributions. Later, once text passages have also been coded with thematic codes or codes for group interactions, these levels can also be included in the Codeline for more in-depth analyses. To create a Codeline for a focus group, first activate the participants' codes in the "Code System"; otherwise all codes, including participants from other focus groups, will be visible in the first column. Figure 15.4 depicts a Codeline, compressed to window width, for a television

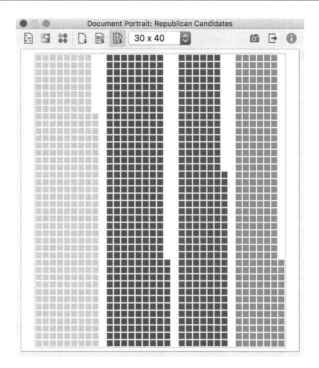

Fig. 15.3 Document Portrait (ordered by color frequency) for a focus group (yellow, Trump; blue, Rubio; red, Cruz; green, Kasich)

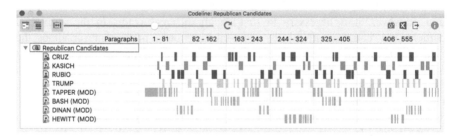

Fig. 15.4 Visualizing the progression of a discussion in a Codeline

discussion with four presidential candidates in the USA. The individual participants are listed in the rows and the successive sections of the discussion in the columns, such that its progression is clearly visible in the Codeline. Apart from the expected short contributions of the moderators, you can see here that the breaks between the contributions made by Cruz, Kasich, and Rubio tend to be longer than the breaks between contributions from Trump, who speaks more frequently and makes multiple short statements. When you double-click on a colored section, the corresponding text passage is displayed in the "Document Browser," where you can check and refine any potential hypotheses by reviewing the original text.

Word Clouds: Identify Frequently Used Words of Selected Participants

As described in Chap. 5, word clouds also provide explorative access to the contents of texts and can be used for one or more focus groups. For an individual focus group document, a word cloud can be opened via the document's context menu in the "Document System." In the list of word frequencies that opens, you can fill the stop list with words that are not relevant to your analysis, thus displaying only relevant words in the resulting cloud.

If you only want to analyze the contributions of selected participants, you need to activate the corresponding focus group documents in the "Document System" first. Then, activate the relevant participants in the "Code System." MAXQDA will then display these participants' contributions in the "Retrieved Segments" window. Here you can also click on the icon in the header of this window to open a word cloud based on the displayed text segments.

Lexical Searches in Focus Group Contributions

MAXQDA's specialized features for the analysis of focus group data allow you to search for words and strings within the contributions of selected participants. For example, if you have identified certain words of interest with the help of a word cloud and want to see them in context, you first need to activate all the desired participants in the "Document System" and then go to *Analysis* > *Lexical Search*. In the dialog box that opens, you can restrict your search by selecting the *Only in activated documents/activated focus group contributions* option.

Coding Focus Group Transcripts

Once you have completed the explorative stage of the analysis process, you will typically progress to examining the focus group transcript more closely and begin coding it, for which all of MAXQDA's coding functions described in Chap. 6 are at your disposal. Due to the special characteristics of focus groups (moderated discussion with several participants; focus on a given topic or theme; group interaction), different analysis levels can be defined for the discussion, which should be reflected in different sections in the "Code System":

- A topic level
- A participant level
- A group interaction level
- A moderator level

At the group interaction level, for example, we can refer to the coding system developed by Morgan and Hoffman (2018), which is shown in Fig. 15.5. An evaluative, scaling qualitative content analysis (Kuckartz, 2014; Mayring, 2014) will add evaluative codes to measure, for example, the degree of endorsement of a new product or service. If you are conducting a study on the method and

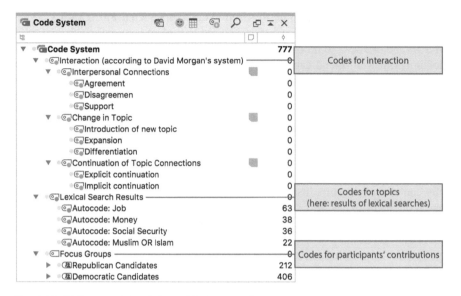

Fig. 15.5 Different code levels in the "Code System"

methodology of focus groups, additional code areas will also be required in the "Code System."

For the sake of clarity, we recommend defining separate parent codes in the "Code System" for all of these levels, so that, as in Fig. 15.5, topic and interaction codes are clearly separated from each other. Subcategories can be defined for all of them. MAXQDA's analysis tools then allow you to make connections between these various levels and to compare them once you have finished coding the data, e.g., by displaying them together in the Codeline or by compiling coded segments according to selected criteria, as we will describe in the next section. Since the focus group codes can be moved and rearranged like normal codes in the "Code System," it is also helpful to combine these under a higher-level code too, so that these can be collapsed at any time (Fig. 15.5).

Retrieving Coded Segments from Focus Group Transcripts

Once the data has been explored and coded based on your research questions, these coded text passages can be systematically compiled for further analysis in the "Retrieved Segments" window. For this, MAXQDA's activation functions can be used to select the relevant focus group transcripts and contributions of individual participants in the "Document System" and then combine them with activated codes in the "Code System." For each question you want to answer, you will need to use a different activation logic:

What Did a Specific Participant Say in One or More Focus Group Discussions?
To compile everything one participant said, activate all of the focus groups in which they were a participant in the "Document System," and additionally activate their codes in the focus groups listed in the "Code System." All the contributions made by this participant will then be displayed in the "Retrieved Segments" window. As soon as you select another participant in the "Code System" by activating them, their contributions will also be displayed here. The status bar will, as usual, inform you about the number of coded segments found—in this case the number of contributions.

If you are only interested in what one participant said within one focus group, you can right-click on their name in the "Document System" or "Code System" at any time and open the *Overview of Contributions* entry from the context menu. MAXQDA then opens a window containing that specific participant's contributions in a table overview, which you can operate in exactly the same way as the Overview of Coded Segments and allows you to browse through the details, including a preview, of what they said.

What Did One or More Participants Say About a Specific Topic?
If you want to restrict your search for contributions to a specific topic, you need a different activation logic. Instead of including the entire focus group document in the analysis, activate only the relevant participant (or several, if required) in the "Document System," and additionally activate the relevant topics in the "Code System." The contributions pertaining to the selected topics, made by the selected participants, will then appear in the "Retrieved Segments" window. To assist you in matching these contributions to the speakers, the source information in this window contains the name of the respective focus group and respective participant (Fig. 15.6). This information is also included when exporting these results as a table overview.

The *Analysis > Complex Coding Query* function also allows you to perform more complex searches and compile coded segments where, for example, several codes or only specific codes have been assigned. To limit the analysis to the currently activated participants, make sure that you have selected the *Only in activated focus group contributions* option in the dialog box.

What Did Participants with a Shared Characteristic Say About a Topic?
Just as the function *Mixed Methods > Activate by Document Variables* allows you to select individual documents for analysis based on variable values, you can also activate individual participants in focus groups based on their variable values. To do this, first open the function *Activate Focus Group Participants by Variable* from the

Fig. 15.6 Participant's name displayed in the source information in the "Retrieved Segments"

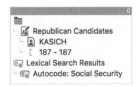

context menu at the top level in the "Document System." Then, as described in Chap. 13 on MAXQDA's mixed methods functions, set a condition in the middle area of the dialog box which the participants you want to activate must fulfill, such as "Age > 45" or "Occupational group = Nursing staff." MAXQDA will then activate all participants in all focus groups to which the entered condition applies. If you want to restrict the selection to one focus group, you can specify its name as an additional condition. By default, MAXQDA automatically offers you the variables "Focus group," "Contributions," and "Characters" as conditions for activating participants based on their variable values. With the last two, you can easily activate only those participants who contributed more or less than the average for the whole focus group.

Comparing Participants and Groups of Participants

Further questions typical to focus group analyses concern the comparison of individual participants and groups of participants. As already mentioned above, the Codeline can be used for this purpose—once the data has been coded—to visually examine the progression of discussion topics covered by one or more participants. Additionally, MAXQDA's Code Matrix Browser, Interactive Quote Matrix, and Crosstab functions offer further ways to compare the contents and frequencies in your focus group data on an individual or group-based level.

Visualize Code Assignments per Participant with the Code Matrix Browser
To answer the question of who spoke about which topics and how often, we recommend making use of the Code Matrix Browser to visually compare focus group participants. Before you open this function, as usual via the *Visual Tools* ribbon tab, you first have to activate the relevant participants in the "Document System" and the appropriate topics in the "Code System." In the Code Matrix Browser options dialog box, select *Focus group participants* as your columns, and make sure that you select *Only for activated focus group participants* and *Only for activated codes*. Consider the example in Fig. 15.7: after exploring several topics in a presidential debate between four candidates using the lexical search and then automatically coding the search hits along with their surrounding paragraphs, a

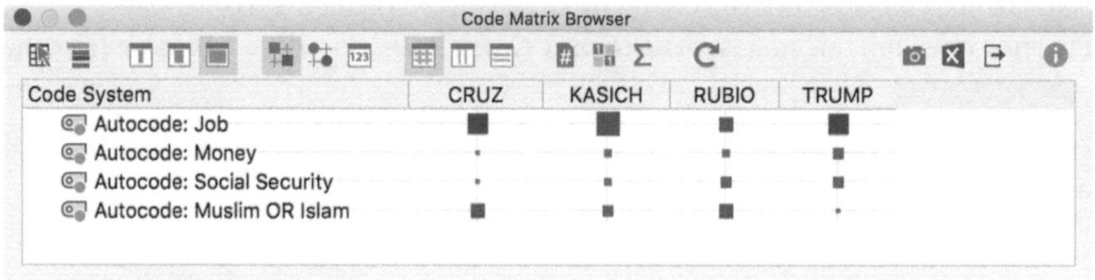

Fig. 15.7 Participants (columns) × Topics (rows) in the Code Matrix Browser

Participant × Topic matrix was created using the Code Matrix Browser. It shows the distribution of topic codes across the four candidates.

The larger the square on a node, the more frequently the respective topic code has been assigned to that candidate. So, in this example you can see that, for Kasich, the largest number of his contributions was coded with the topic "Job." Of course, the results of automatic coding processes and the resulting code frequencies should be interpreted with a certain degree of caution. First, it helps to switch the display in the Code Matrix Browser to a numerical format to see how pronounced the differences between the code frequencies that resulted in squares of varying sizes are. Second, we also recommend that you look at the codes behind the numbers in their original context. Double-clicking on one of the squares lists the corresponding segments in the "Retrieved Segments" window, where you can examine them in detail. For smaller tables with a maximum of four to six columns, the results can also be displayed as an Interactive Quote Matrix, which you can open via the first icon at the far left of the Code Matrix Browser toolbar. This provides a condensed comparison of the coded segments behind the displayed squares by listing these in a table format. Optionally, the source information, code comments, and memos attached to the segments can also be displayed.

By default, the Code Matrix Browser is configured to display the largest square for the cell(s) with the most code assignments and the smallest square for the cell(s) with the least code assignments. You can switch between row or column calculations to determine the square size depending on whether you want to compare the distribution of coding frequencies per topic or for each individual participant. If you switched to a row calculation in Fig. 15.7, that is, per topic instead of per person, you would be able to see which presidential candidate had the most contributions coded for each topic and which had the least.

Compare Groups of Participants with the Crosstab
The Crosstab function allows groups of participants from one or more focus groups to be combined on the basis of their previously assigned variable values and compared in terms of their code frequencies per topic. You could think of the display as follows: the columns of the Code Matrix Browser are grouped together, and the sums of the frequencies per group are calculated.

If you want to limit the group comparison to certain focus groups, you should activate the corresponding participants in the "Document System" before opening this function. The fastest way to do this is in the context menu of a focus group transcript with the entry *Activate all participants*. In any case, you should also activate just the codes in the "Code System" for which you want to conduct the comparison, because otherwise the Crosstab will take irrelevant data into account when calculating the percentages.

Once you have activated the relevant participants and codes, you can open this function via *Mixed Methods* > *Crosstab* > *Crosstab for Focus Groups*. In the dialog box that appears, select the variables, and set the conditions for your comparisons in the *middle* area, e.g., "Age < 50" and "Age ≥ 50," to compare under-50s with those who are 50 years or older. The Crosstab will then contain a

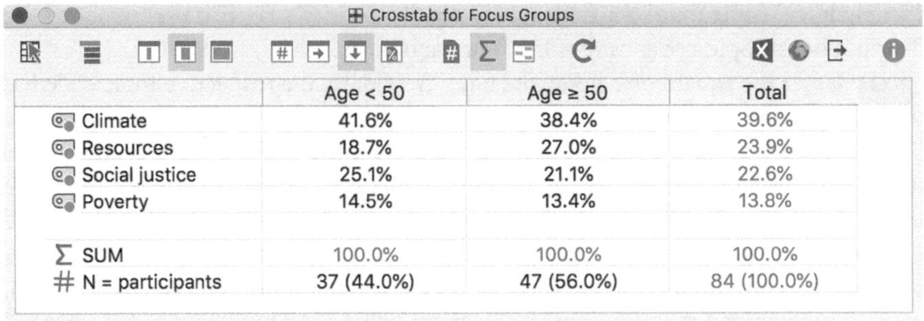

	Age < 50	Age ≥ 50	Total
🗨 Climate	41.6%	38.4%	39.6%
🗨 Resources	18.7%	27.0%	23.9%
🗨 Social justice	25.1%	21.1%	22.6%
🗨 Poverty	14.5%	13.4%	13.8%
Σ SUM	100.0%	100.0%	100.0%
# N = participants	37 (44.0%)	47 (56.0%)	84 (100.0%)

Fig. 15.8 Crosstab for comparing two groups of participants

separate column for each defined condition, in which only those participants are considered who fulfill the respective condition. To be able to compare several groups, you must enter at least two conditions. Since MAXQDA does not check whether a person fulfills several of the defined conditions, and thus could be assigned to several groups, you should check these conditions carefully. Moreover, you should make sure that the options *Only for activated focus group participants* and *Only for activated codes* are selected in the dialog box, which will be suggested by default if you have activated the relevant participants and codes before opening this function.

Figure 15.8 depicts a Crosstab that divides the members of several focus groups into two groups according to their age. Column percentages have been chosen as the cell display setting, so that the distribution of the discussed topics within these two groups can be compared. While the topic "Climate" takes the lead for both groups, there are clear differences regarding the topic "Resources": only 18.7% of the contributions of the under-50s refer to this topic, while in the older group, it occurs in 27.0% of their contributions.

Answering Typical Analysis Questions

The literature on focus groups often mentions lists of questions that are typically addressed when analyzing focus group data. These questions result from the features of focus groups already mentioned above and may be seen as complementary to the specific research questions at the center of a study, insofar as they have not already been incorporated into the development of the study. Here, we will discuss some of the analysis perspectives of Krueger and Casey (2015, p. 147), Stewart and Shamdasani (2015, pp. 120–123), and Liamputtong (2011, pp. 173–178), which are peculiar to focus groups, and conclude with an overview of how their associated questions can be meaningfully analyzed with the aid of MAXQDA.

Frequency and Extent: How Often or Rarely Was a Concept or Topic Mentioned? How Many Different Participants Mentioned a Given Topic or Point of View? How Extensively Was a Topic or Point of View Discussed?

Once you have coded the relevant topics, concepts, and viewpoints in your focus group transcripts, the best way to determine their frequencies is to use the Code Matrix Browser, including the sums available per participant/per focus group and per topic. It is possible to include the entire focus groups as well as individual or all participants in the visualization by activating them in the "Document System." Dictionary-based word counts using MAXDictio also make it possible to perform frequency analyses for larger data sets and compare the results for individual participants, groups of participants, or entire focus groups.

The visual representation of topics in the Codeline can be used to assess the extent to which certain topics and views are discussed, as it allows you to see the relative time period over which individual topics are discussed or mentioned. More analytically valuable, however, because it provides precise figures, is the function *Analysis > Code Coverage > Texts, Tables and PDFs*, which you can use for activated focus group documents and activated topic codes. The results table provides information on the extent to which the individual topics are discussed, and in which focus groups, based on the number of characters coded.

Stewart and Shamdasani (2015, p. 121) point out that it may also be important to investigate what the participants did *not* say. This could include relatively mundane, self-evident matters but also issues that are difficult to address in the context of a group discussion, such as topics concerning a person's own body. The analysis of the unsaid can be carried out in MAXQDA with the help of a deductive code system, designed on the basis of previous knowledge: topics and viewpoints not coded in focus group data were obviously not discussed by the respective group. Alternatively, you can perform searches for words of interest to find out for which ones there are no hits.

Sequence: In What Order Were Topics and Points of View Mentioned? What Was Said First?

For the analysis of temporal aspects, the Codeline is usually quite useful, as you can see which topics and points of view are "top-of-mind" (Stewart & Shamdasani, 2015, p. 120) and are mentioned first in response to open questions. Of course, in order to assess the relative importance of topics, one should consider more than merely the order in which they are mentioned. Each respective response's relevance vis-à-vis the research question, its content, and also the intensity with which the response is presented should all be included in this analysis.

Intensity and Specificity: With What Level of Fervor and Emotional Content Were Statements Made? What Level of Detail Did Participants Provide in Their Contributions?

If these aspects of your analysis are to be given a high priority, it makes sense to create a separate "intensity" and "specificity" top-level code with ordinal values in the "Code System"—as you would for an evaluative, scaling qualitative content analysis—in order to be able to make a scaled assessment of individual statements. Various MAXQDA functions then allow you to analyze the co-occurrence of intensity codes and topic codes. In the Code Relations Browser, or with the help of function *Analysis > Code Configurations > Complex Code Configurations*, you can examine the frequencies of the co-occurrences (see Chap. 12), and in the Codeline, you can also view them in terms of their chronological order.

Alternatively, you can use the weight function, with which you can assign an intensity value of 0–100 to each code assignment and later include or exclude certain coded segments with the help of the weight filter. In the context of a less formal approach, simply surmising the intensity of a statement on a subject when compiled along with other text passages in the "Retrieved Segments" window, and including this information in your analysis report, may prove sufficient.

Reasoning: How Did Participants Justify Their Views and Assessments?
It can also be helpful to create your own codes for reasons and justifications in the "Code System" and to code relevant statements as such. However, an analysis of the co-occurrence of these codes can be problematic, because opinions and their justifications need not necessarily be in the same places in the transcript. It may therefore be more effective to work with document links, memos, and coding commentaries to establish the connections between stated views and their justifications.

Consistency: To What Extent Did the Individual Participants Stick to Their Opinions?
The compilation of an individual's contributions on a topic in the "Retrieved Segments" window is particularly well suited to answering this question. The quickest way to put them together for different participants is to open the Code Matrix Browser, display the participants in the columns, and then double-click on the relevant nodes to display a particular participant's contributions for any one topic in the "Retrieved Segments" window. With the help of links and memos, contradictory statements and amended opinions can be highlighted in the text itself.

Group Dynamics: How Are Topics, Participants, and Interactions Interrelated?
Liamputtong (2011, p. 176) lists a very helpful set of questions by Stevens (1996, p. 172), which divides group interactions into three primary areas, each containing related questions:

- What? (e.g., "Which statements provoked conflict?")
- Who? (e.g., "Were individual participants excluded?")
- How? (e.g., "How did participants react to the ideas of others?")

Many of these questions can easily be translated into categories within a separate code area in the "Code System," such as "conflicts," "agreement," or "dealing with emotions," and then analyzed as described above. However, several of the questions can be analyzed more effectively using other techniques. "Were alliances formed among the participants?" and "Whose interests were more strongly represented in the group than others?" are questions that require a holistic analysis of the entire conversation and are ideally based on exploration results and case summaries, where initial thoughts and hypotheses relating to such questions have been compiled in memos on or within the focus group document.

References

Krueger, R. A., & Casey, M. A. (2015). *Focus groups: A practical guide for applied research* (5th ed.). Thousand Oaks, CA: SAGE.

Kuckartz, U. (2014). *Qualitative text analysis: A guide to methods, practice & using software* Thousand Oaks, CA: SAGE.

Liamputtong, P. (2011). *Focus group methodology: Principles and practices.* Thousand Oaks, CA: SAGE.

Mayring, P. (2014). *Qualitative content analysis: Theoretical foundation, basic procedures and software solution.* Klagenfurt. Retrieved from http://nbn-resolving.de/urn:nbn:de:0168-ssoar-395173

Morgan, D. L. (1997). *Focus groups as qualitative research* (2nd ed.). Thousand Oaks, CA: SAGE.

Morgan, D., & Hoffman, K. (2018). A system for coding the interaction in focus groups and dyadic interviews. *The Qualitative Report, 23*(3), 519–531.

Onwuegbuzie, A. J., Dickinson, W. B., Leech, N. L., & Zoran, A. G. (2009). A qualitative framework for collecting and analyzing data in focus group research. *International Journal of Qualitative Methods, 8*(3), 1–21. https://doi.org/10.1177/160940690900800301.

Stevens, P. E. (1996). Focus groups: Collecting aggregate-level data to understand community health phenomena. *Public Health Nursing, 13*(3), 170–176.

Stewart, D. W., & Shamdasani, P. N. (2015). *Focus groups: Theory and practice* (3rd ed.). Thousand Oaks, CA: SAGE.

Analyzing (Online) Survey Data with Closed and Open-Ended Questions

16

Surveys often contain closed questions with predefined responses and open questions for free text responses to collect both quantitative and qualitative data. The result of a survey like this is almost always a data matrix in a "Cases × Questions" format, which provides one row for each respondent and contains at least one column per question. The issue then arises as to how a data matrix of this kind, which could easily contain several hundred or thousand cases in the rows and a few hundred columns, may be imported—and meaningfully analyzed—in MAXQDA. Since many surveys are conducted online these days, you might also want to import surveys from tools such as LimeSurvey, Qualtrics, or SurveyMonkey. Whether the survey was conducted online or on paper, the great advantage of analyzing survey data with MAXQDA is that qualitative data imported as text and quantitative data imported as case variables can not only be separated but also analyzed in an integrated manner, that is, in the form of a mixed methods analysis.

In This Chapter
- Importing and automatically coding survey data
- Tips for importing data from online tools such as LimeSurvey and SurveyMonkey
- Analysis strategies for responses to open questions
- Analysis strategies for the integration of qualitative and quantitative data

Preparing and Importing Survey Data

A data matrix with the results of a survey can be imported into MAXQDA from the Excel format, which is offered as an export option by many online data collection tools and statistics programs. Before importing an Excel file with survey results, you

U. Kuckartz, S. Rädiker, *Analyzing Qualitative Data with MAXQDA*,
https://doi.org/10.1007/978-3-030-15671-8_16

should check carefully whether any responses need to be removed and whether the remaining responses are plausible. This especially applies to online surveys where the data has not been entered by the analysts. For online surveys, test runs of the finished questionnaire are often carried out, the responses of which must be removed, along with any duplicate entries that may have resulted from multiple submissions by the same person. Valuable information about entries that need to be removed can often be found in the time the responses were submitted, which is usually recorded in a separate column by the online tool in question. Moreover, it is particularly important in the case of online surveys to decide on the extent to which data from people who did not complete the survey in its entirety should be taken into account. The widely used online tool "LimeSurvey" provides valuable information in this regard, i.e., on which page a person ended the survey and the total time taken to complete it. Plausibility checks primarily involve checking whether a person entered made-up information in order to participate in a promised prize draw or because their motivation declined toward the end of the survey. You can often recognize fake data where "no answer" responses have been provided for multiple questions, where the same response option has been selected for every matrix question, or where open questions were not answered at all or only very briefly.

Apart from cleaning up the data records (rows) and variables (columns), there are usually no further precautions to be taken for the import into MAXQDA. However, the import does require that there be a column in the data that can serve as document name in the MAXQDA project. Furthermore, you should always use a unique identifier for each individual case, if possible, to ensure that the correct allocation of cases to respondents can be guaranteed at all times both within MAXQDA and for later exports of the data. This could be, for example, a case ID that was assigned automatically by the online survey tool or a unique name that you assigned to the case yourself. Table 16.1 shows an excerpt from the data matrix of an online survey of students at Marburg University regarding their quality of life; the matrix comprises a total of 1178 cases (rows) and contains 9 columns with answers to open questions, in addition to numerous variables for standardized information.

Table 16.1 Responses to open and standardized questions in a table format

Case ID	What recreational opportunities/facilities do you think are missing? (Open question)	How would you define a good quality of life? (Open question)	Age	Area of residence in Marburg
1007	Good and inexpensive gym near me. Club with good music	When you can find a balance between your responsibilities (studies), socializing (friends), and personal...	27	Marburg district
1008	[empty, because no response]	Time, the space and courage to do things that the person really...	27	Marburg city center
...	...	...	...	...

▶ **Tip** If the data matrix is available as an SPSS file, you can also save it in an Excel format from within SPSS via *File* > *Save As*. Here you should select the option that the value labels are to be exported instead of the values. This ensures that, for a variable like "Area of residence in Marburg," for example, not only the numbers in the data matrix are included in the file but also the assigned response specifications as text. Unfortunately, SPSS does not export the variable labels themselves to the Excel file but rather the often significantly shortened variable names in the headings, which is why you should then manually replace these with suitable short versions of the questions before importing them into MAXQDA.

You can start the import into MAXQDA by going to **Import** > **Survey Data** > **Import Data from Excel Table** and then selecting the Excel file containing the data matrix. MAXQDA analyzes the file and then opens a dialog box that lets you adjust the import settings (Fig. 16.1).

In the upper area of the dialog box, you can select which columns contain the names of the document groups and documents. It is helpful to select a grouping variable that can form the document groups, within which the documents based on each case can be organized in the "Document System." For the quality of life data set above, for example, you could organize the data according to area of residence.

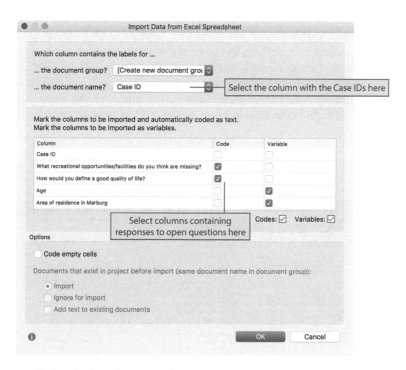

Fig. 16.1 Settings for importing survey data

However, since the standardized data can later be used to compile documents into any number of document sets to conduct group comparisons, it is usually sufficient to accept the default settings and allow MAXQDA to automatically create a single new document group for all the imported documents. That said, for performance reasons ideally document groups should not contain any more than 1000 documents. For the document name, as shown in Fig. 16.1, it is essential that you select the case ID to make sure it can be associated with the original data set. This also ensures that each document name occurs only once.

During the import, MAXQDA automatically creates a separate document for each case, i.e., for each row in the Excel table. The responses to the open questions form the content of the respective case, and they are automatically coded with the respective column heading, usually the shortened version of the question. One possible result is illustrated in Fig. 16.2: in the "Document System," each row of the Excel table has been converted into a separate text document. One of these text documents is open in the "Document Browser," indicating that two open responses have been coded with a question each, for which two codes were automatically added to the "Code System." In addition, the imported variable values are always visible in the Data Editor for Document Variables.

Returning to the import dialog box in Fig. 16.1: in the middle area, MAXQDA lists all the columns from the Excel table. For each column, you have to decide whether the content of the column is to be included in the document as pre-coded text or imported as a document variable. By default, MAXQDA places a check mark in the column "Variable" for all questions, because usually there are more standardized quantitative answers in a data set than responses to open questions. What is important for the import is to change the check mark to the "Code" column for all *open questions*. In addition to the open questions, you can also check the "Code" column for some standardized information, such that the contents of the column are both included in the document as text and imported as variables. This is

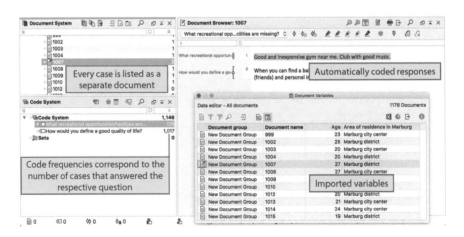

Fig. 16.2 Imported survey data in MAXQDA

especially helpful if you not only want access to the variable information for a document via its name's tooltip or via the Data Editor for Document Variables but want to be able to see within the text itself how old the respondent is, for example, and where he or she lives in Marburg.

The option ***Code empty cells*** should normally remain unchecked, because otherwise it ensures that cells without content are also coded with the respective column header. The great advantage of deselecting this option is that, after you have completed the import, you will be able to see immediately from the code frequencies in the "Code System" in how many cases a code has been assigned, i.e., how many people actually answered each open question. You can see an example of this in the "Code System" in Fig. 16.2, which illustrates the view in MAXQDA just after survey data has been imported: while only 129 people responded to the question about recreational opportunities/facilities, 1017 people responded to the question about quality of life.

The options in the lower area of the dialog box in Fig. 16.1 are intended for studies involving several survey cycles and, among other things, enable you to attach the contents of a data matrix to texts which you already imported at an earlier point in time. Remember that the document group and document name must match in both data sets, which is why the imported data should always contain these two columns to ensure that the documents can be correctly assigned.

The import process is quite fast for 1000–2000 respondents. The precise time required depends on the number of open questions the survey contains and how many variables need to be generated, so you may need to allow for a few minutes waiting time for, say, 5000 cases and 10 open questions; after all, imports of this size may generate up to 50,000 code assignments. There is no limit to the number of cases in MAXQDA, but for technical reasons, it is best to avoid exceeding a total of 200,000 code assignments in MAXQDA projects—a number you should keep in mind when dealing with several thousand cases and multiple open questions.

Importing Survey Data from LimeSurvey

LimeSurvey is a convenient and free open-source software tool for conducting online surveys, which you can easily install on your own web server. This has the great advantage that you can determine the server location yourself and are not dependent on countries with questionable regulations when it comes to data privacy and data security.

Once all the data has been collected in LimeSurvey, you can log in to your LimeSurvey account and save the data as an Excel file via the ***Export > Export results to application*** button in the "Responses & Statistics" section. You can define numerous settings for the export:

- *Format*: Should be set to Microsoft Excel.
- *Range*: IDs of the cases you want to export—this will usually be all the cases.
- *General > Completion state*: Usually all rows and not only the filled-out rows should be exported, because you can easily remove duplicate or implausible data rows in Excel.

- *General > Export language*: For surveys conducted in several languages, the export can be restricted to one of the languages used.
- *Headings*: Here simply leave the default settings as they are, because it is usually helpful if the full question text is included in the heading.
- *Responses*: Here we also recommend sticking to the default settings. The complete responses will then be entered in the individual cells, instead of numerical codes that may be difficult to interpret.
- *Columns*: Here you can specify which information you want to export. There is a risk here of clearing your entire previous selection of columns with one wrong click, so it is much easier to export all the columns and later, in Excel, delete those that are not important, such as the response times for individual questions.

Importing Survey Data Directly from SurveyMonkey

SurveyMonkey is currently one of the world's most widely used online survey tools, offering a very large selection of ready-made questions from a variety of subject areas. The company is headquartered in California and offers a free basic plan with limited functionality and a limited number of cases, as well as several fee-based plans with additional question formats and unlimited cases. MAXQDA allows you to import responses directly from a SurveyMonkey survey, saving you the intermediate step of exporting the data into Excel. The import procedure is as follows:

- Step 1: Go to **Import > Survey Data > Import Data from SurveyMonkey**.
- Step 2: The SurveyMonkey website will then open in your web browser, where you will need to log in with your SurveyMonkey account and grant MAXQDA access to the survey responses.
- Step 3: Once you have successfully granted it access, MAXQDA will display an overview of all the surveys in your SurveyMonkey account, from which you can select one by clicking on it. The options also allow a random selection of cases if you only want to analyze a subset of them.
- Step 4: Just as with the import via Excel, you can determine which elements of the data are to be imported as open questions and which ones as document variables. MAXQDA will have already made an automatic selection based on the question types.

▶   **Please Note** SurveyMonkey's basic plan does not allow you to import data directly into MAXQDA or export it into Excel. This requires a paid plan. You can find an overview of all the plans and their features here: https://www.surveymonkey.com/pricing/details/. The "Extract data" row in the "Partner Integrations and APIs" section tells you whether a given plan lets you import data directly into MAXQDA or not. The "Analysis & Reporting" section lists the export options for each plan.

Analyzing Survey Data

Exploring the Data

Once the survey data has been imported into MAXQDA as described above, you can begin your analysis. Usually you will want to get an overview of the survey data first, both of the scope of the free text responses, which are much shorter in comparison to interview transcripts, and of the standardized variable information available. Kuckartz, Ebert, Rädiker, and Stefer (2009) describe one possible procedure for exploring survey data using the example of an online evaluation and also provide tips on how to use MAXQDA in this context. The procedure they describe for exploring qualitative data makes use of many of MAXQDA's data exploring capabilities, as described in Chap. 5: case summaries in bullet point form can be prepared for a random selection of about 5–10% of cases, taking into account particularly relevant standardized data. To do this, open the List of Document Variables via the **Variables** ribbon tab, and choose a selection of variables as tooltip variables so that the information stored in them is displayed in the small preview when you hover your cursor over the document in the "Document System" (see Fig. 16.3; details on tooltip variables can be found in Chap. 10). Case summaries are stored in the document memo and are given a title that briefly describes the case in question and may also contain certain quantitative information, such as age and area of residence. Analysis ideas, theses, hypotheses, and ideas for helpful analysis categories can be noted in a free memo or more easily in a memo at the top level of the "Document System." This exploration can be complemented with a lexical search for words of interest or with word frequency analyses, which you can open in MAXQDA via the word cloud function: simply right-click on a document group to generate a word cloud containing the most frequently-used words within the texts in this group, as described in detail in Chap. 5.

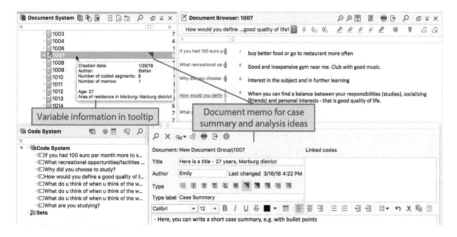

Fig. 16.3 Data exploration screen (with more imported questions than in the previous figure)

To explore the quantitative data from surveys, stored in the form of document variables, once you have completed the import, you can perform a basic count in which frequency tables are generated for each closed question containing their respective responses and absolute as well as percentage frequencies. You can perform a basic count of this kind in MAXQDA via *Variables > Document Variable Statistics* and browse through the frequency tables question by question. A more efficient method is available in MAXQDA's add-on Stats module, in which you can create frequency tables for document variables via *Descriptive Statistics > Frequencies*. You can save meaningful groupings of cases based on their variable values in the form of document sets using MAXQDA Stats. But you can only create new memos to record further analysis ideas once you have closed Stats, since all other MAXQDA functions are locked while Stats is open.

Categorize Responses to Open Questions
Once you have explored the survey data, the issue arises as to how you can meaningfully analyze the comparatively short responses to open questions. As a rule, each question is analyzed individually, and the respective response texts are systematized and described using thematic categories such that, among other things, conclusions can be drawn about frequently and less frequently mentioned topics after the analysis has been completed. The categories for the analysis of responses can be formed using both an a priori approach or based directly on the data. For example, forming categories based on the data is the ideal option if you want to avoid pre-categorization and you want to use the responses themselves as your starting point, if the range of possible responses is unknown, or if the questions to be answered in the survey have a rather more exploratory character. A priori category formation, on the other hand, is to be recommended if information on the survey topic is available in advance, if only specific aspects of the responses are of interest and the responses contain information that does not need to be coded, or if the analysis categories are to be derived directly from the survey questions.

MAXQDA offers you a function especially designed for the analysis of responses to open questions and the associated formation of categories. If you go to *Analysis > Categorize Survey Data,* a window will open into which you can drag a code with the responses to an open question from the "Code System," and this will in turn open the analysis view. In Fig. 16.4 you can see the view of the Categorize Survey Data function for the question "How would you define a good quality of life?". In the left window area, the "Code System" is reduced to the codes corresponding to question you want to analyze, and in the "Responses" column, you can see the texts written by all the respondents for that question. You can use your mouse to select response texts, or parts of them, and drag them onto a code, after which that code will be displayed in the "Assigned Codes" column. The fourth column "Comment" lets you record notes, comments, and reminders for each individual response. Whether you have decided to form your categories a priori, based on the data, or by applying a combination of these two approaches, you can click on the *New code* icon to add new subcategories either in advance or as your analysis progresses.

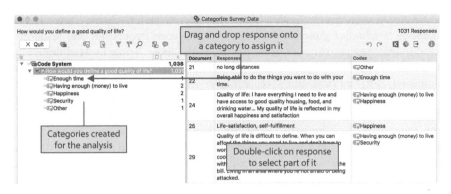

Fig. 16.4 Analysis view for categorizing responses to open questions

Sometimes responses to a given question also address topics relating to other questions than the one answered—topics which then also need to be coded here. By activating the option ***Display all codes*** in the toolbar, you can briefly display the complete "Code System" and perform such "external coding" and then hide the unnecessary codes again by deactivating this option.

▶   **Tip** The shortcuts you can set by right-clicking on a code and opening its properties menu are also available for coding survey responses. By right-clicking on a response and selecting ***Create and Assign New Code***, a new subcode can be added directly below the code associated with the open question and assigned to the selected response.

Once all the responses have been categorized, you can generate an overview of the individual categories and their code frequencies. What is helpful here is that the subcodes can be sorted by frequency—you can do this simply by right-clicking on the code of the open question and then selecting the corresponding function. To get an overview of the coded segments of a particular category, click on the code in the displayed code system; only the responses corresponding to the selected category will then be displayed in the "Responses" column.

Analyses of Interrelationships and Mixed Methods Analyses

While the "Categorize Survey Data" window is open, MAXQDA's other functions are locked. Only once you close the window, when you have completed the categorization process, are further functions available once again for analyzing the interrelationships between categories and for mixed methods analyses involving document variables. Since several hundred, even several thousand cases are often analyzed in surveys, strategies that are based on the frequencies of code assignments can produce very interesting results. Although individual cases are not the focus in this situation, you can still review them at any time and compile responses based on groups or topics. The following are some particularly noteworthy strategies:

Group comparisons based on imported variables—Using the **Mixed Methods > Crosstab function**, you can compare code frequencies and responses for different groups of respondents, for example, those living in Marburg's city center and those living in the countryside. These groups may, for instance, have completely different expectations regarding leisure activities in and around Marburg.

Group comparisons based on categories applied to open responses—Groups can also be formed that are based on the coded responses resulting from the categorization process. In the simplest case, at least two groups can always be compared, namely, those who gave a specific response and those who did not. In the Marburg student study, for example, you could compare respondents who mentioned "friends" when asked about quality of life with those who did not write about "friends." The first step here is to add the code "Friends" as a new document variable, which you can do via the function **Transform into Document Variable** in the code's context menu. The newly formed variable then indicates how often the code "Friends" was assigned to each case, which means that this variable can also be used to generate a crosstab. Additionally, the **Mixed Methods > Statistics for QUAL Groups** function lets you create a so-called joint display (Guetterman, Creswell, & Kuckartz, 2015), in which you can compare the statistical values of groups formed for that purpose. A joint display of this kind can be used to answer questions such as "How old on average are the respondents who named friends as an aspect of quality of life?". If you use the MAXQDA add-on module Stats for statistical analysis, you can dispense with the intermediate step of converting codes into variables and simply use code frequencies as grouping variables to generate descriptive statistics and crosstabs, and for performing variance analyses.

Combinations of categories—Which categories often co-occur in the same case? To answer this question, you can use the functions listed under **Analysis > Code Configurations**. In a simple configuration analysis, several codes are selected—usually the subcategories of an open question formed in the course of your analysis, where you have used a "code all that apply" approach. MAXQDA then presents a list containing the combinations of subcategories and displays the number of cases in which each combination occurs. For an open question about the respondents' understanding of quality of life, this function could be used to investigate whether the aspects "friends," "family," and "leisure time" are often mentioned in combination. In the case of complex configuration analyses, at least two top-level codes of different open questions must be selected. MAXQDA then analyzes the frequency of all possible combinations of their respective subcodes and presents the occurring combinations, together with their respective frequencies, in a table. With regard to the study involving Marburg students, this technique could be used to analyze how strongly the lack of recreational opportunities and facilities correlates with certain notions about quality of life. Finally, both simple and complex code configurations can also be analyzed to create a typology with types of respondents.

References

Guetterman, T., Creswell, J. W., & Kuckartz, U. (2015). Using joint displays and MAXQDA software to represent the results of mixed methods research. In M. T. McCrudden, G. J. Schraw, & C. W. Buckendahl (Eds.), *Use of visual displays in research and testing: Coding, interpreting, and reporting data*. Charlotte, NC: Information Age Publishing.

Kuckartz, U., Ebert, T., Rädiker, S., & Stefer, C. (2009). *Evaluation online: Internetgestützte Befragung in der Praxis*. Wiesbaden: VS Verlag für Sozialwissenschaften.

MAXMaps: Creating Infographics and Concept Maps

17

As early as the 1990s, American methodologists Miles and Huberman dealt with the topic of "visualizing social science research" and made many practical suggestions in their seminal book *Qualitative Data Analysis: An Expanded Sourcebook*. The visualization tool MAXMaps builds on these principles and offers a wide range of possibilities for graphically representing data and interrelationships. Visualizations can serve different roles in the research process: they can be used both for exploratory and diagnostic purposes as well as for presentational purposes. Importantly, they also facilitate better communication with scientific audiences in research and with the wider public. Often the latter especially requires aesthetically pleasing visualization options.

> **In This Chapter**
> - Learning to visualize interrelationships with MAXMaps
> - Discovering which project elements can be integrated into a map
> - Designing a map and its elements
> - Working with layers and creating a presentation
> - Synchronizing maps with MAXQDA project data
> - Using model templates for special visualizations

Visualizing Interrelationships

Infographics are everywhere, and today journalism, textbooks, and television would be quite unimaginable without them. In the humanities and social sciences, however, visualizations are still comparatively rare. Ebert (2013) demonstrated that leading social and educational science journals contain very few visualizations. In other branches of science and scholarship, the situation is the reverse: disciplines such as medicine, physics, or climate research rely heavily on all sorts of visual

© Springer Nature Switzerland AG 2019
U. Kuckartz, S. Rädiker, *Analyzing Qualitative Data with MAXQDA*,
https://doi.org/10.1007/978-3-030-15671-8_17

representations. Imagine, for example, if climate research could only be presented and argued for using texts; surely it is precisely the images that "show" these dramatic developments in the truest sense of the word.

But why should relationships be visualized at all? The proverbial phrase, "A picture is worth a thousand words," is not only true in everyday life but also applies to the humanities and social sciences, which can often be rather text-heavy. In general, two functions can be distinguished regarding the role of visualizations in research: on the one hand, visualizations are a valuable tool in the analysis process and a vital means of diagnosing phenomena in the data; on the other, they help to communicate, present, and publicize results. These two functions are perhaps best illustrated by the example of medical imaging methods (e.g., ultrasound examinations or magnetic resonance imaging). The ultrasound examination during pregnancy serves to obtain information about the "child in the womb" and to detect deviations from normal values. That is the diagnostic function of this imaging procedure. However, standard ultrasound machines are also capable of taking photos of the ultrasound image, which the parents-to-be can then proudly present to friends and family.

Visualizations as a means of presenting scientific discoveries and information are very widespread today, but it is mostly quantitative information that is presented in this way. Bar and pie charts, for instance, that show the results of survey research, are not only featured in specialist literature but can also be found in a great many articles in magazines such as *Time* and *The New Yorker*.

MAXQDA offers you a variety of visualization options. The visualization tools *Codeline*, *Code Matrix Browser*, and *Document Portrait* have already been described in Chap. 12; this chapter focuses on MAXMaps, MAXQDA's most comprehensive visualization tool. This is a special tool that allows you to graphically display concepts, research designs, the conditions present during field research, as well as the relationships present in the empirical data.

But what does this mean more specifically, that is, what types of relationships can you display with MAXMaps? The following illustration contains some simple examples of possible visualizations of the relationship between two elements, here the relationships between Code A and Code B.

You can visualize relationships as shown in Fig. 17.1 using MAXMaps; A and B can represent any element of your analysis, including categories. Moreover, beyond

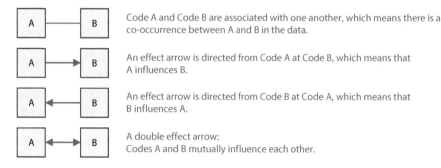

Fig. 17.1 Visualizing the relationship between two elements

MAXQDA's standard elements, you can also insert photos, charts, or images into the map. You can also meaningfully arrange these individual elements in the MAXMaps workspace and—if there is a connection or relationship between them—link them via connecting lines. A diagram like Fig. 17.1 is called a "map." A map is generated in the (initially empty) MAXMaps workspace, to which any number of elements can be added.

At this point, a distinction needs to be made between *"free" representations* and *data-based representations*. *Free representations* are graphics that could in principle also be created with other software such as OmniGraffle or even Microsoft Word. These programs allow you to create diagrams, organize charts, graphs, and more. *Data-based representations*, on the other hand, are graphics that consist of the elements of a MAXQDA project and can visually represent relationships present in the data, such as the co-occurrence of certain codes.

The following visualizations may be useful as *free representations* in the context of a research project:

- Overviews of fieldwork conditions, e.g., spatial settings, exterior views of buildings, or organizational charts
- Contextual elements such as photos of research participants or research settings
- Representations of the research methods used in the project
- Representations of the different content units of an interview
- Geographical information on fieldwork locations and conditions
- Temporal progressions of research projects and much more

Hence, MAXMaps can be used to generate graphics that are not directly related to the *empirical data* in a MAXQDA project. The real highlight of MAXMaps, however, is that the icons and objects displayed in a map *can* also be linked to the data of a MAXQDA project. A graphic created with OmniGraffle or Word may be aesthetically pleasing and informatively designed, but it is never directly linked to empirical data. In contrast, the connection between the project data and the graphics in MAXMaps makes it possible, for example, to click on the icon of a code and see its definition or to view all the text passages coded with this particular code in table form.

Primarily, MAXMaps is intended as a way of visually representing the various elements of MAXQDA ("objects") on a workspace, connecting them with each other, and thus visually rendering complex content-related relationships. Elements that can be imported into such a map are, for example, the icons for codes, documents, coded segments, and memos, as well as free elements and text fields the designs of which are freely definable. Photos and user-made graphics can also be inserted into a map.

MAXMaps can be used for a wide variety of tasks. Maps can be used exploratively to develop ideas and communicate them within a team. Maps can also be used to visualize very complex interrelationships or to create overviews of a project or partial aspects of a project. For example, they can visualize:

- The cause-effect relationships between different categories
- The memos belonging to specific documents or document groups
- Intersections and overlaps between codes
- The subcategories of codes
- The constellation of codes in a given document in the shape of a so-called case map

Furthermore, MAXMaps can help create interesting presentations. Different layers of a map can be successively displayed or hidden, providing a variety of design options for visual demonstrations. MAXMaps can be used in several ways during the research process, especially for diagnostic purposes and for identifying relationships. And MAXMaps also lets you organize and group codes (see the section "Creative Coding, a Tool for the Visual Development of a Coding Frame" in Chap. 8); visually represent links between codes, documents, and memos; and much more.

MAXMaps is interactive, i.e., the objects displayed in the map have a direct connection to the MAXQDA project when the Sync Mode is switched on. For example, you can open a document simply by clicking on its icon in the map, you can read memos and if necessary amend them, and you can open selections of coded segments from different groups to conduct group comparisons.

MAXMaps enables you to make existing connections in the data visible. For documents imported into MAXMaps, for example, all the memos attached to them can also be automatically imported. Similarly, for a code displayed as an icon in MAXMaps, the memos linked to this code, the codes intersecting with it, as well as its subcodes can also be inserted into the map. This creates a completely new way of looking at the data: interrelationships that might otherwise have remained hidden in tables and lists become *obvious*. The display of the relationships between individual elements in these maps—for example, between two or more codes—is not limited to hierarchical list-like relationships; complex networks between these elements can be represented too.

This visual access to the data is additionally supported by the flexible design options in MAXMaps. The wide range of these options offers you a great deal of creative freedom. This applies above all to the presentation of the visual elements, which are not fixed in their shape or size. Codes, memos, and documents need not necessarily be displayed with the same icon or same color; instead, they can be freely designed by the user. Images and labels can easily be customized, and you can even import your own photos or icons.

The Basics of Working with MAXMaps

You will find MAXMaps in the *Visual Tools* ribbon tab. The MAXMaps window (Fig. 17.2) is initially divided into two areas, on the left you can see the "List of Maps" and on the right, the workspace in which you will design your map. You can create any number of maps, and these are automatically saved to your MAXQDA project file, so you do not have to worry about saving the map yourself.

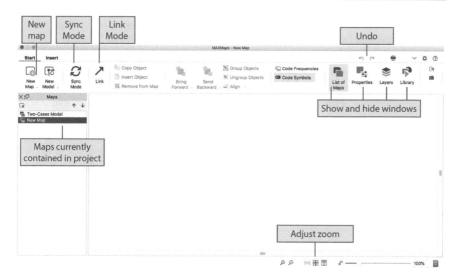

Fig. 17.2 The workspace in MAXMaps

Maps can be exported as graphic files in PNG, JPG, or SVG (scalable vector graphics) formats, so that you can insert them as images into other programs such as Word or PowerPoint. At the top of the workspace, you will see a ribbon menu with two tabs. The *Start* tab contains all the important tools for creating and editing your map. Use the *Insert* tab to insert new codes, texts, images, and shapes into it. And you can create a new map by clicking on *New Map* in the Start menu.

In the upper right corner of the MAXMaps window, there are two arrow icons for undoing and restoring your most recent actions. These undo functions always apply only to the currently open map. The "undo memory" is deleted as soon as another map is opened or the MAXMaps window is closed. The global undo function of MAXQDA has no effect on the stored maps in MAXMaps.

Using the zoom options at the bottom right of the window, you can zoom in and out and jump directly to the first object you added, the "origin" of the map.

Designing a Map

Once you have created a new empty map, you can start designing it, i.e., you can add various elements to the workspace. This is easily done by dragging elements from your project into the MAXMaps workspace with the mouse or by double-clicking an element while holding down the *Alt* key (Windows) or *option* ⌥ key (Mac). Alternatively, you can right-click on the element and select the *Insert into Map* option. MAXMaps recognizes three types of objects:

- *Standard objects.* These are MAXQDA project elements (codes, documents, memos, coded segments) and can each only be inserted once into the same map. Changes made to these objects have no retroactive effect on the MAXQDA project:

if, for example, the name of a document inserted from MAXQDA is changed in a map, the name remains unchanged in MAXQDA's "Document System."

- *Free objects.* These are graphic objects; they are called "free" because they are not connected to any elements in your MAXQDA project, i.e., they exist independently of the analyzed data.
- *Linking objects.* This refers to the lines that link two objects in a map to each other.

Standard objects and free objects consist of two parts: an object label and an object image. The linking lines can also be labelled.

Several options—available via the ***Preferences*** icon in the top right-hand corner of the MAXMaps window—are important when designing a map:

- ***Apply grid***—This activates a grid displayed in the background of the workspace that facilitates a more precise positioning of individual elements. The objects snap into fixed positions against this grid.
- ***Reduce imported images to this size***—This option controls how large images are imported. You can select between 300, 600, 1200 pixels, and "original size." The longer side of the image is reduced to the specified size. Background images are always imported in their original size.
- ***Visualize document links***—If this option is selected, existing document links between two documents are represented by a blue line.

The following MAXQDA elements can be inserted into a map—brackets indicate where these elements are located in MAXQDA:

- Documents ("Document System")
- Document groups ("Document System")
- Document sets ("Document System")
- Codes and subcodes ("Code System")
- Code memos ("Code System")
- Memos attached to places within a document ("Document Browser")
- Memos attached to documents ("Document System")
- Memos attached to document groups ("Document System")
- Free memos (Overview of Memos)
- Coded segments ("Retrieved Segments" window, Overview of Coded Segments, "Document Browser," or "Multimedia Browser")

Graphics with Style

With a little creativity, you can turn your map into something rather special that will make an excellent impression on a conference poster or in a presentation. You can edit the appearance of the elements in your map in various ways in the Properties window. You can open this window by clicking on the icon of the same name in the

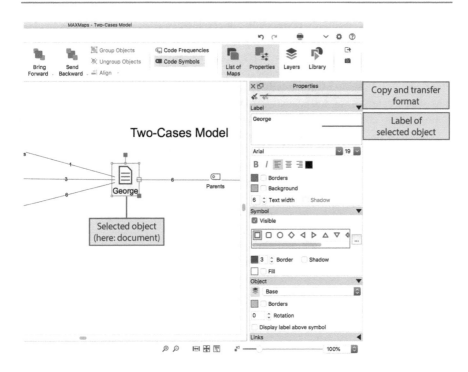

Fig. 17.3 Selected document icon and the Properties window

Start ribbon tab. As soon as an object is selected in the map, you can edit its label, font, and font size and adjust many other settings in the Properties window (Fig. 17.3). For example, in the "Symbol" section of the window, you can determine whether the icon or symbol of the object or only its label should be visible. It may also be useful or interesting for you to insert your own symbol or a photo instead of the standard available symbols and icons. In the "Links" area, you can add either an external link or a geolink to the element. Then, when you double-click it later, the linked file is opened or, in the case of a geolink, the corresponding geo-reference is opened. This linking function lets you create a link to the image of a person, for example, or to make their place of residence visible on a geographical map.

MAXMaps allows you to transfer the applied format of one object to another, thus giving them a uniform appearance. To do this, follow these steps: first, select the object whose format you want to transfer and then click on the *Copy Format* icon in the Properties window. Now select the object you want to apply this format to and click the *Apply Format* icon.

Creating a Case Map

Free representations refer to infographics created with MAXMaps that are independent of the data in a MAXQDA project, i.e., they can in principle also be created with Corel Draw, OmniGraffle, Adobe Illustrator, or other design programs. Only rarely

will you generate graphics completely independently of a MAXQDA project—
although this is certainly possible: you can even create impressive birthday
invitations with MAXMaps. Free representations and data-based representations
cannot be separated in a strict sense anyway; often as not they blend into each
other, as the following example will show. Let us look at Fig. 17.4, in which a case
map was created for an interview with James K. The purpose of the visualization is
to present the characteristics of this interview at a glance.

The steps below were used to create this map:

1. Click on *New Map* and provide the map with a name, e.g., "Case James K."
2. Switch on the grid view via Preferences (the gear icon the top right corner of the
   MAXMaps window).
3. Drag the document James K. onto the workspace with the mouse. The document
   icon will appear just as in the "Document System."
4. Draw this element out with the mouse to make it larger, and add "Case" to the
   label after double-clicking on the label.
5. Drag the codes "Biggest world problems," "Individual behavior," "Consumption and climate," "Personal views," "Causes for discrepancies," and "Influence" into the workspace.
6. If necessary, change the labels of the codes as shown in Fig. 17.4. For the code
   "Consumption and climate," uncheck "Visible" in the Symbol section in the
   Properties menu.
7. Place the five codes on the workspace as shown in Fig. 17.4.

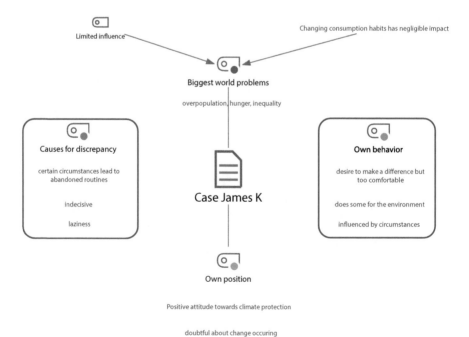

Fig. 17.4 Example of a case map: "Case James K."

8. In the **Start** tab, click on **Link,** and draw the connecting lines from one object to another by clicking and dragging with the mouse.

9. In the **Insert** tab, click on **New Text,** and enter "Overpopulation, hunger, inequality" in the text field inserted in the upper left corner of the workspace. Move the text field below "Biggest world problems."

10. Insert a new free object "Rectangle—rounded corners" by double-clicking on the corresponding symbol in the **Insert** tab. Draw the rectangle out with the mouse, large enough to serve as a frame. Set the line width to 10 in the Properties window; the background color remains "white." Click **Add to Library** in the context menu for the newly inserted rectangle.

11. Drag the object you just added to your Library onto the workspace so that you now have two identical free objects.

12. Move both objects to their intended position, where they cover the codes located there; select one after the other and click the button **Send to Back** in the **Start** tab.

13. Now only the thematic summaries in the two rectangles are still missing. These are inserted as text fields, so click the button **New Text** in the **Insert** tab. The text appears in the upper left corner and can be moved to the appropriate position in the rectangular frame. Now you can enter the respective thematic summary in the text field, e.g., "certain circumstances lead to abandoned routines."

14. After you have entered all thematic summaries in this way, you can optimize the map as a whole, i.e., move the elements individually or select several objects and distribute them with **Start > Align,** so that the layout is optimally arranged.

Working with Layers and Designing a Presentation

Anyone who has ever worked with image processing programs like Adobe Photoshop will be familiar with the term "layer." In Photoshop, layers are compared to transparent foils that are laid one on top of the other, i.e., you can see the layer below. MAXMaps also lets you to work with layers; the elements of a map can be assigned to different layers. With the help of these layers—which can be displayed in sequence, one on top of the other—you can design a detailed and informative presentation that progressively becomes more complex and reveals an evolving structural thesis.

To distinguish layers from each other, they are given a name. If you have not created additional layers, all newly inserted objects are assigned to the default layer "Base." You can access the layers function via the corresponding icon in the **Start** tab. A window will then open where the existing layers are listed and where you can create new layers by clicking the **New** icon in the top left corner of this window.

The first step is to set up as many layers as you need. In the Single-Case Model shown in Fig. 17.5, for example, you could work with three layers: first, the center of the map with the document name and the map title; then a second layer with the inner circle of the codes; and third, a layer with the outer circle (currently hidden).

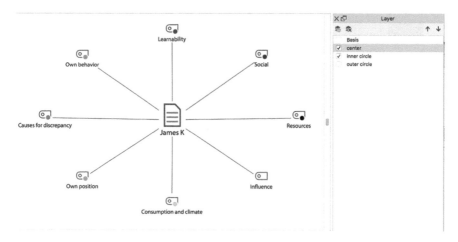

Fig. 17.5 Working with different layers

Accordingly, the layers should be named "center," "inner circle," and "outer circle." The "Base" layer is always present and cannot be renamed or deleted.

In the second step, all elements of the map are assigned to a specific layer. This works as follows: right-click on the element, select the "Layer" option, and assign it to one of the three layers—initially all elements are assigned to the "Base" layer, which is then gradually cleared as they are assigned to other layers.

By activating or deactivating the checkmark in front of the respective layer, the elements of the layer are displayed or hidden. In Fig. 17.5 you can see the map where only the layers "center" and "inner circle" are switched on.

Visualizations are very often created for presentations. In a live presentation as part of a lecture, you could reveal the distinct layers one after the other, starting with "center" followed by the "inner circle" and then the "outer circle." Another possibility is to create three images of the map: (a) map only with the "center" layer, (b) with the two layers "center" and "inner circle," and (c) with all the layers. If you export the map as an image file (e.g., in PNG format) after each step, these three files can be integrated into a PowerPoint or Prezi presentation. This enables you to create a dynamic presentation using layers, independently of MAXQDA.

Synchronizing MAXMaps with the MAXQDA Project Data

MAXMaps' great strength is that it allows you to connect and synchronize its infographics with your MAXQDA project file. In the simplest case, this connection means that elements, e.g., codes, memos, or documents, can be dragged into a map from MAXQDA's various overviews and windows whereby their icons and colors are also adopted. Many MAXQDA context menus, for example, in the "Document System" and in the "Code System," also contain the entry *Insert into Map*. There are also two further ways of connecting map and project data: (a) via the context menu of individual elements in a map and (b) via Sync Mode.

Synchronizing via Context Menus in MAXQDA

One way to synchronize project data and maps is via the context menus of elements in MAXMaps. If you right-click on a code in the MAXMaps workspace, the Overview of Coded Segments, Overview of Memos, and Overview of Variables are all available, just as they are in MAXQDA's "Code System." For details on how to work with these overviews, see Chap. 6.

Using the *Import Memos* option available in MAXMaps, via the context menu for documents, you can insert all the memos attached to this document into the workspace (Fig. 17.6); these are automatically linked, graphically, to the document icon by nondirectional lines.

The *Import Subcodes* function is available in the context menu for inserted codes; it imports all the subcodes on the level immediately below the selected code and links them to the code by connecting lines. If required, the thickness of these linking lines can be set to correspond to the frequency of the subcodes. Other options in the context menus allow you to:

- Import intersecting codes: here, all codes are inserted into the workspace that intersect with the selected code within the documents in your MAXQDA project and are linked to the code in the map by dashed connecting lines.
- Import linked memos: all memos linked to the code are inserted into the workspace. Linked memos already displayed in the map are not inserted a second time but are instead also graphically linked to the code by a line.
- Import the text of a coded segment: right-click on the coded segment icon in the workspace to insert the segment's complete text as a label.

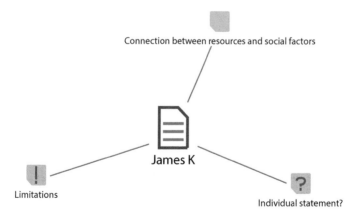

Fig. 17.6 Memos of a document displayed in MAXMaps having been automatically imported

Table 17.1 Available actions in MAXMaps' Sync Mode

| Icon | What happens when you... | | |
	Hover	Single-click	Double-click
Document group or document set icon	Displays memo attached to document group or document set in tooltip (if a memo exists)	Selects document group or document set in the "Document System" window	
Document icon	Displays document memo in tooltip (if a memo exists)	Selects document in the "Document System"	Opens document in the "Document Browser"
Memo icon	Displays memo in tooltip	Selects memo (depending on the memo type) in the "Document System," "Code System," "Document Browser," or "Multimedia Browser"	Opens memo
Code icon	Displays code memo in tooltip (if a memo exists)	Selects code in the "Code System"	Opens the Overview of Coded Segments for this code
Coded segment icon	Preview of coded segment in tooltip	Selects code in the "Code System," corresponding document is opened in the "Document Browser," or media file in the "Multimedia Browser," at the location or time position of the coded segment	

Synchronizing via Sync Mode

Sync Mode synchronizes the map with the MAXQDA project; you can activate and deactivate this mode in the *Start* tab by clicking on the corresponding icon. For example, hovering the cursor over a document icon in the map reveals the memo assigned to this document in a tooltip, and double-clicking the icon opens the document in MAXQDA's "Document Browser." Table 17.1 provides an overview of the actions available in Sync Mode.

It is important to note that there is intentionally no backward synchronization between a map and the MAXQDA project data. Hence, changing the name of a document or code in a map does not affect the name of this document or code in MAXQDA. The same applies if the text of a displayed coded segment is shortened or summarized; even in this case, the segment remains unchanged in the MAXQDA project file.

The Model Templates: Prepared Maps for Special Tasks

The ready-made model templates provided in MAXMaps are particularly useful. These templates create specific visualization formats with a single click. They can save you a considerable amount of time and effort compared with manually implementing the same analyses.

There are several different model templates to choose from. Table 17.2 provides an overview of the nine variants and the concepts behind the individual models.

Table 17.2 Overview of the model templates in MAXMaps

Description	Focus	Meaning and purpose
Single-Case Model	One document, document group, or document set	This model produces a map of the assigned codes, memos, and coded segments for a selected document from the "Document System"
Single-Case Model for Focus Group Participants	A participant in a specific focus group	This model produces a map of the assigned codes, memos, and coded segments for a specific participant in a selected focus group
Single-Case Model with Code Hierarchy	A document, document group, or document set	This special variant of the single-case model produces a map in which the code hierarchy is also displayed
Two-Cases Model	Two documents, document groups or document sets and their respective codes	This model visually displays which codes occur in both documents, document groups, or document sets and those which only exist in one of the two "cases"
Single-Code Model	One code with coded segments and subcodes	This model displays a selected code and its corresponding coded segments in a map, as well as the code memo and the memos linked to this code
Code Theory Model	The memos linked to a code	This model can assist you in developing theories and testing hypotheses. A selected code, and if necessary also its corresponding subcodes, and the memos linked to this code and its subcodes are displayed in the workspace
Code-Subcodes-Segments Model	A code with its subcodes and coded segments	A selected code and its subcodes are displayed in a map. Each code and subcode is linked to its corresponding segments
Hierarchical Codes-Subcodes Model	A code and its subcodes	A selected code and its subcodes are displayed in a map. The hierarchical structure of the subcodes is visualized in the form of several "levels"
Code Co-occurrence Model	Intersections of codes	For selected codes, the intersections between them and other codes are mapped out. Including the subcodes in this map increases its complexity

With all the available models, you can control the selection of documents or codes by activating them before creating the map. In the Code Co-occurrence Model, you can also select the coded segments by specifying the weight variable range (see Chap. 6). One-click graphics can be edited like normal maps, i.e., you can change the position of elements in the workspace, insert or delete links between them, and add additional elements, text fields, and free objects.

All models are created by clicking on *New Model* in the *Start* tab and selecting the model that suits your analysis. The following will describe some selected models in greater detail and give examples of what the corresponding visualizations look like.

Single-Case Model: Displaying All the Codes and Coded Segments in a Document

The basic questions underlying this model are "Which codes and subcodes have been assigned to a specific document?", "Which coded segments correspond to these codes?", and "Which memos have been assigned to the document or text passages of this document?".

In the case of an interview, you might ask: "What issues did the person's interviewed mention? What exactly did they say, what words did they use? What dimensions did they address?". A map of this kind, created for a specific document, is called a Single-Case Model in MAXQDA. Once you have opened this model, you can drag any document (or, alternatively, a document group or a document set if multiple documents represent a single case) from the "Document System" into the workspace with the mouse. The following options are at your disposal regarding the automatic selection of elements in the map:

- Memos: you can select the type of memos included (document memo, memos within the document, code memos, and memos linked to codes)
- Codes: you can restrict the map to activated codes or restrict it to a certain maximum number of codes.
- Coded segments: you can choose whether coded segments are displayed (yes/no), restrict the maximum number of segments displayed per code, and set a priority regarding the display of coded segments, either by weight or by size.

Figure 17.7 provides an example of a Single-Case Model: the selected document "James K." is located at the center of the map; the document's codes, beginning with "Influence" at the top, are linked to it with lines within the inner circle. In the outer circle, you can see the coded segments, each linked to its code. This Single-Case Model is taken from an interview study that was conducted by following a guideline. For many of the codes, there is only one coded segment linked to it, which is explained by the fact that there is only one text passage which was coded with this code—the code that corresponds to the respective question in the guideline.

In the upper left corner of the map, there is a memo with the title "Restrictions." You can open this memo in Sync Mode by double-clicking on it. The document "James K." will then be opened in the "Document Browser" at the same location in the text where the memo is attached.

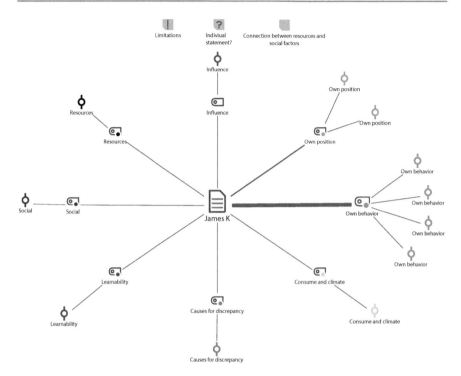

Fig. 17.7 Map for the document James K. created using the Single-Case Model

What can we take from this map? First, you can see which codes are assigned to the document. Second, the width of the linking lines indicates which codes have been assigned more frequently to the document and which have been assigned less frequently; here, the codes that have been assigned the most frequently are the codes "Own behavior" and "Own position." Third, the number of segments assigned with a code is visually displayed in the map, and, fourth, the map can be used to explore content: if you hover your mouse cursor over a coded segment icon when Sync Mode is switched on, the corresponding text of the segment is revealed.

Further design options allow you to replace the icons for the coded segments with their texts, insert images to represent elements in the map, change the size of elements, and insert memos, free text fields, and external links—such as a geolink from the document symbol for "James K." to his place of residence.

The Single-Case Model with Code Hierarchy creates a similar model for a document. However, the code hierarchy is displayed here, and you can choose how many subcode levels are displayed.

Single-Case Model for Focus Group Participants
The Single-Case Model for Focus Group Participants is structured in the same way as the regular Single-Case Model, but instead of featuring a document or document group at the center of the map, there is a single focus group participant (Fig. 17.8).

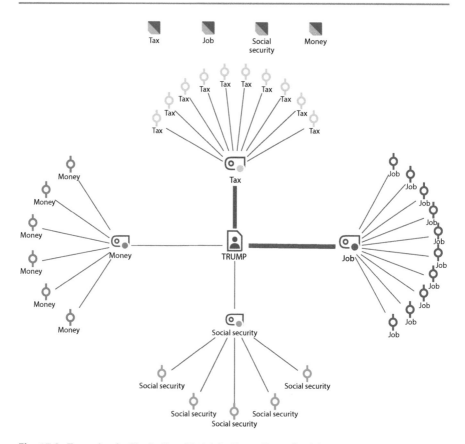

Fig. 17.8 Example of a Single-Case Model for Focus Group Participants

Single-Code Model: Placing the Focus on One Category

The key questions associated with this model are, for example, "In which documents has a certain code been assigned?", "What is the content of the text passages assigned with this code?", and "Which memos are associated with this code?". To a certain extent, this model is the counterpart to the Single-Case Model, but instead of a certain document, a specific code is the focus here.

Figure 17.9 shows a very simple Single-Code Model for the code "Nature and the environment as a global problem," i.e., respondents named "nature and environmental problems" among the world's current biggest problems. For the sake of clarity, the example illustration is limited to ten coded segments.

This map contains the code "NA—Nature and Environment" at the center, and the ten selected coded segments are linked to it by lines. As can be seen by their labels, these segments stem from interviews 6, 7, 9, 11, etc. The segment texts have been inserted in place of their icon for two coded segments, using the context menu option *Insert Text of Coded Segment as Label*. You could also insert the texts of the other segments to gain a more complete overview of what was said on this particular

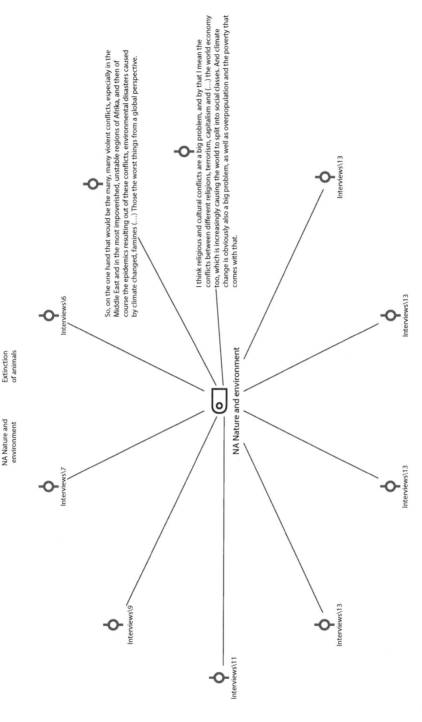

Fig. 17.9 Focused display of a code using the Single-Code Model

topic. At the top of the screen, you can see two memo icons: one is the code memo, which contains the code definition, and the other is simply another memo which has been attached to this code. This map, created as a Single-Code Model, can be customized, as required: elements can be changed, new elements can be added, and new linking lines drawn.

This map is also synchronized with the MAXQDA project data. Double-clicking on a coded segment opens the document in the corresponding location in the text—provided that Sync Mode is switched on.

Code Theory Model: Using Memos for Theory Development

This model effectively supports the development of theories and the testing of hypotheses. In this model, the focus is placed on the memos attached to a particular code and its subcodes, and so this will be most useful if you have previously written detailed and thoughtful memos. The map first includes the code memos that are normally used to record the respective code definition as well as ideas and hypotheses referring to the category; secondly, the map also includes further memos linked to these codes. For a selected code and its subcodes, the code memos and linked memos are automatically inserted into the workspace. The memos are visually linked to their code or subcode by lines.

Figure 17.10 provides an example of a Code Theory Model. At the center is the code "Biggest world problems," its subcodes (inner circle), and their memos (outer circle). As usual, the display in the map can be limited to activated codes. Only the code "NA—Nature and Environment" is linked to two memos: its code memo (this contains the code definition) and a linked in-document memo entitled "Animal extinction," which is attached to a passage in the text and contains reflections on this topic.

The map is interactive (when Sync Mode is switched on): double-clicking on a memo opens it and selects the corresponding code in the "Code System." Double-clicking on a text memo opens the corresponding document in the "Document Browser," precisely at the location in the text where this text memo is attached.

Code Co-occurrence Model: Discovering Interrelationships Between Codes

Some key questions associated with this model are "In what way are two or more codes related?", "Which codes occur together?", and "Which codes appear in which documents in combination with which other codes?".

These questions can be answered using the Code Co-occurrence Model; Fig. 17.11 illustrates its basic structure using a simple example. In an open interview, the question was asked as to which problems are currently regarded as the biggest problems worldwide. Inductive, data-driven categories were then formed from the answers. The visualization in Fig. 17.11 now indicates which subcodes were assigned to the interview in combination with which other subcodes, and how often this occurred. The width of the connecting lines indicates the frequency of this co-occurrence.

The map demonstrates that "NA Nature and environment" and "SO Social affairs" are mentioned together particularly often. The combinations of "NA Nature

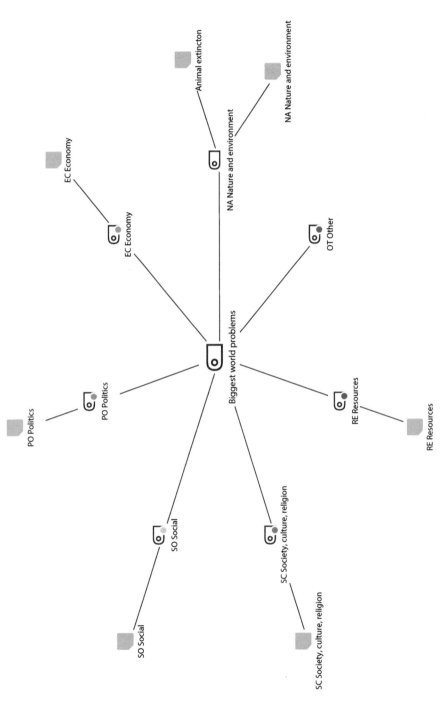

Fig. 17.10 The Code Theory Model with a code, subcodes, code memos, and linked memos

and environment" and "RE Resources" as well as "NA Nature and environment" and "PO Politics" are also quite common. By comparison, however, the combination of "EC Economy" with other subcodes is quite rare. This means that problems associated with economics are usually mentioned alone and comparatively rarely in combination with other topics, as the biggest world problem.

There are several options available for customizing this model:

- The analysis of intersections can be limited to activated documents.
- The frequency of intersections can be represented by the width of the linking lines between codes, as shown in Fig. 17.11.
- Subcodes can be included, making graphics much more complex.
- You can specify a minimum number of intersections that must be present in the data before they are represented in the map.
- You can include weight scores, i.e., only coded segments whose weight scores lie within a specified range are displayed in the map.

Code-Subcodes-Segments Model: Placing the Focus on a Category, Its Subcategories, and Coded Segments
Like the Code Co-occurrence Model, this model has the capacity to display extensive information; in other words, these maps run the risk of quickly becoming quite unwieldy and confusing. In many respects, this model is similar to the Single-Code Model, but unlike it in that this model focuses not only on one particular code and its coded segments but also includes its subcodes.

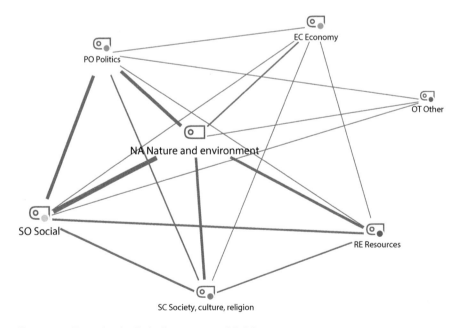

Fig. 17.11 Example of a Code Co-occurrence Model

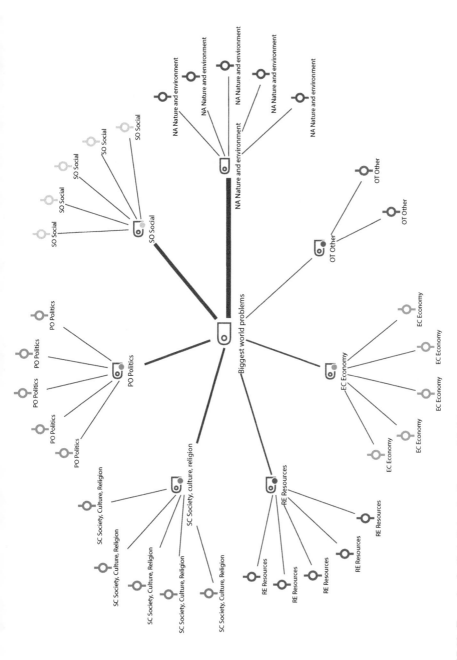

Fig. 17.12 Example of a Code-Subcodes-Segments Model

So, what does this model do? It visually portrays the coded segments of a code and its subcodes. It offers you a visual impression of the distribution of frequencies (by line thickness). And it can also be used to explore statements on specific topics. If you hover your cursor over a coded segment icon, the corresponding text is displayed—provided that Sync Mode is switched on.

You can generate this map by first selecting a group header code from the "Code System" and dragging it to the center of the workspace. You can then select further options, including the maximum numbers of subcodes and coded segments to be displayed per subcode. It also makes sense to select the option *Line width reflects frequencies*, because you can then tell at a glance which codes occur most frequently.

The model in Fig. 17.12 contains the selected code "Biggest World Problems" in the middle. It is linked to its subcodes by nondirectional arrows. The outer circle contains the segments for each subcode, up to a maximum of five (previously selected as an option in the model dialog box). By applying weight scores to the most significant segments during coding work, you can ensure that these are the selected elements for this model. The segments are each connected to their subcode by linking lines.

The map can easily be expanded if required: the elements can be rearranged, and new elements, such as code memos, can be added to suit your analysis.

Reference

Ebert, T. (2013). *Die Systematisierung visueller Darstellungsformen in der sozialwissenschaftlichen Forschung*. Marburg: Philipps-Universität Marburg. Retrieved from https://archiv.ub.uni-marburg.de/diss/z2013/0712/

Collaborating in Teams

18

You will have no doubt come across two types in your research career: the passionate solo researchers, in the style of Stephen Hawking, who work at a problem day and night largely by themselves, and the team players, who are convinced that challenges are best tackled together. Teamwork is becoming increasingly common in empirical social research. As one example, calls for research proposals often explicitly request multidisciplinary working groups, often in collaboration with various partners. The question this raises is how you can most effectively organize and map out collaborative analysis work involving software. A project not only needs an agreed plan as to who does what and at which point in time; it also demands strict rules and guidelines—to avoid chaos ensuing. It may be, for example, that not every team member is allowed to delete codes, reorganize the category system, or change memos. Rules like these require a user management system, in which project leaders can define detailed permissions for each team member.

In This Chapter
- Understanding teamwork and differentiating between various ways of sharing research work
- Managing and distributing externally stored files
- Organizing and implementing the division of work: merging two projects together and transferring analysis work from one project to another
- Reviewing analyses as a team
- Allocating permissions to individual team members participating in a project

© Springer Nature Switzerland AG 2019
U. Kuckartz, S. Rädiker, *Analyzing Qualitative Data with MAXQDA*,
https://doi.org/10.1007/978-3-030-15671-8_18

Different Forms of Teamwork and Division of Work

The roles collaboration and the division of work on projects play are different between qualitative and quantitative research. While the analysis procedures for quantitative data are largely standardized and can sometimes even be entirely "outsourced"—complete with the data collection process—to external service providers, the qualitative data analysis process involves a more time-consuming examination of the data. Hence, teamwork is arguably more important for the analysis of qualitative data than for quantitative data. Collaborative data analysis and interpretation has a long tradition in qualitative research; this is reflected in the regular calls for joint analysis groups through specialist mailing lists as well as the many workshops at qualitative methods conferences in which participants discuss, interpret, analyze, and comment on research data using variously formalized techniques. The frequently debated topics of "intersubjectivity," "consensual validation," and "reflexivity" provide further evidence that teamwork is central to qualitative research. Against this background, several questions arise as to how the division of work can be efficiently and effectively designed for qualitative and mixed methods research projects involving the software MAXQDA.

The more people are involved in a research project and the more complex the required analysis, the more important it is to define guidelines that serve to structure the collaborative work with MAXQDA. Which transcription rules need to be observed? Which analytical information should be recorded in memos and which in code comments? Which memo icons are to be used to identify certain issues and contexts? How extensively should the data be coded; do the questions asked by the interviewer also have to be coded or are the interviewee's responses sufficient? How should repeat occurrences of the same information in the data be dealt with; should they be coded several times or just once? How extensive should summaries be and at what level of abstraction? These and other questions must be clarified with the team and recorded in writing, e.g., in the logbook of the MAXQDA project (see Chap. 3).

Working in teams and sharing the analysis work can be organized in different ways using MAXQDA. However, please note that MAXQDA is not a multiuser system, which means that several people cannot access and edit the same project file at the same time. MAXQDA instead offers numerous functions for simultaneous work with project copies, and you can merge these copies together or transfer analysis work from one project to another at any time. There are three different ways a collaborative project might start out, each of which are accompanied by distinct technical approaches in MAXQDA:

Model 1 *Several people work with the same project file at separate times in succession. Team members pass the project file on to the next person after each step.*

first person 1   then person 2   then person ...

This model is the simplest for working collaboratively, and it is ideally suited to projects in which different team members work on the data at different stages. For example, the project leaders first develop a code system and coding guideline, another team member then uses these specifications to code the data, and the project managers finally evaluate the completed coding work. With the help of MAXQDA's User Management system, which we will explain in detail at the end of this chapter, you can define and restrict the permissions of team members according to their responsibilities during the analysis process. This is recommended to prevent inadvertent changes being made to the code system or the texts being analyzed.

The project file can also be stored centrally on a network drive or can be distributed across several computers via cloud services such as Dropbox, Google Drive, and OneDrive. With this procedure, however, you need to define a rule system which ensures that the file is only ever opened by one person at a time to avoid subsequent file conflicts. We would also advise against opening the project file directly from a folder synchronized with Dropbox or other cloud-based systems. That said, to be on the safe side, you could create a copy of the project file in a local folder before you start working on it and then save the file with a new timestamp when you have finished editing it. This will ensure that slow network connections do not hamper your work or cause cloud services to synchronize only fragments of your MAXQDA project file, which could potentially damage it.

For this model of collaborative work, it is not necessary for all team members to have a MAXQDA license. You can pass a MAXQDA Portable License round on a USB stick, for instance, or share a computer on which MAXQDA is installed.

Model 2 *Several people work on different cases of a project at the same time. Your project files contain different documents, and these are later merged together to form one project.*

When sharing the workload in this way, project's cases are divided among the team members such that each of them receives a project file with the documents they need to process. This model is especially suitable when the team members do not necessarily need to be able to view all the documents at all times, for example, to compare them, or when the volume of data is very large and needs to be distributed. The team often works with the same code system for this type of work, which can be easily protected against changes with the help of MAXQDA's User Management function. However, the use of an entirely identical code system across all project files is not mandatory; MAXQDA's teamwork options will still work later in the process, since these options allow you to work with differing or partially overlapping code systems. Once all the project's team members have completed their cases, the individual project files are merged into a single project, which will then contain the complete set of documents and can then be made available to all or selected team members so that the project data can be analyzed further as a whole.

If your team plans to work according to this model, i.e., simultaneously, then several MAXQDA licenses are required.

Model 3 *Multiple people work on the same cases at the same time. The project files contain identical documents and the codes, variable values, memos, and summaries applied to one, several, or all documents are later merged into one of the projects, which from then on functions as the "master project."*

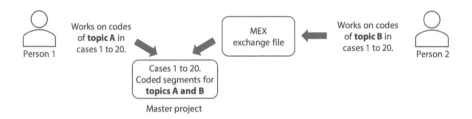

This collaboration model is very common, as it allows all team members to have all the material in front of them at all times. Often individual team members work on different topics in the documents, adding existing and sometimes new codes and writing memos and summaries for their respective topic area. Once the individual work on the documents has been completed, the coded segments, memos and summaries, as well as any variable values and links contained within individual documents, document groups, or all documents are transferred from the various projects into a "master project" via an export file in the MAXQDA exchange format.

To ensure a smooth transfer of the analysis work, it is essential that the documents in all of the projects are identical. This is usually guaranteed for PDF and image documents as well as for videos, since their contents cannot be changed in MAXQDA. The situation is different for text and table documents: as these can be changed in Edit Mode, they should at least be set to "read-only," which you can do by selecting the ***Properties*** option in the document's context menu. It is quicker and safer, however, to deactivate the permission to change text and table contents for all team members in MAXQDA's User Management system.

Several MAXQDA licenses are also required for simultaneous work to follow this model.

The three models of collaborative work are by no means mutually exclusive and can be combined with one another. There is no reason why team members should not be able to work on one project file one after the other, before a further analysis round sees the data divided among them. Moreover, for model 3 it is not absolutely essential for all the documents to be available in every project. The relevant documents only need to exist in the target project, which you can do by merging projects if needed. Experience suggests that it is a good idea to designate one person as the "file master," who can ensure that individual team members are working with the right data and are sticking to the agreed rules for the collaborative work process.

Regardless of which variant of teamwork you choose, you should make sure that you log in to MAXQDA with the same user name each time you start work, so that all changes you make to the project are tagged with your name. This ensures that even after merging projects, or transferring analysis work to another project, the performed work can be attributed to the correct team member.

Merging Two MAXQDA Projects

The MAXQDA function used in the second teamwork model to merge two projects together is always suitable where both contain different documents that need to be combined to form one project. From a technical perspective, the merging process takes place in such a way that the data of one project is integrated into another already open project. It therefore makes sense to open the larger of the two first, because then less data needs to be imported. To start the merging process, open the *Merge Projects* function in the *Home* ribbon tab, and then select the project file you want to add to the open project. As a MAXQDA project can contain only one logbook, only one memo per code, and only one project memo (this is the memo at the top of the "Document System"), MAXQDA will ask you before merging the two whether any existing data should be retained or replaced by the data in the imported project.

Figure 18.1 illustrates the principle of the merging process. Imagine a simple project A with the document group "Interviews" and the three documents "Interviews 1, 2, and 3," into which you import project B with the "Interviews 4 and 5." The merged result can be seen on the right: by default, all document groups of the imported project are added to the "Document System" of the open project. A

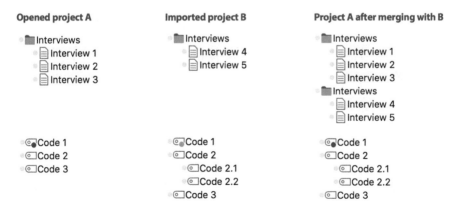

Fig. 18.1 "Document System" and "Code System" before and after two projects have been merged

second document group called "Interviews" has been created, which contains interviews 4 and 5 from the second project. The code systems of both projects have also been merged. Codes 2.1 and 2.2 were only included in project B and have been added to the code system of the open project A. During the merging process, codes bearing the same name at the same location are considered identical. The code color, if assigned, is not taken into account, which is why in this example, MAXQDA considers the red "Code 1" from project A to be identical to the green "Code 1" from project B.

If the projects you want to merge contain document groups or document sets of the same name, you can select the option *Merge document groups/document sets with same name* in the import dialog box. In the example above, this would mean that no further "Interviews" document group would be added to the "Document System"; instead, interviews 4 and 5 would be added to the existing document group. And if you want to combine several projects, some of which contain identical documents, the option *Don't import already existing documents* is also quite useful. This ensures that documents with the same name and document group are skipped during the merging process, so you can avoid ending up with annoying duplications of the same documents.

When merging two projects, all the data from the imported project is transferred to the open project, including summaries, internal and external links, and graphics created with MAXMaps. Variables are also transferred, that is, variables that do not exist in the open project are also added from the imported project.

Transferring Codes, Memos, Summaries, Variables, and Links from One Project to Another

The "Teamwork Export/Import" functions described in this section elaborate further on third model above for sharing analysis work. These functions are particularly useful if you have identical documents in several MAXQDA projects and want to transfer analysis information like codes and memos between these projects. Suppose Jacob and Emily are both working on the same five documents in their respective MAXQDA projects. Jacob codes topic A in the documents and Emily codes topic B, with corresponding codes for each topic included in the code systems of their individual project files. In this case, we are looking at the scenario illustrated in Fig. 18.2.

To transfer all 195 coded segments that Emily has made in her project to Jacob's project, Emily first opens the function *Teamwork > Export Teamwork: Export Data to Exchange File* in the context menu for the document group "Analysis of documents" and then selects the name and location for the export file. MAXQDA records all information required for the exchange of the five documents in this file, which is stored in the format "MAXQDA Exchange File" with the file extension . *mex*. This exported file can then be sent to Jacob by e-mail or via a cloud service. Jacob opens his existing project file as usual and then selects the counterpart to the export function in the context menu for the document group "Analysis of

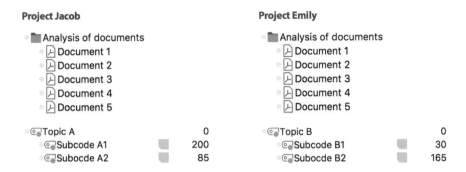

Project Jacob		Project Emily	
Analysis of documents		Analysis of documents	
Document 1		Document 1	
Document 2		Document 2	
Document 3		Document 3	
Document 4		Document 4	
Document 5		Document 5	
Topic A	0	Topic B	0
Subcode A1	200	Subcode B1	30
Subocde A2	85	Subocde B2	165

Fig. 18.2 Initial scenario before the teamwork transfer

documents," namely, ***Teamwork > Import Teamwork: Import Data from Exchange File***. In the file dialog box that opens, he then selects the file he received from Emily, whereupon MAXQDA opens a further dialog box in which he can check whether the source and target documents are correctly matched. Provided that the documents have not been renamed in the target project, MAXQDA automatically assigns the source documents to the correct target documents based on their names.

▶ **Tip** To ensure that your teamwork runs smoothly, documents and document groups should not be renamed during the course of a project or assigned to other document groups. Additionally, you should always ensure that your documents and document groups are assigned unique names, that is, that these names are assigned once only. Only then will identical documents actually be recognized as such.

In the options dialog box, you can also specify which elements of the data you want to import and how to proceed in the case of conflicts with code assignments and summaries. A coding conflict occurs when a code assignment is to be added to a document which has already been assigned with the same code at the same location, since MAXQDA functions according to the rule that the same code can only be assigned once per segment. A summary conflict arises if the opened project and the imported data contain a summary for the same code in a document. The following list describes how MAXQDA processes different data types during a teamwork import and explains which options are available for dealing with conflicts. The options specified apply to the entire import process; you cannot instruct MAXQDA to proceed differently for individual coded segments or variables.

- *Coded segments*—All coded segments including the corresponding comments and weight scores are inserted into the target project. Four variations are available in the options dialog box for dealing with conflicts in which an identical code has already been applied to a segment: (1) the existing code assignment is retained; (2) the imported code assignment "wins" and overwrites the existing code assignment; (3) with the "OR combination," the outermost limits of the overlapping code assignments are taken; and (4) with the "AND combination," only the intersecting area of the overlapping assignments is coded.

- *Codes*—The codes from the imported file are added to the bottom of the code system, if they are not included here already. Codes with the same name, and at the same position in the code system, are interpreted as identical, but any assigned colors are ignored in this process.
- *Variables*—Here the same procedure is applied as when importing a data matrix for variables: variables that do not yet exist are added, and existing variable values are updated.
- *Memos*—The memos in the "Document System" and the "Code System" are imported if no memo has already been assigned at the corresponding location. Memos within documents are imported if no memo with the same title has been assigned at the same location in the respective document. Free memos (these are memos that are not linked to any MAXQDA elements) are always added.
- *Summaries*—If there is no summary at a given location, the summary is added directly from the import file. If a summary has already been created at that location, MAXQDA offers you the option of specifying whether (1) the new summary from the import file is additionally attached to the existing one, (2) the new summary overwrites the existing one, or (3) the new summary from the import file is ignored.
- *Links*—Links within a document leading to external files or web pages are transferred if there is no link at the same location. If there is a link at the same location, the links in the import file are not accepted.

During the import, MAXQDA checks each document individually to see whether it is identical to the document from the export file. This ensures that the import is free of errors, e.g., if the source and target documents were incorrectly assigned to each other by mistake or they don't match for any other reason. If MAXQDA discovers a difference between two documents, you will see a warning message. If this happens, skip the import process for the document in question, and then compare the two documents for differences. You can do this quite easily for text documents with the "Compare" function in Microsoft Word, which lets you see the differences between two documents.

In the example at Fig. 18.2, the Import Teamwork process adds the code "Topic B" and its two subcodes, as well as the two corresponding code memos, to the code system in Jacob's project. The coded segments of these subcodes are also transferred to the documents in Jacob's project. The project has 285 existing coded segments + 195 transferred = 480 code assignments after the import.

You can transfer teamwork using MAXQDA exchange files from individual documents, from document groups, or from all the documents in your project. If you start the process from a single document's context menu, only this specific document's information will be included in the export file. If, on the other hand, you start this process at the very top row of your "Document System," the relevant information will be exported for all the documents in your project. If you have done the latter but want to complete the import process for only certain individual documents in the target project, you can start the import process from the context menu of a document in the target project and then, if necessary, adjust the individual allocations of source and target documents. To transfer analysis data between two projects, these projects do not need to contain the same complete data set; it is important, rather, that those documents whose information you want to transfer are identical in both projects. However, as Fig. 18.2 demonstrates, not all codes need to be identical.

Box 18.1 describes the procedure for transferring analysis data from one project to another:

Box 18.1: Transferring Analysis Data from a Source Project to a Target Project

- Open the source project from which you want to transfer the data.
- Right-click either on an individual document, document group, or the top line in the "Document System"—depending on the documents for which you want to transfer the analysis data. From the context menu, select *Teamwork > Export Teamwork: Export Data to Exchange File*.
- Select the codes to be exported and click *Next >>*. Assign a file name, and select a location to save the file with the transfer information—and make sure you remember this location.
- Close the source project and open the target project.
- Right-click on the document, document group, or the top row in the "Document System"—depending on the documents to which you want to add the analysis data. From the context menu, select the option *Teamwork > Import Teamwork: Import Data from Exchange File*.
- Select the file you saved earlier.
- Then, in the dialog box that opens, check whether the source and target documents have been correctly matched, and specify which information you want to transfer. Click *Import* to start the transfer.

Managing External Files When Collaborating in Teams

With all of these various approaches to collaborative work, you need never worry about whether your team members are using Mac or Windows computers; MAXQDA's teamwork functions can be used seamlessly across both platforms. What you should give some thought to, however, is how to go about saving and transferring external files if you are working with projects where not all the documents displayed in the "Document System" are included in the actual project file.

As discussed in Chap. 3, audio and video files are not imported into the project file by default—images and PDF documents may also optionally be saved externally. In these cases, the files in question are instead stored in the "Folder for external files." You can freely designate a folder on your system as this external files' folder via MAXQDA's global preferences. If you are working in a team with a project that contains externally stored documents, it is very important that these files are available in the designated external files folder on each computer the MAXQDA project is being worked on. To make sure of this, you can distribute these files via a USB stick or shared network drive to the individual team members, who can copy them to the appropriate folder on these computers.

We always strongly recommend that you use a local folder for the external files so that MAXQDA can load these files quickly. Network drives are therefore not an ideal location, since they can cause annoying delays when opening or browsing a document. A shared Dropbox, on the other hand, or similarly synchronized folder, can be used to distribute external files between team members, because these folders store copies of the files locally on each respective computer.

▶   **Tip** If the local storage space is not sufficient, e.g., because you need to analyze very large video files, you can also store the external files on an external hard disk connected via a fast USB 3.0 port.

If you are unsure whether a project contains external files, go to *Home > External Files*: this function gives you an overview of all your external files, and you can easily identify any files not included in your project file. If the overview is empty, you don't need to worry about any external files for this project.

Communicating About the Analysis in a Team

A great advantage of working collaboratively is that it gives you the chance to talk about the analysis work as a group, discuss uncertainties, and thereby improve the quality of the analysis. This applies to each step of the research process: from the development of suitable survey instruments and appropriate analysis categories for the collected qualitative data to the interpretation and publication of the analysis results. Particularly when it comes to the coding process, which is often at the core of the analytical work of qualitative research projects using MAXQDA, the team can define review procedures to systematically check completed coding work. Alongside the use of the functions for determining the level of intercoder agreement (cf. Chap. 19), this includes the successive checking of code assignments by different team members. The code weight function and the code comments are particularly well suited to these review processes. These functions allow team members to log the status of individual coded segments in the data and to communicate this status with other team members throughout the analysis process.

Using Weight Scores of Coded Segments for Teamwork

Working with the weight function involves two very simple steps. First, all the coders in the research team set a default code weight in MAXQDA's global preferences—this could be any weight but should be uniformly agreed upon, e.g., 20—such that all future coded segments are automatically provided with this weight. Of course, depending on your project's requirements, your team may instead agree that coders should only apply a weight of 20 to code assignments they are uncertain about or want to discuss further.

In the second step, a second team member, e.g., the project manager, checks the coded segments and sets them to 100, or another agreed weight score, to indicate that these assignments have been successfully reviewed. To check the coded segments with a particular weight score, you can compile them in the "Retrieved Segments" window using the weight filter. To do this, right-click in the gray area of the window, select the function *Edit Weight Filter*, and enter a minimum and maximum value for the codes to be displayed. You can then click on the weight icon in the status bar along the bottom edge of the MAXQDA interface to switch the weight filter on or off. Alternatively, you can also sort the Overview of Coded Segments table according to the "Weight score" column to gain quick access to the coded segments you are interested in reviewing. This function also offers you the major advantage of being able to change the weight scores directly in this table once you have finished reviewing them.

You could also apply various other types of "status" to coded segments using these weight scores. In unclear cases, for example, it may be helpful to specify a number for a "discuss as a team" status. The meaning of these respective numbers should be available for everyone to see in the logbook or a project memo at the top level of the "Document System" window.

Using Comments of Coded Segments for Teamwork

While the code weights only allow you to communicate with other team members using numbers, you can also record textual information during the coding process in the form of comments on specific coded segments. As described above for the weight function, different statuses of coded segments can be recorded in comments with the aid of agreed abbreviations—and they can be supplemented with additional notes for the other team members.

Managing Permissions and Restrictions for Team Members

For each MAXQDA project, you can define a separate user management system, which allows you to provide individual team members with specific permissions for working on or editing a project. It is important to emphasize, however, that this user management system does not offer increased data security by encrypting the data; instead, limits placed on permissions in MAXQDA are intended to ensure a good workflow in the team and to prevent individuals from inadvertently changing a predefined code system, which would hinder the collaborative process. The procedure for activating MAXQDA's User Management system for a currently opened project and assigning permissions to users is described, step by step, in Box 18.2.

Box 18.2: Activating MAXQDA's User Management System and Assigning Users

- Go to *Home* > *User Management* > *User Management*.
- Enter a password in the dialog box that opens. MAXQDA then adds a new user to the system with the name that you are currently logged with. The new user is automatically assigned the highest permission level.

The User Management window shown in Fig. 18.3 will then open, in which you can assign different permission levels to four different user groups. The default settings are based on a typical research team with a project manager ("Admin" group), research staff ("Level 1"), and assistants ("Levels 2 and 3").

- Check whether the predefined permissions of these respective groups meet the requirements of your project. Once you have clicked on a group in the left window area, you can switch this group's individual permissions on and off in the right window area by clicking on either the tick or stop sign.
- Select one of the levels with your mouse, and then add as many users as necessary to it using the first icon at the bottom of the dialog box. When you click on a user, you can subsequently change which group they are assigned to. The user name is sufficient for logging in to the project, but you can also enter additional information about the user in the "Name" and "Comments" fields, if required.
- Distribute the project to all your team members and tell them their respective user names.
- When a team member opens the project file, he or she enters their assigned user name. The password field must remain empty the first time you log in. Clicking on *OK* opens a dialog box in which each user must create their own password with which they can access the project from then on.

▶   **Please Note**   Once you have switched on the User Management system for a MAXQDA project, the project can only be accessed if you log in with one of the user names listed in this system. If the default permissions of the user groups have not been changed, only users of the highest permission level can access the User Management system. These users should therefore take extra care to remember their passwords.

In Fig. 18.3 you can see that the user "Camilla" was automatically added to the "Admin" group when the User Management system was opened for the first time. The key on her user icon indicates that a password has already been assigned to her

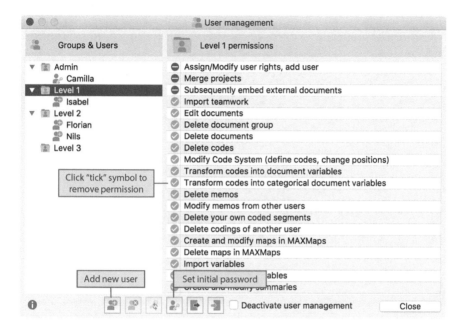

Fig. 18.3 Assign permissions for respective user groups, in this case "Level 1"

user name. For all the other users, however, the plus sign indicates that they are yet to "log in to the project" and have not entered their own passwords. As an additional security measure, you can define a password in the User Management window, by clicking the **Set initial password** icon. All new users must then enter this password the first time they log in to the project and before they can choose their own password as a next step.

The permissions system for a project can be switched off at any time by selecting the corresponding option at the bottom of the User Management window. Here you will also find an icon that allows you to export the complete User Management system of a MAXQDA project, including its user names, passwords, and permission settings, as a single file. The complementary **Import** function lets you import this system into another MAXQDA project. This transfer option can save you a lot of work when setting up new team projects.

Analyzing Intercoder Agreement

19

In qualitative research projects, questions often arise about the intersubjectivity of the analysis. Given the same interview passage, for example, does my fellow researcher see the same topics addressed as I do, and do they draw the same conclusions? To what extent do we agree on our understanding of categories? With these questions we are entering the field of quality criteria, which should not be neglected in qualitative research. In category-based approaches, the focus is placed on the question to what extent two people identify the same topics, aspects, and phenomena in the data and assign these to the same categories. It is quite possible for two people to agree in terms of content, but assign different categories to a phenomenon, because the category definitions have not yet been clearly formulated. MAXQDA offers numerous (partly interactive) functions, which enable systematic analysis, improvement, and verification of the agreement between coders. Problematic categories, misleading instructions, and blurred category definitions can be identified to improve the quality of analysis step-by-step.

In This Chapter
- Getting to know the objectives and areas of application of agreement testing
- Understanding the procedures for testing intercoder agreement in MAXQDA
- Conducting document-level and segment-level agreement tests
- Calculating percentage agreement and setting useful thresholds
- Taking agreement by chance into account

© Springer Nature Switzerland AG 2019
U. Kuckartz, S. Rädiker, *Analyzing Qualitative Data with MAXQDA*,
https://doi.org/10.1007/978-3-030-15671-8_19

Objectives and Areas of Application for Analyzing Agreement

The extent to which different researchers produce the same result is an important quality criterion of empirical studies. Hence, qualitative research involves the question of intercoder agreement: "To what extent do different coders agree when assigning categories to texts, images and videos?" Checking and improving intercoder agreement is closely linked to the research tradition of qualitative content analysis and is considered a central factor of quality (Kuckartz, 2014; Mayring, 2014; Schreier, 2012). In qualitative methods that follow a more interpretative approach, the question of intercoder agreement rarely arises, or not at all, since categories play a subordinate role or even none at all as tools for analysis. Although research projects following the grounded theory approach involve intensive work with codes and categories, it is not common to perform any intercoder agreement tests in this context. The focus in grounded theory is explicitly on the continuous development of concepts and categories and not their application to the material according to precisely defined rules.

So, what exactly is the benefit of an agreement analysis and for what purpose is it used? Well, there are many answers to this: just as new employees in the control departments of Facebook have to learn the rules for assessing contributions to delete inappropriate ones, it is also the task of new coders in a research project to understand the guidelines for applying categories. A test of agreement with a model example of code assignments reveals to what extent a coder's training has been successful. Intercoder analysis can be used not only to determine the effects of training for coders but also to sharpen the category system and coding instructions. With the help of intercoder analysis, problems with individual categories and their definitions can be identified and reduced, problems concerning the delimitation of categories can be traced, and, in addition, coders can be identified whose work differs systematically from those of the others. Thus, intercoder analysis can be used equally as a tool for checking, improving, and ensuring the quality of coding processes.

If several people are to code the same data for the purposes of an agreement analysis, questions about how best to organize the workflow inevitably arise. In principle, you can distinguish between three separate variations:

Coding at Two Different Times Here the data is first coded by one person, and then their code assignments are checked by one or more people subsequently. For example, as a first step a student assistant codes the texts, the project manager then looks through their code assignments, makes corrections, and discusses doubtful cases with the assistant or in the research team. This procedure is only suitable in the situation where well-developed category definitions already exist. When working alone, sometimes it can also be helpful to repeat the coding process at a later stage; 2–4 weeks later, the same person checks their own coding work again, or the same person codes the data again without looking at the coding work done previously.

Simultaneous Collaborative Coding   In the case of concurrent coding, the data can be discussed throughout the whole research team or in pairs of two, and suitable categories can be collectively assigned to data segments. This approach is particularly suitable for initial examinations of the data and the development or initial testing of coding frames. It is, however, exposed to the risk of the influence of research team hierarchies or the dominance of particularly extroverted personalities.

Simultaneous Independent Coding   The most frequently used method involves researchers code the data independently of each other and then comparing their results. Independent coding is generally mandatory for the calculation of the percent agreement and for chance-corrected agreement coefficients such as Cohen's kappa or Krippendorff's alpha (see below). In our opinion, however, it is important and desirable for qualitative research that more than just coefficients of agreement are calculated and published. Rather, they should, together with the places where inconsistencies have occurred, form the basis for a systematic discussion of the inconsistencies and the consequences for the category system and coding instructions. Based on this aspiration for qualitative-oriented analyses, we consistently prefer the term "intercoder agreement" to that of "intercoder reliability" in this chapter. Reliability is one of the three classical quality criteria of quantitative research; it stands for the claim of accuracy and replicability of measurements and is mainly located within the context of quantitative content analysis. In addition, the transferability of classical quality criteria to qualitative research must be critically questioned (Kuckartz, 2014, pp. 151–155).[1]

It is striking that simultaneous independent coding is particularly suitable for carrying out *systematic* agreement analyses. The first two analysis variations above represent further ways of increasing the coding quality and can be profitably combined with the third.

MAXQDA offers specially developed functions that support the determination of intercoder agreement, the control of disagreements, and the improvement of agreement. We will describe these functions with regard to different coders and therefore use the term "intercoder" throughout this chapter. However, these methods can also be used in the case of repeated coding by one and the same person, which is always useful if you want to analyze the stability of your own coding work, the so-called intracoder agreement.

Before you can start analyzing intercoder agreement in MAXQDA, you must first clarify for which documents (and in which order) the analysis is to be carried out. If the amount of data to be analyzed is small, all the documents can be coded by a second person. This is the case, for example, if you have conducted ten half-hour interviews that have been thematically coded using a simple category system. Most

---

[1]Krippendorff consistently differentiates between agreement and reliability in the context of content analysis (in his case rather classically oriented): "To be clear, agreement is what we measure; reliability is what we wish to infer from it. In content analysis, reproducibility is arguably the most important interpretation of reliability" (2004, p. 414).

of the time, however, the data will be more extensive than that, in which case you will require a sample. It is sometimes suggested in the literature on the subject that a certain percentage of the data should be coded by a second person. Such a percentage rate of perhaps 10% may provide an initial indication, but due to potentially very different amounts of data and the diversity of conditions between projects, further criteria should definitely be included in the decision:

- The expected number of coded segments—for example, it makes no sense to limit yourself to very few documents if you only expect a few of the available categories to be used in the selected documents.
- The diversity of cases—the sample should include a broad spectrum of available data. A well-considered selection of documents according to the principle of maximum contrast (e.g., short vs. long texts or interviews with storytelling vs. short answering interviewees) or a random selection is recommended.
- The stage of development of the category system—especially when applying a newly developed coding frame for the first time, the intercoder agreement analysis should be started relatively early in order to be able to detect deficiencies in the coding frame.
- The available resources—intercoder analyses take time. Projects are often conducted under time pressure, and there are not always people available who are willing and able to do a second round of coding. However, when performing a qualitative content analysis, you should never go completely without an intercoder check. Sometimes the amount of effort involved is overestimated, but the motto "a little is better than nothing at all" clearly applies here.

In general, it is best to check the coding consistency with a manageable data set at an early stage to avoid finding out late in the project that the coding instructions were incomplete or misleading. To be able to report improvements regarding the coding process, you need to perform multiple checks, i.e., start with two very different documents, discuss any inconsistencies that have occurred, and then continue with two further documents.

Before starting the analysis in MAXQDA, it makes sense not only to think about the selection of documents but also the codes you want to include. When analyzing intercoder agreement, it usually makes no sense to check all the codes at the same time. First of all, codes such as "Interesting text passage," "Suitable quotation," and potentially also the code "Other" are often excluded from the analysis. Then, the analyst who has carried out the coding in two steps—by first applying broad-brush themes before subsequently differentiating them—should proceed with the agreement analysis in two equivalent stages: firstly for the broad-brush segments, followed by further analysis of the subcode assignments. In addition, the types of the assigned codes must be taken into account. Simple factual codes (e.g., whether a person claims to be a supporter of a party or not) should only be mixed with sophisticated codes in the context of a complex argumentation analysis if you are not interested in the calculation of an overall value of agreement.

The Procedure for Analyzing Intercoder Agreement in MAXQDA

MAXQDA allows you to determine the agreement between two coders for selected documents. To perform the analysis in MAXQDA, the documents need to exist twice in the project—once coded by person 1 in one document group or set, and once coded by person 2 in another document group or set. In addition, a coding frame and corresponding instructions for the coders must have been defined in advance. What is the best way to organize the agreement analysis process? The following steps illustrate an appropriate procedure:

- Step 1—Create a project with all the relevant documents and the complete code system. Specify the coding instructions for individual categories in the code memos. If the units that both people should code have been defined in advance, they can be tagged with a code called "Segments to be coded." If the data material has a uniform structure, it may be sufficient to instruct both coders to always code the entire paragraph or the entire answer to a question.
- Step 2—Activate write protections for the code system and document texts in MAXQDA's User Management system in the case of each coder to protect the project from unwanted changes (see Chap. 18). The selection of documents that are to be coded by a second person can easily be made visible, for example, by assigning a certain color to the document in the "Document System" window.
- Step 3—Provide a copy of the master project file to both coders.
- Step 4—Both people then code the selected documents and add their abbreviations or names to the name of a document group (or set) to be able to identify their code assignments later.
- Step 5—Merge the two project files into one, which will then contain two copies of all the documents to be compared, using the ***Home > Merge Projects*** function described in Chap. 18. Select the option ***Don't import already existing documents*** here, so that only documents coded by the second person are added. Once the import has been completed, the document names will indicate who has coded which document.

Once a project contains the selected documents that have been coded by both people, the analysis of the intercoder agreement can be done *for two document groups or sets*. To start the procedure, first select the codes you want to include in the analysis by activating them and then open the function via ***Analysis > Intercoder Agreement***. The dialog box that appears (Fig. 19.1) allows you to specify the two document groups or sets you want to analyze and to distinguish between three types of agreement.

MAXQDA can check the selected documents for consistent coding on three different levels, where the first two consistency types refer to the "document level" and the third to the "segment level":

- ***Code existence in the document***—A match is counted if both coders have assigned the same code to the document. It does not matter in this case whether one person assigned the code three times and the other only once. The location of the code in the document is also irrelevant, as long as the code exists somewhere in the document. Disagreement regarding a given code therefore only occurs if one person has assigned the code *once or several times* and the other person has *not assigned it at all* in the document. This level of agreement check is interesting, for example, for categories that refer to the entire document. If a code "Previous rehab experience" is to be assigned in a study with rehabilitation patients, it may not matter where and how often the code was assigned in the document—the main point is that both coders *have* assigned it.

- *Code frequency in the document*—A match is counted if both coders have assigned the same code in the document the same number of times. If one person has assigned the code "self-confidence" three times in the document and the other only twice, there is no agreement for this code. Again, the locations of the coded segments in the document do not play a role here.
- *Min. code overlap between segments [%]*—A match is counted if both coders have assigned the same code to a given data segment. The segments do not have to be 100% identical in their position; you can set a tolerance range.

To correctly analyze intercoder agreement in MAXQDA, the compared documents need to be identical. If this is not the case, MAXQDA displays a warning message including a reference to the first location where the documents differ. In this case, we recommend abandoning the procedure to first examine the differences between each document to avoid producing incorrect results.

The agreement analysis can be carried out for all document types, i.e., for texts, PDFs, tables and images, as well as audio and video files.

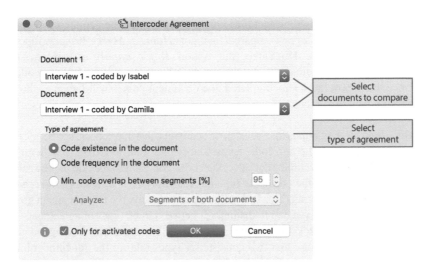

Fig. 19.1 Options dialog box for intercoder agreement analyses

Document-Level Intercoder Agreement

You can see an example of the result of an intercoder analysis in Fig. 19.2. Camilla and Isabel independently coded interview 1, and then an intercoder check was performed using the second option above, that is, where a match is counted when the code has been assigned the same number of times. To compare their code assignments, MAXQDA uses the Code Matrix Browser, in which the two documents are displayed side by side in two columns. In Fig. 19.2, the numbers display was switched on to provide an accurate comparison: for example, Isabel and Camilla have both assigned the code "Interests" twice, which means there is an intercoder agreement for this code. In the title bar, MAXQDA displays the percent agreement between the two coders in relation to all codes displayed in the Code Matrix Browser. The percentage value is calculated by the number of codes for which there is intercoder agreement divided by the number of all analyzed codes. This is the same as the number of rows with concordances divided by the total number of rows when all codes are expanded. The 60% agreement shown in the title of the example is calculated as follows: for three codes ("Interests," "Money and Financial Issues," "Religion and Spirituality") the two coders agree, and for the other two codes, they do not. The number of matching codes divided by the total number of codes is $3/(3+2) = 60\%$. This value indicates that the two coders agree on 60% of the codes, and they differ accordingly on 40% of the codes. Incidentally, the analysis variation "code existence in the document" would result in a percentage of agreement of 100% between these two coders, since both completely agree that the same four codes apply to this document and one does not.

▶ **Please Note** By default, only the activated codes are displayed in a linear list without their parent codes. When selecting the option ***Display Codes with Hierarchy*** in the toolbar, non-activated parent codes that are necessary for the correct display of the code tree may also be listed. The calculation of the percent agreement ignores these codes.

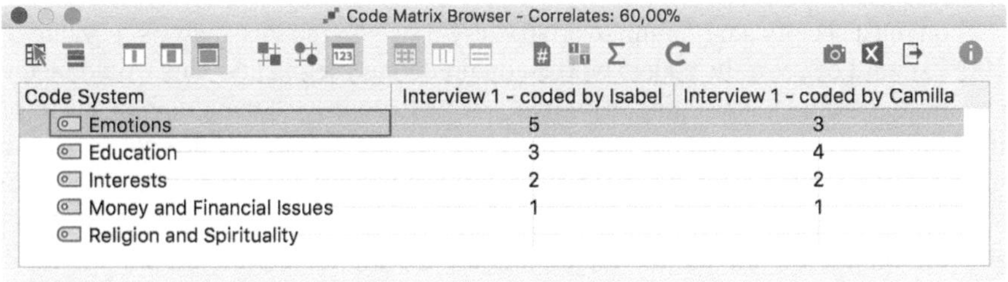

Fig. 19.2 Results table for an intercoder agreement analysis at the document level

Usually, the interesting aspects of an intercoder analysis are the disagreements, which can reveal problems concerning individual codes, the coding instructions, or the approaches of individual coders. MAXQDA supports the analysis of disagreements through its interactive display of the results: double-clicking on a cell lists all the corresponding coded segments in the "Retrieved Segments" window. Hence, in the example, you can see which segment Camilla has coded with "Emotions," but Isabel has not.

Segment-Level Intercoder Agreement

Although a document-level analysis provides initial indications of systematic differences in the use of categories, in most cases a segment-specific agreement check will be necessary. You can do this by selecting the third type of agreement in the options dialog box (***Min. code overlap between segments [%]***, Fig. 19.1). In practice, coders often not only assign categories to predefined segments but in fact define the segments that need to be coded as they go. In other words, if the latter approach is taken, it can often happen that one person codes an extra character or word compared to the other, and it is just as if not more likely that two coders will differ by 1 or 2 seconds when coding the same scene in a video. In order to ignore these minor, inconsequential differences in segment boundaries during the intercoder analysis, you can set a minimum overlap of two coded segments to be compared in the options dialog box as a percentage value. A code overlap of 100% means that the segment boundaries must match precisely to be counted as identical segments in MAXQDA.

▶   **Please Note** The percentage set in the options dialog box should not be confused with the percent agreement that is displayed as the result of the analysis. The options dialog box only lets you set the minimum overlap for which two coded segments are considered to be identical.

You must specify a minimum overlap every time you run this analysis. A value of 100% should be set if the coders worked on predefined segments. This would be the case if, for example, the coding instructions were to code each paragraph of a text, or if all the segments to be coded were previously tagged with a specific code and were then assigned to thematic codes. In most cases, however, you would be advised to start with a minimum overlap of about 95% as a test and reduce this value step-by-step if it results in an inordinate number of *insignificant* disagreements.

After starting an intercoder agreement analysis at the segment level, MAXQDA first processes the code assignments of the first document and then the ones of the second document. Each coded segment is checked to see if the other person has

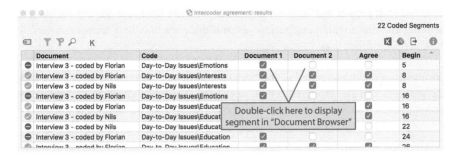

Fig. 19.3 Results table for an intercoder agreement analysis at the segment level (segment table)

assigned the same code to this segment. Assuming one person has coded 10 segments in the document and the other person has coded 12 segments, then $10 + 12 = 22$ segments are checked for agreement. Figure 19.3 shows part of the results table MAXQDA produces for this analysis. Each row contains the result of the check of a single segment, where green check marks represent agreements and stop signs represent disagreements. The following information is provided in the first row: in paragraph 5, Florian (Document 1) assigned the code "Emotions," but Nils (Document 2) did not. Accordingly, the check mark is missing in the "Agree" column, and a stop sign is displayed in the first column.

▶ **Tip** By clicking on the column heading "Agree", the table can be sorted for that column, so that all disagreements are displayed at the top of the table.

In qualitative research in general, especially at the beginning of the analysis process, all disagreements are investigated and their causes identified. Did the second person miss something? Should two codes be more clearly separated or even merged? Did the two people assign the same code but diverge on where to place the segment boundaries? The interactivity of the result table supports you in identifying these and similar problems. Double-clicking in either the "Document 1" or "Document 2" columns opens the respective documents at the corresponding location in the "Document Browser" and lets you examine the differences between the coders.

The question of how to deal with disagreements swiftly follows. As we emphasized above, qualitatively oriented research projects aim to use these differences as an occasion for discussions concerning code assignments, the coding frame, and the document segments. To reach an agreement on problematic coded segments, it is sometimes helpful to include the whole case as contextual information or to investigate other coded segments under the same category. As a rule, it is worth logging this problem-solving and consolidating process as well as the arguments and points of view put forward, because these discussions can often result in valuable information. Not infrequently you can make very interesting discoveries relevant to your research project and analysis process as a whole while solving the problem of defining and demarcating categories—even if these are only hypotheses that need to be tested on further data.

To optimize the coded segments in the MAXQDA project file, one of the two documents should be defined as the "master document." In this document, the code assignments can be improved where necessary, so that it contains the optimized version. Once you have finished the intercoder analysis, you can delete the second version of each document to continue working in the optimized, merged project.

Code-Specific Results Table

MAXQDA not only displays the segment results table but also a so-called code-specific results table. The latter shows not only the percentage of agreement across all codes but also for each code individually (Fig. 19.4). The percentage of agreement results from the proportion of agreements in the evaluated code. In Fig. 19.4, in the row "<Total>", with 18 agreements and a total of 22 coded segments, the overall percentage is 81.82%.

The percent agreement provides valuable information for the identification of problematic codes, but you should evaluate its size with a good degree of caution. Particular attention should be paid to the absolute number of segments evaluated per code in the "Total" column and the number of disagreements. For example, if each coder created five segments, a single disagreement would already reduce the percentage of agreement by 20 percentage points. And with two segments (as with the code "Money and Financial Issues" in Fig. 19.4) the table would only include the values 0% and 100%. Moreover, in addition to the absolute number, the total number of segments per coder should also be considered. If it is very unequal, there will usually be a systematic difference between the coders, for instance, because one of them coded the data in smaller, broken-down parts than the other, which will lead to a small percentage of agreement.

If you include the percent agreement for a qualitative study in a report or publication, you should always also state which segments caused the remaining differences and what relevance these have to the study. It is not particularly helpful to present only the "overall percentage" for all your codes. It might, instead, be better to provide at least the minimum and the maximum percentages regarding all tested codes or, better still, to include all the information in the code-specific results table in

Code	Correlates	Doesn't corr...	Total	Percent
Day-to-Day Issues\Emotions	6	2	8	75.00
Day-to-Day Issues\Education	6	2	8	75.00
Day-to-Day Issues\Interests	4	0	4	100.00
Day-to-Day Issues\Money and Financial Issues	2	0	2	100.00
<Total>	18	4	22	81.82

Fig. 19.4 Results table for an intercoder agreement analysis at the segment level (code table)

the publication. This is advisable because, for the reasons mentioned above, the absolute number of evaluated codes and disagreements should also be stated. During the analysis it is therefore necessary to document problematic codes and discrepancies to be able to include them in reports and publications later.

The question remains as to what is to be regarded as a low and what as a high percentage of agreement. Unfortunately, this question cannot be answered with established thresholds, because the percent agreement between coders not only depends on the number of absolute coded segments as described, but also on other factors. These include, in particular, the number and variance of different (sub) categories as well as the degree of difficulty of the coding process itself (it is more difficult to code an interviewee's argument, e.g., than it is to assign factual or thematic codes). A simple inversion of the conclusion will usually help you evaluate whether the percentage is too low: if a code has 80% agreement, for example, this means that 20% of the code assignments differ. Usually this level of disagreement would not be considered ideal, and you would need to set stricter thresholds. However, how you determine suitable values should ultimately always be related to the content of your data.

Coding Units vs. Coded Segments
When conducting an intercoder analysis using MAXQDA, it is important to distinguish between coding units and coded segments. In many approaches for the analysis of intercoder agreement, it is assumed that a single code is assigned to each coding unit. This is the case, for example, if physicians rate an x-ray image for the presence of a disease or if entire newspaper articles are rated low, medium, or high on a scale of "latent racism." Then exactly one code has been assigned by each coder to each coding unit.

This is not the case in many analyses performed with MAXQDA. It is quite possible that the two coders have assigned different numbers of codes to the same passages in the document. Furthermore, it is common for the coding units not to have been predefined, and the coders quite often decide about which passages to code on their own, which may result in overlapping coded segments or coded segments contained within other segments. To perform an intercoder analysis in such cases, MAXQDA follows the same process described above: first the codes of coder 1, then those of coder 2, are checked for agreement with the other person, respectively. Figure 19.5 shows some examples that illustrate how many matches result from this procedure in different cases. The first row, in which both coders assigned only "Code A" to the same segment, indicates that two agreements have been counted here. The case where the coders assigned one code to the segment each, but these codes are not the same, results in two disagreements, as shown in the second row.

When you open the ***Intercoder Agreement*** function, a drop-down menu labeled ***Analyze:*** is visible in the options dialog box that opens (Fig. 19.1), where you can instruct MAXQDA to analyze only the coded segments in a single document, i.e., the document coded by only one of the coders, to assess their level of agreement with the other coder. This setting can be used where both coders have coded predefined

			Coded segments	Agreements	Disagreements	Percent
A	Text segment	A	2	2	0	100%
A	Text segment	B	2	0	2	0%
B, A	Text segment	A, B	4	4	0	100%
B, A	Text segment	A	3	2	1	67%
B, A	Text segment	C	3	0	3	0%
B, A	Text segment	C, D	4	0	4	0%

Fig. 19.5 Number of agreements, in different constellations, between two coders

segments with a single code. In this case, the number of coded segments evaluated corresponds to the number of coding units in the results table.

Calculating Chance-Corrected Agreement Coefficients like Kappa

"My supervisor told me to calculate kappa. How do I do this in MAXQDA?" "I need kappa for my analysis, don't I?" These questions are not only on the minds of the many doctoral candidates we advise in workshops, they are also regularly asked in the discussion forum on the MAXQDA website. This is often based on the desire to legitimize one's own qualitative approach to a scientific community that primarily adheres to the tradition of quantitative research. Here kappa is a known coefficient, which is why supervisors often demand it. A coefficient like kappa quantifies the quality of qualitative analysis as a figure and translates the work into a comprehensible (and familiar) form. Calculation of such measures helps to keep you connected to some scientific communities and increases the chance of publication in certain journals.

Even if an excessive emphasis on a chance-corrected coefficient at the expense of other important quality criteria for qualitative research should be called into question, the calculation of chance-corrected coefficients does have its place. When determining the percent agreement, the question arises as to how likely it is that agreement could have arisen by chance. To answer this question, chance-corrected coefficients were developed that subtract possible random matches from the raw agreement. Their central idea involves determining to what extent human coders can code a text or video, with an existing set of categories, better than a randomly working machine.

The following basic formula is often used to calculate chance-corrected coefficients: (Po − Pc)/(1 − Pc), where Po is the observed percentage of agreement and Pc is the expected agreement by chance. Following this method of calculation, the resulting value indicates how much the agreement of the coders exceeds the agreement by chance. Coefficients such as Kappa (Cohen, 1960), Pi (Scott, 1955), and Alpha (Krippendorff, 1970) differ primarily in how the expected agreement by

Table 19.1 "Code by code" table; the agreements are on the diagonal line (a, e, i)

	Coder 2			
Coder 1	Cat. 1	Cat. 2	Cat. 3	SUM
Cat. 1	a	b	c	a + b + c
Cat. 2	d	e	f	d + e + f
Cat. 3	g	h	i	g + h + i
SUM	a + d + g	b + e + h	c + f + i	N

chance is computed. Usually a matrix "categories by categories," as shown schematically in Table 19.1, is used as the basis for calculating these coefficients. The cells indicate how often the respective categories have been assigned to a coding unit by the two coders. The primary diagonal contains the cells with the agreements between the two coders (the cells a, e, i). The agreement by chance is computed using the marginal sums. For the following explanations, it is important to emphasize that generating a table of this kinds usually requires that the coders have assigned only one category to each segment.

Here we will limit ourselves to the calculation of chance-corrected coefficients for agreements at the segment level, since they are seldom determined at the document level and cannot be performed automatically in MAXQDA. To request the calculation of a chance-corrected coefficient at the segment level in MAXQDA, click on the kappa symbol in the results table (Fig. 19.3) after performing the intercoder analysis. MAXQDA then generates a set of results as shown in Fig. 19.6.

What information is included in the results MAXQDA produces and how can it be interpreted? In practice in qualitative research projects, you will rarely be able to

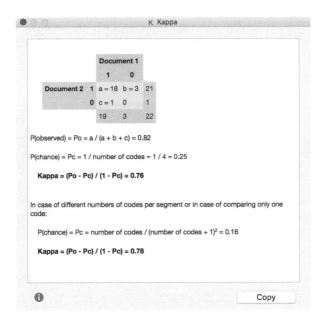

Fig. 19.6 Results window for calculating kappa according to Brennan and Prediger (1981)

create a matrix as shown in Table 19.1, since coders often assign more than one code to a segment, and, furthermore, it also happens that one person assigns one or more codes to a segment where the other person assigns no category at all. This is the reason why MAXQDA goes through the coded segments of one coder, and then the segments of the other, as described above, and counts them as matches if the other person has assigned the same code to the same segment. In order to determine a chance-corrected coefficient for this procedure, MAXQDA generates a 2×2 table as shown in Fig. 19.6. The upper left cell (a) indicates how often the two coders have assigned the same code to a segment. The upper right cell (b) and the lower left cell (c) indicate for how many segments the two coders differ in their assignment. The fourth cell (d) is always zero, because due to the method used, there are no predefined segments that were not coded by either coder.

Below this table, both the raw agreement Po and the expected agreement by chance Pc are calculated. Po corresponds to the value output in the "<Total>" row of the code-specific table. Since the marginal distributions of the 2×2 table are always unequally distributed due to cell d = 0, agreement by chance cannot be calculated as for Cohen's Kappa, Scott's Pi, or Krippendorff's Alpha. Unequal marginal distributions can lead to abstruse and paradoxical values in Cohen's Kappa, which is a frequently articulated point of criticism (e.g., in Feinstein & Cicchetti, 1990; or Gwet, 2008). When calculating Pc, the calculation in MAXQDA therefore follows a concept proposed by Brennan and Prediger (1981).[2] Instead of determining the expected agreement by chance using the marginal distribution, the number of categories is used here. You can see quite easily that the probability of agreement decreases as the number of categories increases. Computationally, Pc is $1/n$, where n corresponds to the number of categories used. This is graphically illustrated in the left table in Fig. 19.7: the number of gray cells with coincidences on the main diagonal corresponds to the category number n, and the total area of the table corresponds to n^2 cells, resulting in a random coincidence of $n/n^2 = 1/n$.

In the frequently occurring case that the coders differ in the number of categories assigned per segment, the expected random agreement can be slightly corrected downward. As the middle table in Fig. 19.7 shows, another category "X" is added in this case, which represents "not coded." Since the number of cells with coincidences (by chance) still corresponds to the category number n, Pc is now calculated with $n/(n+1)^2$. MAXQDA also displays the value calculated in this way. In the example, it is 0.78, slightly greater than the "normal" Kappa value of 0.76. As the table at the far right in Fig. 19.7 illustrates, this way of calculating must also be used if only a single code is evaluated for an agreement analysis.

---

[2]Krippendorff (2004, p. 417) points out that this proposal was already formulated in the 1950s and was later "reinvented" with slight variations by several authors, including Brennan and Prediger (1981).

	Cat. 1	Cat. 2	Cat. 3
Cat. 1			
Cat. 2			
Cat. 3			

	Cat. 1	Cat. 2	Cat. 3	X
Cat. 1				
Cat. 2				
Cat. 3				
X				0

	Cat. 1	X
Cat. 1		
X		0

Fig. 19.7 Determining the agreement by chance (gray); "X" stands for "not coded"

> **Please Note** MAXQDA does not provide Cohen's Kappa, but kappa according to Brennan and Prediger (1981), who named their coefficient with a Greek kappa with subscript n: κ_n. If you use the results of a MAXQDA calculation in a publication, you should make a reference to Brennan and Prediger to avoid confusion.

Clearly, as the number of categories increases, the agreement by chance calculated in this way will decrease. Let us assume that there is a 90% match. Then the random correction for two categories leads to a Brennan and Prediger's Kappa of 0.80, and for ten categories, Kappa would be as high as 0.89.

But how should the level of Kappa be evaluated? Brennan and Prediger's Kappa can take values between −1.00 and +1.00; a value of 0 corresponds to a parity with chance, and a value of +1.00 corresponds to perfect agreement of the coders—this is as far from agreement by chance as you can get. 1.00 is reached if the percent agreement between the two coders is 100%. The interpretation of the value can be based on the established benchmark notes for Cohen's Kappa: according to Landis and Koch (1977) one can label a result as good ("substantial") from 0.61 and as very good from 0.81 ("almost perfect"). However, any such threshold could be misleading. First, in many cases Cohen's Kappa can never reach the value of 1.00 due to its calculation method, which is why the threshold values for Brennan and Prediger's Kappa might be raised but should never be lowered. Second, as previously explained for the percent agreement, the definition of this threshold and the interpretation of its value should also be justified in relation to content, for example, by explaining which remaining inconsistencies were accepted by the researchers.

We want to conclude this section with two important notes: *firstly*, we think that the calculation and publication of a chance-corrected coefficient should by no means distract qualitative researchers from the process of improving their category system. *Secondly*, it is necessary for the calculation of chance-corrected coefficients that the segments to be coded, i.e., the coding units, are defined a priori. If the coders are free to set the segment boundaries, there is no sense in calculating chance-corrected coefficients of agreement. The reason for this is obvious: even for a one-page text of 2000 characters, the probability Pc that two coders will randomly select exactly the same characters and assign the same code to them tends to zero. A random correction is therefore not necessary.

References

Brennan, R. L., & Prediger, D. J. (1981). Coefficient kappa: Some uses, misuses, and alternatives. *Educational and Psychological Measurement, 41*(3), 687–699. https://doi.org/10.1177/001316448104100307.

Cohen, J. (1960). A coefficient of agreement for nominal scales. *Educational and Psychological Measurement, 20*(1), 37–46. https://doi.org/10.1177/001316446002000104.

Feinstein, A. R., & Cicchetti, D. V. (1990). High agreement but low Kappa: I. The problems of two paradoxes. *Journal of Clinical Epidemiology, 43*(6), 543–549. https://doi.org/10.1016/0895-4356(90)90158-L.

Gwet, K. L. (2008). Computing inter-rater reliability and its variance in the presence of high agreement. *The British Journal of Mathematical and Statistical Psychology, 61*(Pt 1), 29–48. https://doi.org/10.1348/000711006X126600.

Krippendorff, K. (1970). Bivariate agreement coefficients for reliability of data. *Sociological Methodology, 2*, 139–150. https://doi.org/10.2307/270787.

Krippendorff, K. (2004). Reliability in content analysis: Some common misconceptions and recommendations. *Human Communication Research, 30*(3), 411–433. https://doi.org/10.1111/J.1468-2958.2004.TB00738.X.

Kuckartz, U. (2014). *Qualitative text analysis: A guide to methods, practice & using software*. Thousand Oaks, CA: SAGE.

Landis, J. R., & Koch, G. G. (1977). The measurement of observer agreement for categorical data. *Biometrics, 33*(1), 159–174. https://doi.org/10.2307/2529310.

Mayring, P. (2014). *Qualitative content analysis: Theoretical foundation, basic procedures and software solution*. Klagenfurt. Retrieved from http://nbn-resolving.de/urn:nbn:de:0168-ssoar-395173

Schreier, M. (2012). *Qualitative content analysis in practice*. Thousand Oaks, CA: SAGE.

Scott, W. A. (1955). Reliability of content analysis: The case of nominal scale coding. *Public Opinion Quarterly, 19*(3), 321–325. https://doi.org/10.1086/266577.

Documenting and Archiving the Research Process

20

When it comes to quality criteria and standards in qualitative research, the criteria of plausibility, confirmability, reliability, credibility, and auditability each play a significant role. Ensuring these criteria are met involves comprehensively documenting the research process throughout every stage of a project—from its conception, through the data collection phase, to the final analysis. MAXQDA lets you do all this easily and effectively. Every stage of the data analysis process can be documented: the original recordings of interviews, the transcriptions, videos and source material synchronized with these recordings, records of the interview conditions, the developed categories and their definitions, the category system and its development, and much more. On the one hand, you have the analysis and presentation of the results, and on the other you have a record of the complete research process. This chapter focuses on the latter: how the progression of a project can be documented and archived. We will therefore examine some of the features and functions of MAXQDA that we have already covered from this fresh perspective and introduce some additional functions designed specifically for this purpose.

In This Chapter
- Using memos throughout the research process: project descriptions, postscripts, and code definitions
- Using the Logbook as a research diary
- Getting to know MAXQDA's documentation functions
- Documenting the category system with the Codebook
- Compiling code assignments using the Smart Publisher
- Creating an audit trail: how did everything develop during the analysis process?
- Archiving the data and analysis work and passing these archives on

© Springer Nature Switzerland AG 2019
U. Kuckartz, S. Rädiker, *Analyzing Qualitative Data with MAXQDA*,
https://doi.org/10.1007/978-3-030-15671-8_20

Fig. 20.1 Functions included in the "Reports" ribbon tab

The Duty to Document the Research Process

Plausibility, credibility, and auditability are key quality criteria for qualitative research. Adequate documentation of the research and analysis process plays a vital role in this context. The recipients of this documentation should be able to see which method was chosen and how it was implemented in the project. A study involving the analysis of open interviews or expert interviews using the qualitative content analysis method, for example, should document the following (Kuckartz, 2014, pp. 155–158):

- The process of selecting research participants
- The interview guidelines
- The accompanying questionnaire, if one was used
- Information about the length of the individual interviews as well as the range of interview lengths
- The rules according to which the interviews were transcribed
- At least one transcript as an example of the collected data and style of transcription (if required by the assessors of a thesis, research paper, etc.)
- The category development process over the course of the analysis
- The category system, including examples, i.e., coded segments of individual categories

You can access an overview of your project via **Reports > Project Information** (Fig. 20.1), which includes—among other information—the project description provided in the project memo, as well as the total numbers of documents, document groups, categories, and code assignments.

Both the "Code System" and the "Document System" can be exported and printed to help you keep a record of your category system and processed cases. You can do both via the **Export** or **Print** options, likewise provided in the **Reports** ribbon tab.

Memos as Important Documentation Tools

Ideally you should start documenting the research and analysis process from the very beginning of a project. MAXQDA's memos are one of the key tools available for this purpose. Table 20.1 provides an overview of the different types of memos and how they can be used to help document your work.

Table 20.1 Overview of different memo types for documenting a project

Memo type	Available where?	Role in documenting a project
Project memo	The highest-level entry, "Documents," in the "Document System"	Project description: design, sample, surveys
Document group memo	Each respective document group in the "Document System"	Description of document group and, if applicable, the criteria for the selection of research participants and/or the sampling strategy
Document memo	Each respective document in the "Document System"	Postscript, information about the process of this interview, possibly also a case summary
Code memo	Each respective code in the "Code System"	Category definitions with examples extracted from the data
Free memo	The Overview of Memos in the "Reports" tab; or create a new memo via "Free Memo" in the "Analysis" tab	Any information not linked to specific documents, document groups, or codes, e.g., the interview guideline

Chapters 3 and 5 describe in detail how to work with memos. The export options, which you can access via **Reports** > **Overview of Memos**, are also important in this regard; these allow you to export a selection of memos as files in RTF format for Word, or as Excel files, so that they can serve as the basis for the documentation section of a project report, thesis or research paper.

The Logbook as a Digital Research Diary

The practice of keeping a research diary has its origins in ethnology and field research, but merits being adopted by other disciplines, too. The research diary is your constant companion throughout the research process, ideally from the very beginning. Not only should you record everything that happened throughout the project, and what you learned from research participants in the field, you should also note down your own reflections as well as plans for further surveys and analyses. In other words, the research diary has a dual function; on the one hand, it is an instrument that serves as a documentary and memory aid, that is, it is in effect a self-referential tool; and on the other hand, it is the optimal basis for creating a comprehensible and detailed description of the research process for others, e.g., the scientific community. In the latter respect, the research diary is also directed outward, as a form of "presentation."

MAXQDA enables you to create and continuously maintain your research diary using the "Logbook" function. The word "logbook" is in fact a borrowed nautical term. In the seafaring context, it is used to record significant events and observations in a daily diary. The MAXQDA logbook has a similar function. Here you can record all the events and processes surrounding the project and data analysis work. You can open MAXQDA's Logbook via the **Home** ribbon tab. A window will then open with a toolbar below the header. The symbols are largely self-explanatory; they serve to format the text of the Logbook, i.e., to select a font, font size, or font color—and this Logbook can also be printed and exported as a file.

You can add a new entry by clicking on the *New logbook entry* icon 🗓 at the far left of the toolbar. This causes the current date, time, and user name to be recorded in the Logbook. The Logbook is structured like a scroll, i.e., new entries are always added at the top of the chronological list.

Exporting and Printing a Text Together with Codes and Paragraph Numbers

There will only very rarely be a need to prepare a complete record of your raw research data, as just 20–30 open interviews would produce a considerable amount of text, enough to quickly fill a filing cabinet if printed out. Very often, however, one or more examples of the raw data collected are included in the appendix to a research paper or thesis—especially for doctoral and master's theses. In these cases, it is helpful to create a version of the text with paragraph numbers. To do this, follow these steps:

- Open the relevant text.
- Click on the *Export displayed document* icon in the "Document Browser."
- In the dialog box that opens select RTF as export format, which is recognized by Word and other word processing programs.
- Be sure to check the option *As table with paragraph numbers*.

The exported text is always saved as a table, the first column containing the paragraph numbers. You can also export several texts at the same time by selecting *Export documents* in the context menu of a document group in the "Document System" window.

If you need a printed version of the text, you can either print the generated and saved export file or click the *Print document* icon in the "Document Browser." When you print directly from MAXQDA, you can adjust the following settings in the print dialog box:

- Number of copies
- Individual page selection
- Portrait or landscape format
- Page margins
- Headers and/or footers
- Printed page numbers
- Printed visual display of coded segments
- Printed visual display of memos
- Maximum width of the coded segments column

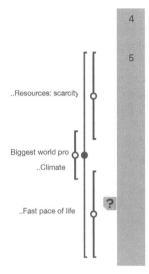

4   I: Ok, good, then let's get started with the first question. So, what are, in your view, the biggest world problems in the 21st century?

5   R: Well, those would be the problems we're all facing now. There are the material problems, so we're facing energy challenges, how do we ensure our energy supply in the future? What are we going to do in terms of that? Fossil fuels are going to run out at some stage. And what alternatives are there? Like biofuels and solar energy, what are the pros and cons of those? We're not there yet with hydrogen, it's not ready for the market yet. I think that's as a pretty big problem. And then, of course, there's climate change, although there's a lot of hysteria at play there too. It's not as if we need to turn the ship around and just reverse the last 60 years of emissions within a single year, so I don't think we need to take such a hectic, hasty approach. We've also got quite a big, I guess, emotional problem going on now which is that life has become much for fast-paced. We take far too little time for the important things in life like spending time with family and things like that. All the modern technology that we have, so for instance cellphones that ring round the clock (...) we just don't get a moment of peace anymore. That's a problem where I think we might see some related illnesses developing.

Fig. 20.2 Text excerpt with visualized code assignments and memos

To document your analysis procedure and the coding work performed, it is often useful to prepare a sample text or text excerpt in which the coding stripes are displayed at the edge of the page, and, if necessary, the coded text passages are also highlighted in color. Figure 20.2 shows a prepared text excerpt like this. Instead of a printout, you can also export a PDF file to archive or distribute electronically by choosing this file type in the export dialog box.

Documenting the Coding Frame and the Coded Segments

Category-based analysis methods naturally focus on categories and their definitions. You can easily generate an overview of your codes via *Export > Code System* or *Print > Code System*, both of which are available in the *Reports* ribbon tab. The export function allows you to specify the output format, and, if needed, you can also export the corresponding code memos. Please note that the function *Codes > Export Code System* creates a MAXQDA-specific file that can be used for transferring the code system to other MAXQDA projects and is not suitable for purpose of documentation.

The *Reports > Codebook* function lets you automatically generate a codebook with all categories and their definitions. All or only selected codes are listed in the Codebook in the same order as they appear in the "Code System," and the corresponding code memo is provided for each of them. Further options allow you to include code and subcode frequencies and to standardize the memo font type. The generated Codebook then contains the category definitions of the individual codes as recorded in their respective code memos. Hence, the Codebook function can save you a lot of work when creating an appendix for your dissertation or for research reports.

The Codebook is exported in RTF format and can be easily edited and adapted further using standard word processing programs. It contains a cover sheet with the title "Codebook," the project name, and the creation date. The second page lists the code system in a table format. The main section contains each respective code with its corresponding memo in the order listed in the "Code System."

The Smart Publisher, accessed via **Reports > Smart Publisher,** is another convenient tool that automatically generates a report of the code assignments in your project. We described this function in detail in Chap. 9, including its various options. In the context of documenting a project, however, the Smart Publisher can generate a list in a uniform layout of the coded segments for one or more selected categories as well as their source information.

Audit Trail: How Did the Project Develop During the Analysis?

An audit trail is generally defined as a chronological record of performed actions and procedures. In empirical social research, this trail might record the development of a category system, for instance. In quality criteria stipulations, you will often find the term "auditability," which refers to the same thing in practice.

A simple, yet very effective way to ensure that you leave an adequate audit trail for your project is to duplicate and save copies of your MAXQDA project files at regular intervals. You can do this using the **Save Project As** option in the **Home** ribbon tab. The current date should be added to the suggested file name, and then click "no" to the question whether you want to continue working with the newly saved copy.

To specifically document the development of your category system during the analysis process—or of individual categories and subcategories—we recommend that you create a visual representation of these at various intervals, using MAXMaps as described in Chap. 17. You can access MAXMaps via the **Visual Tools** ribbon tab. Drag the codes whose development you want to trace onto the workspace, and then add their subcodes. You can set the width of the linking lines between them such that they indicate the frequency of the subcodes. If you create maps like this at several points during the analysis process, you can visually illustrate the development of the code system later, e.g., in a PowerPoint presentation. You can find a detailed description of working with MAXMaps in Chap. 17.

Sharing and Archiving MAXQDA Projects and Data

Suppose the supervisor of a master's thesis or dissertation wants to gain an impression of the analysis work completed so far and look at what has been coded with which codes, what the code system looks like, and so on. This raises a few questions for the student, including "Which elements do I leave in the project, and which do I take out?", "Can I just pass on the raw data as it is?", and "Moreover, my supervisor may not have a MAXQDA license. What then?".

Let us answer these questions one by one. Personal notes, unfinished ideas, and so on should not be included in the shared project. And, if you have not done so already, you must render the data completely and consistently anonymous prior to passing it on to others. Since every case needs to be anonymized, you should complete this process with your project, first. Then click on *Save Project As* (in the *Home* ribbon tab) to create the version you are going to share. The elements not required, e.g., personal memos, will have to be removed from this copy. In this form, the project can then be passed on to supervisors and assessors. A MAXQDA project usually consists of only a single file—but this is not the case if it includes multimedia files. These files, including PDF files over a certain size (which can be adjusted in MAXQDA's global preferences), are saved externally. The function *External Files* (in the *Home* ribbon tab) provides an overview of the number, size, and location of these external files (Fig. 20.3).

External files can be compiled in a zip archive using the *External Files > Bundle External Data Files* option, available in the *Home* ribbon tab. This zip file is named "projectname.mx18.zip" and is saved in the same folder as the project file. You can then pass it on along with the MAXQDA project file, and, provided it is contained in the same folder as the project, it will automatically be unpacked in the folder for external files when the MAXQDA project is opened at its destination.

But what if your assessors do not have a MAXQDA license? In this case they would presumably not be able to do much with the project file. However, the "MAXQDA Reader" is available for this purpose. The Reader is a free MAXQDA version, which can be used to browse through projects and trace completed analytical work. This version does not allow the user to edit or process the data or to

File name	Path	Size	State
1700016.pdf	/Users/stefanraediker/Documents/MAXQDA/Externals/1700016.pdf ...	118.24 KB	Original location
1700029.pdf	/Users/stefanraediker/Documents/MAXQDA/Externals/1700029.pdf ...	473.65 KB	Original location
1700044.pdf	/Users/stefanraediker/Documents/MAXQDA/Externals/1700044.pdf ...	1.19 MB	Original location
1700071.pdf	/Users/stefanraediker/Documents/MAXQDA/Externals/1700071.pdf ...	138.82 KB	Original location
1700123.pdf	/Users/stefanraediker/Documents/MAXQDA/Externals/1700123.pdf ...	136.76 KB	Original location
1700130.pdf	/Users/stefanraediker/Documents/MAXQDA/Externals/1700130.pdf ...	129.64 KB	Original location

Fig. 20.3 List of externally stored files

actively code it; instead, it makes projects accessible to specific target groups—it can also be used in museums and libraries, for instance.

In the case of final theses, such as bachelor's and master's theses or dissertations, the question arises as to what should be documented and whether it should be included in the text of the thesis itself or separately, for example, in the form of an appendix or an accompanying DVD. It is difficult to set out any universal rules for this, since there are often institution-specific conventions and/or special requirements made by assessors. In other words, we recommend you first find out what is expected in your specific case and only then start working on the corresponding documentation. As a general rule, the central codes of your project or your developed category system—depending on the analysis method used—should be documented in the text of the thesis itself, while the category definitions should be included in its appendix. It is usually also a good idea to document examples of the raw data—such as some of the transcribed interviews—in the appendix. The way to do this is described at the beginning of this chapter.

There has been a debate for many years over whether it also makes sense for qualitative data to be archived for secondary analyses and made available to further researchers (Corti, Witzel, & Bishop, 2005; Medjedović, 2011). In the UK, a special data archive at the University of Essex called ESDS Qualidata, which is part of the UK Data Service, has been in place for some time. However, if you want to make your own data available to such archives, you should check in detail whether the data you can provide is suitable for archiving purposes, and whether this transfer of data is covered by the consent you obtained from your research participants, which you usually would have done at the beginning of the data collection process. This may be particularly difficult in the case of video data, which cannot easily be rendered anonymous.

References

Corti, L., Witzel, A., & Bishop, L. (2005). On the potentials and problems of secondary analysis: An introduction to the FQS special issue on secondary analysis of qualitative data. *Forum Qualitative Sozialforschung/Forum: Qualitative Social Research, 6*(1). https://doi.org/10.17169/FQS-6.1.498.

Kuckartz, U. (2014). *Qualitative text analysis: A guide to methods, practice & using software.* Thousand Oaks, CA: SAGE.

Medjedović, I. (2011). Secondary analysis of qualitative interview data: Objections and experiences. Results of a german feasibility study. *Forum Qualitative Sozialforschung/ Forum: Qualitative Social Research, 12*(3). https://doi.org/10.17169/FQS-12.3.1742. Qualitative archives and biographical research methods.

Printed by Printforce, the Netherlands